The Demographics of Innovation

The Demographics of Innovation

Why Demographics is a Key to the Innovation Race

JAMES LIANG

WILEY

This edition first published 2018
© 2018 James Liang

Registered office
John Wiley & Sons Ltd, The Atrium, Southern Gate, Chichester, West Sussex, PO19 8SQ,
United Kingdom

For details of our global editorial offices, for customer services and for information about how
to apply for permission to reuse the copyright material in this book please see our website at
www.wiley.com.

Wiley publishes in a variety of print and electronic formats and by print-on-demand. Some
material included with standard print versions of this book may not be included in e-books or in
print-on-demand. If this book refers to media such as a CD or DVD that is not included in the
version you purchased, you may download this material at http://booksupport.wiley.com. For
more information about Wiley products, visit www.wiley.com.

Designations used by companies to distinguish their products are often claimed as trademarks.
All brand names and product names used in this book are trade names, service marks,
trademarks or registered trademarks of their respective owners. The publisher is not associated
with any product or vendor mentioned in this book.

Limit of Liability/Disclaimer of Warranty: While the publisher and author have used their best
efforts in preparing this book, they make no representations or warranties with respect to the
accuracy or completeness of the contents of this book and specifically disclaim any implied
warranties of merchantability or fitness for a particular purpose. It is sold on the understanding
that the publisher is not engaged in rendering professional services and neither the publisher nor
the author shall be liable for damages arising herefrom. If professional advice or other expert
assistance is required, the services of a competent professional should be sought.

Library of Congress Cataloging-in-Publication Data

Names: Liang, James Jianzhang, author.
Title: The demographics of innovation : why demographics is a key to the
    innovation race / James Jianzhang Liang.
Description: Hoboken : Wiley, 2018. | Includes bibliographical references and index. |
Identifiers: LCCN 2017044554 (print) | LCCN 2017051971 (ebook) | ISBN
    9781119408932 (pdf) | ISBN 9781119408949 (epub) | ISBN 9781119408925
    (hardback) | ISBN 9781119408932 (ePDF) | ISBN 9781119408963 (e-bk)
Subjects: LCSH: Technological innovations–Economic aspects. |
    Population–Economic aspects. | BISAC: BUSINESS & ECONOMICS / Banks &
    Banking.
Classification: LCC HC79.T4 (ebook) | LCC HC79.T4 L5345 2018 (print) | DDC
    338/.064–dc23
LC record available at https://lccn.loc.gov/2017044554

A catalogue record for this book is available from the British Library.

ISBN 978-1-119-40892-5 (hardcover)   ISBN 978-1-119-40893-2 (ePDF)
ISBN 978-1-119-40894-9 (ePub)   ISBN 978-1-119-40896-3 (obook)

10 9 8 7 6 5 4 3 2 1

Cover design: Ctrip
Cover images: Leaves image: © Teia/Shutterstock; People image: © Leremy/Shutterstock

Set in 10/12 pt ITCGaramondStd-Lt by Thomson Digital, Noida, India
Printed in Great Britain by TJ International Ltd, Padstow, Cornwall, UK

Contents

Acknowledgments

First, and most importantly, I am very grateful to my advisor, Edward Lazear, who first introduced me to the field of labor economics at Stanford; special thanks also go to the late Gary Becker, who encouraged me to work on this topic during my postdoctoral study under his guidance at the University of Chicago. I benefited immensely from the collaboration with my fellow researchers, Wenzheng Huang and Hui Wang, who co-authored many articles with me on this topic. I am grateful to my research and executive assistants, ZhengYu Fang, Xiaomeng Xu, and Xinxin Wang, who helped with data gathering and analysis, and also to my friends, Wei Gu and Ted Fishman, who gave thoughtful feedback throughout the process.

About the Author

James Liang is both a prominent business leader and an accomplished economist. He is the co-founder and Executive Chairman of the Board of Ctrip. com (NASDAQ: CTRP), the largest online travel company in the world in gross merchandising volume in 2016, and the largest online travel company in China since 2003. Dr. Liang also served as Chief Executive Officer from 2000 to 2006 and from 2013 to 2016.

Dr. Liang is a Research Professor in Economics at Peking University. He received a PhD in Economics from Stanford University in 2011. He publishes academic papers in top economics journals (such as *The Quarterly Journal of Economics* and the *Journal of Political Economy*) on a broad range of labor economic topics such as demographics, innovation, entrepreneurship, and productivity. He has also written extensively on policies related to demographics and innovation. He is the author of *China Needs More Babies*, the first book published in mainland China that criticizes the "one-child policy."

Prior to Ctrip.com, Dr. Liang held a number of technical and managerial positions with Oracle Corporation from 1991 to 1999 in the United States and China, including Head of the ERP Consulting Division of Oracle China from 1997 to 1999. He received his master's and bachelor's degrees from Georgia Institute of Technology. He also attended the "China Gifted Youth Class" at Fudan University at the age of 15.

Introduction

Since the Industrial Revolution, human society has undergone tremendous economic and social change. Economically, average per capita income grew more than 10 times, and people in developed countries are 100 times wealthier than they were 200 years ago. Historically, innovation has always been the driving force for economic development, but it is only recently that technology companies have become the main engine of wealth generation. In 2011, Apple overtook Exxon, an oil producer, to become the most valuable company in the world. In 2015, five of the top 10 most valuable companies were technology companies founded in the last 40 years. The Chinese Internet giant Alibaba.com is now the most valuable company in China, with over US$250 billion in market capitalization, and is ranked only after the big five U.S. technology companies.

Equally dramatic has been the rise of China over the last 40 years. China has transformed from a backward country to the second largest economy and the largest exporter in the world. Much more significantly, China is catching up as a hotbed of innovation, even more quickly than its near miraculous emergence as a dominant exporter a few decades ago. China's overall spending on research and development is growing at 15% a year (Figure I.1). This is much faster than its GDP growth. China already spends more on research and development than all the European countries combined, and will outspend the United States by 2020 on a purchasing power parity (PPP) basis. Wealthy, developed nations such as the United States, Japan, as well as many of the European countries are naturally concerned whether they can continue to reign supreme in the race of innovation that is set to shape the twenty-first century. These established players are all striving to uncover what the best strategies for competing with emerging innovation powerhouses like China and India are. For technology companies, the key success factor is human resources; analogously, it is the view of this book that demographics, more than any other factor, is the ultimate determinant of success in innovation. This view has huge policy implications in areas such as education, immigration, as well as social policies such as, for example, support offered to growing families.

The largest social change of the last 100 years is in demographics. First, people today live longer lives. In the last 200 years, life expectancy in developed countries has doubled from 40 to 80 years and is still increasing.

FIGURE I.1 The United States is still the world leader in R&D spending, but China is catching up

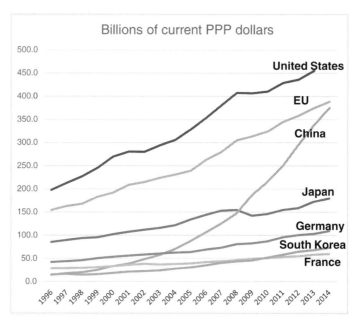

Data Source: World Bank, 2015.

A more recent and abrupt social change is the dramatic reduction in family size over the last 50-year period. The world's average fertility rate has dropped from 4.9 in the 1950s to around 2.5 in the 2010s.

As shown in Figure I.2, fertility rates dropped not just in high-income countries, but also in middle-income and low-income countries. The replacement total fertility rate, defined as the fertility rate required in order for each generation to remain the same size, is 2.1 children per woman (this figure is slightly more than 2, because a small fraction of children die before adulthood). For the first time in human history, the fertility rates in most developed countries as well as in East Asia have fallen below the replacement level. The fertility rates in many developing countries have also been declining rapidly, although they are still above the replacement level. Fertility rates have remained high only in some of the poorest countries, particularly in Africa. Despite the fact that people are living longer, the world's population growth rate has dropped sharply from 1.92% (1960–1965) to 1.18% (2010–2015).

The first country to experience this dramatic social change was Japan. The fertility rate in Japan has been below the replacement level for the last 40 years, and currently is only around 1.4. In 2005, Japan became the first country in the

FIGURE I.2 Fertility rates

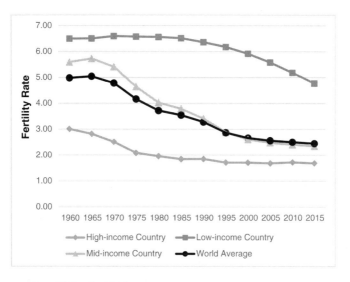

Data Source: World Bank, 2015.

modern era to experience natural negative population growth. In Europe, the total fertility rate is about 1.6, slightly higher than in Japan. In China, the fertility rate dropped below the replacement level in the 1990s and is now only 1.4. Over the next 20 years, China will experience negative population growth and a rapidly aging population. It is estimated that in 10 years' time, India will replace China as the world's largest country in terms of population, but India's fertility rate is also decreasing. The country's total fertility rate has dropped from 5.49 in 1970 to 2.48 in 2013. In some cities in India, such as Delhi, the fertility rate has already fallen below the replacement level. Overall, therefore, the world's population will continue to age rapidly, and many countries will experience negative population growth in the near future. This is a new problem confronting the world, and will have profound implications economically, but particularly in the race of innovation, which is the subject of this book.

This reversal of population growth is unexpected. Two hundred years ago, Thomas Robert Malthus published his influential book *An Essay on the Principle of Population* (Malthus, 1798), in which he argued that productivity improvements always lead to an exponential growth in population size, simply because people have more children when they have more food available to them. A period of plenty results in unchecked growth, and the resulting overpopulation will wipe out the productivity gain by way of famine, war, and other manmade disasters. The net result is that productivity improvement will only lead to growth in population but not in per capita income. Malthus' ideas have very stubbornly retained currency, perhaps because examples of population fluctuation have been so well documented in the natural world. In 1972, for example, a report entitled *The Limits to Growth* by the Club of Rome predicted that a population explosion would lead to energy depletion and resource exhaustion in the subsequent decades.

These predictions have all been proven wrong. Over the last 200 years, both human productivity and population growth have increased. At the same time, natural resources have not run out, as alternative resources and energy sources have been developed. In fact, the price of natural resources has remained relatively stable, and the value of natural resources relative to other assets has declined rapidly. In addition, most developed countries, following the initial stage of swift industrial development, have solved or made significant steps in solving the problems of environmental pollution—once thought to be another potentially disastrous outcome of industrial growth.

Surprisingly, human society has encountered a situation that seems to be completely opposite to what Malthusian economists predicted. In recent decades, as a result of increased urbanization, industrialization, and resulting affluence, people have started to have fewer children. This new demographic scenario has created a different set of social problems, such as labor shortages, aging populations, and a decline of economic dynamism.

There are, of course, many reasons why people choose to have fewer children. The main ones seem to be: a significant increase in the level of women's education, as well as their labor participation; the rising cost of raising children; the reduction in the need for children to directly support their parents in old age; and a modern lifestyle that focuses on individual fulfillment, which itself often competes with the time and effort required to raise children. These topics will be elaborated on in Chapter 1.

How will this unprecedented demographic development affect the global economy (or economies) and society as a whole? Research on the impact of depopulation and aging is very limited, partly because this is a very new phenomenon. The mainstream economic view is that aging is mostly a public finance problem, as the aging population will impose a heavy burden on the public pension system. First, in an aging society, there will be more retirees relative to the working population and expenditure on old age support per worker will increase. The increased expenditure will have to be financed by higher taxes on the current workforce, or simply by postponing retirement. Moreover, consumption among the elderly is different from that of younger people. Older people spend less on houses and cars, but more on medical services and travel. Consequently, a change in the overall industry and economic structure is inevitable. Finally, because an older population has lower income levels, but a higher consumption rate (i.e. a net negative savings rate), capital markets are significantly impacted. Overall, therefore, an aging population will have a profound impact on many industries and the macro-economy as a whole.

It is the view of the author that many negative aspects of an aging population will be mild and manageable. For example, extending the retirement age can largely alleviate the problem of the burden on public pensions in a country where a large segment of the population is older but healthier and more active than it would have been in the past. People today are not only living longer but they remain, for the most part, willing participants in and contributors to the economy. As the majority of jobs in the present day are not physically intensive, it becomes far less challenging to raise the retirement age by a few years.

I will argue in this book that the most fundamental and irreparable problem of aging is the weakening of entrepreneurship and innovation, and a sort of degradation in the vitality of the human population taken as a whole. A 50-year-old may be just as productive as a 30-year-old, particularly when it comes to non-physical labor, but in terms of the ability to learn new skills, or the willingness to take risks such as starting a new venture, the 30-year-old is a much more productive individual. Although medical advancements have allowed people to live longer, humans are still physically most capable in their 20s, and mentally most innovative and energetic in their 30s. More importantly, as Chapter 2 will show, inventors and scientists are most productive in their 30s; most entrepreneurs start their firms at this age.

My research shows that the negative effect of aging on innovation and entrepreneurship can be dramatic. In an aging society, not only is the number of young people reduced, but their vitality itself is diminished. This is mostly because, in an aging society, the opportunities for promotion are blocked by those who are older. In an aging society, because young workers occupy relatively lower-level positions in organizations, they have lower social and political power, fewer skills, and more limited access to financial resources. I will show, consequently, that their entrepreneurship vitality suffers. By analyzing data from Japan and other developed economies, I have found that entrepreneurial activity is much lower in countries with an aging population. For example, in Japan, where the population has been aging rapidly since the 1990s, entrepreneurship and innovation have declined dramatically. This has been, in my view, a contributing factor to a prolonged economic recession experienced by that country over the past 25 years.

In the future, economic competition among the leading countries will mostly be in the fiercely competitive field of innovation. How to boost innovation and entrepreneurship will become the most important problem facing every country. The purpose of this book is to share with the reader my findings regarding the impact of demographic change on innovation and the economy. Furthermore, to help the reader, whether they be a policy maker or simply someone wishing to better prepare themselves for the future, to make good decisions in the present.

The first half of the book (Part I, from Chapter 1 to Chapter 5) will analyze the theories and evidence on the impact of demographics on innovations, as well as their policy implications. After a short overview of global demographic trends in Chapter 1, Chapter 2 strives to demonstrate that demographic factors are the most important drivers fueling innovation capability. The three most important demographic factors affecting innovation are analyzed in this chapter. In addition to aging, the size of the population and the geographical concentration of the population also have a fundamental impact on innovation. Large countries and cities, with easy access to a large consumer market as well as a talent pool, have decisive advantages in innovation.

Chapter 3 discusses how demographics will impact other aspects of the economy, such as public finances, unemployment, and inflation. Chapter 4 clarifies many misconceptions regarding the effects of demographics on various aspects of the economy, including the availability and consumption of resources, as well as the impact on the environment. Chapter 5 discusses the policies that need to be implemented in order to maintain a growing innovative and young workforce. Such policy choices include a pro-fertility policy, an education policy, and an open immigration policy.

The second half of the book (Part II, from Chapter 6 to Chapter 10) will discuss the prospect of future economic competition among the major economic powers, including Japan, China, the United States, Europe, and India. For the major economic powers, demographics and related policy choices are the critical success factors to win the race of innovation.

PART I

Theory and Policy

CHAPTER 1

Global Demographic Trends

In this chapter I will analyze demographic trends globally, as well as trends in different parts of the world, specifically focusing on developed countries, middle-income countries, and developing countries.

Prior to the Industrial Revolution, all countries had a slow population growth that was coupled with high mortality and high birth rates. Because, in pre-industrial societies, the infant mortality rate was high and life expectancy was very low, parents needed to produce as many offspring as possible to make sure that at least one child would reach adulthood.

Let us define some commonly used terms. The birth rate is the number of births per 1,000 people, and the (total) fertility rate is the average number of children per woman, measured by adding up the number of children per woman in each age group at a given time in a country or region.

Over the last 200 years, as a result of the Industrial and Technological Revolutions, the world economy has grown tremendously. Average per capita income grew from just a few hundred dollars to a few thousand dollars globally. As people became wealthier, they had more resources, which in turn enabled them to raise healthy offspring. Advances in medicine and health also resulted in a plummeting infant mortality rate. As a result, life expectancy increased and the world's population grew very rapidly. Although it took some time, people gradually adjusted to the new reality, realizing that, with the lower infant mortality rate, it was no longer necessary to have as many children to ensure that some would survive into adulthood. Consequently, the fertility rate dropped as people became healthier and more affluent, much to the surprise of economists and sociologists, who expected continuous population expansion.

Usually there is a one-generation time gap between decreasing infant mortality and fertility rates. So, when a country begins to become prosperous, a substantially lowered infant mortality rate and a very high fertility rate tend to create a population explosion. Only after 30 to 40 years, approximately one generation later, does the fertility rate begin to decline. Even when the fertility rate falls below the replacement level, the total population will typically continue to grow for one to two generations, simply because people live longer. In most middle- to high-income countries, the fertility rate has dropped below the replacement level at some point in the past, but the total population is still growing, albeit more slowly. However, if fertility rates remain below the replacement level for one to two generations, the population will eventually begin to shrink. That decline will accelerate over time and, meanwhile, with fewer offspring and longer life expectancy, the populations of most countries will age rapidly.

The pattern of demographic transition described above is typical of a post-industrial country. Fertility rates in wealthy European countries began to decline long before the two World Wars, and many of them suffered a heavy population loss during the wars. After a post-war baby boom in the 1950s and 1960s, their fertility rates declined sharply throughout the 1970s and 1980s. By the 1990s their fertility rates had dropped below replacement levels, and it is predicted that their population will begin shrinking (once immigration from different regions is excluded) by 2020. Fertility rates in Russia, Eastern Europe, and Southern Europe have dropped below 1.4, which means that the 0–4 cohort is 30% smaller than the 31–34 cohort. Japan's situation is even worse, with its fertility rate dropping below the replacement level as early as the 1970s, and most recently to only 1.4. Japan was the first major country in the world with a shrinking total population. China had a population explosion during the 1970s and 1980s, as did many other developing countries, but now has a very low fertility rate of 1.3, partly due to its family planning policy. The country's population is expected to begin shrinking by 2030.

As industrialization and urbanization spread globally, more countries are experiencing low and declining fertility rates. India has a fertility rate of 2.5, much lower than it was 10 years ago, and still declining. The only exceptions tend to be the least-developed countries (LDCs) (such as Nigeria), which are still in the very early stages of their demographic transition cycle. Today, more than half of the people in the world are living in a country that has a below-replacement-level fertility rate.

Figure 1.1 shows the population forecasts for the world. The total world population is at 7 billion and counting. However, over the next few decades, the population of many countries—including China—will peak and begin to decline. Even India, which will soon overtake China as the most populous country in the world, will start to have a below-replacement-level fertility rate in 20 years, and its population will peak in 2090. By that time, the world population is likely to peak at around 10 billion people. After that, the world population will start to stagnate or begin to decline.

These population forecasts are based on—and sensitive to—the predictions of future fertility. For example, if each woman, on average, has 0.2 children fewer (or more) than predicted, then the peak world population will be roughly

FIGURE 1.1 Population forecast in major regions of the world: 1950–2300

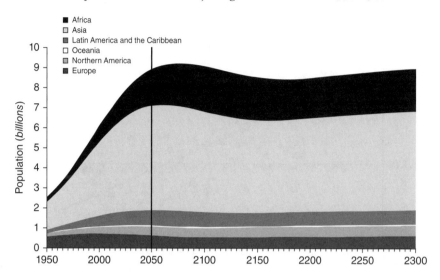

Source: United Nations, Department of Economic and Social Affairs, Population Division (2004). World Population to 2300.

one billion fewer (or more) than predicted. Declining fertility rates can sometimes be surprising in their swiftness; for example, in the 1970s, nobody predicted that China's fertility rate would drop from 5 to only 1.3 by 2010.

The inverse relationship between per capita income and the total fertility rate seems to be strong and universal (Figure 1.2).

I have already mentioned that a decline in infant mortality is one reason why family size has decreased; the other reason is the availability of modern contraceptives. These are the two key factors behind the decline of fertility rates in middle-income countries (with per capita income between US$5,000 and US$20,000) and high-income countries. However, there is not a huge difference between high-income countries and middle-income countries in terms of infant mortality rate and access to contraceptives. One would therefore expect that as a country moves from middle-income to affluent status, the fertility rate should stabilize. What is surprising is that when a middle-income country moves up the economic ladder to become a high-income country, its fertility rate typically continues to drop.

Some high-income countries (and China) have a fertility level below 1.5, an ultra-low level. A 1.5 fertility rate means that each generation is 25% smaller than the previous one, which is clearly not sustainable in the long run. This has become a worrying social problem for many ultra-low-fertility countries,

FIGURE 1.2 The relationship between fertility rate and per capita income in selected countries

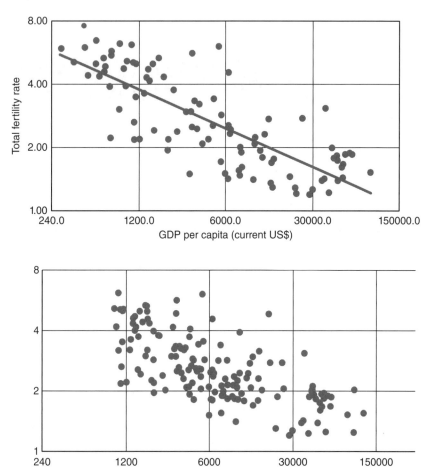

Data Source: U.S. Census Bureau and the World Bank, 2015.

including Southern and Eastern European countries, as well as East Asian countries such as Japan, China, and Korea.

Factors behind Ultra-Low Fertility Rates

First of all, in high-income countries, education is highly valued but also very costly, so it becomes increasingly expensive to raise highly educated offspring. The vast majority of people out there wish not only to be parents, but to also be good parents. And, as a result, will avoid having children unless they are certain that they can assure their children a high-quality education. According to a report published in the *Wall Street Journal* in 2010, the cost of raising a child up until the age of 18 years in the United States is US$222,360, which is four times higher than the average annual income. This figure does not include college tuition. In rich Asian countries, where parents typically put a great deal of emphasis on their children's education, the cost is even higher, because parents usually not only pay for college tuition, but also invest a significant amount of money in tutoring, in order to give their children a competitive advantage in college admission.

Secondly, as a country transitions to a more service-oriented and innovation-driven economy, the education level and labor force participation rate of women increases steadily. In many countries, the college enrollment rate for women is on a par with or higher than that of men (Figure 1.3). In the United States and the United Kingdom, the number of female college graduates is almost 40% higher than that of men. China, though still a middle-income country, also has a higher number of female college graduates than men; moreover, the female labor force participation rate for urban Chinese women is over 60%, which is very high by international standards (Figure 1.4). Naturally, the more time women invest in education and career advancement, the less time they have for raising offspring.

In economies based primarily on agriculture, support in old age is one of the main reasons for raising children. Because agricultural work is physically

FIGURE 1.3 The ratio of female college students to male college graduates in selected countries

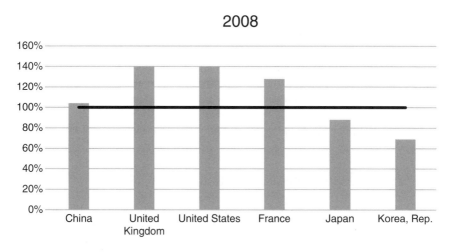

Data Source: World Bank, 2015.

FIGURE 1.4 Female labor force participation rate (% of female population aged 15+)

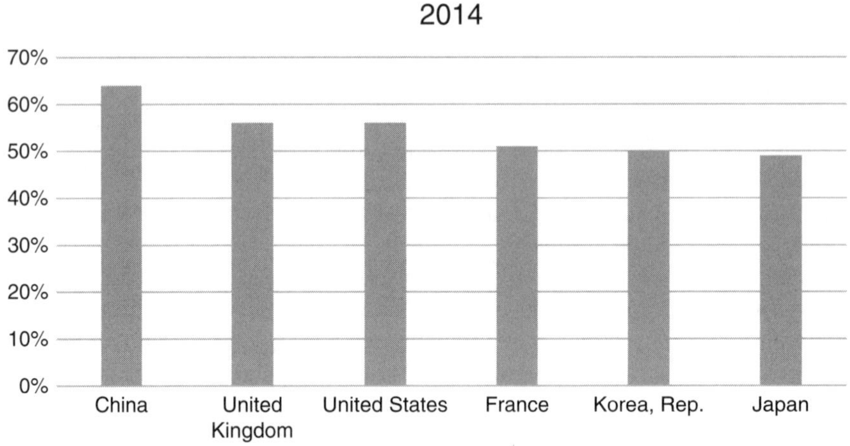

2014

Data Source: World Bank, 2015.

intensive, it is impossible to maintain productivity levels later in life. Having replacement labor available is an important consideration. In contrast, in high-income countries, the elderly rely mostly on their savings and public pension. Children do not, generally, contribute much to supporting their parents, even though they themselves are increasingly costly to raise. Despite governments providing free primary and secondary education, raising highly educated children still requires both considerable time and effort, as well as financial resources. So, from a financial point of view, raising children in a modern economy generates a negative return. Therefore, when high-income countries offer generous pension and medical benefits, the incentive to have children for support in old age decreases.

Lastly, the modern urban lifestyle offers many entertainment and leisure activities, leaving people with less time for raising children. For this and the other reasons mentioned above, it has become a general trend that urban young adults are delaying marriage as well as starting a family at a later age. Some even choose not to have any children, or to remain single for life.

World's Population Forecast by Country

The United Nations, the U.S. census, and the World Bank have all published various population forecasts. Though their assumption and forecast numbers are slightly different, the general patterns and trends are similar. The United Nations forecasts that the world population will continue to grow, but at a

FIGURE 1.5 Fertility map of the world

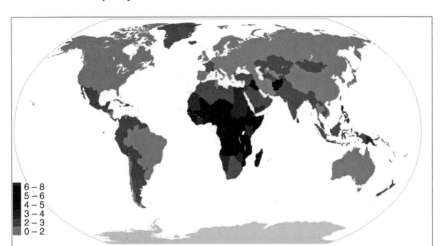

Data Source: Central Intelligence Agency, 2015.

slower rate compared with the recent past. Ten years ago, the world population was growing by 1.24% per year. Today, its growth is 1.18% per year, or approximately 83 million people annually.

Most reports forecast that the world's population will grow to over 8 billion by 2030, and to 9 billion by 2050, peaking late this century or early 2100 at around 10 billion. The population ranking of countries will change. India and China will continue to be the world's most populous countries (each has roughly 18–20% of the world's population). However, it is expected that India will exceed China's population in just five years. Among the current top 10 most populous countries, five of them are in Asia (Bangladesh, India, China, Indonesia, and Pakistan), two in Latin America (Brazil and Mexico), one in Africa (Nigeria), one in North America (the United States), and one in Europe (Russia). Of those top 10 countries, Nigeria has the highest population growth rate, and will surpass the United States to be the third most populous country in the world by 2050. The following six countries are expected to have a population of over 300 million by 2050: India, China, Nigeria, the United States, Pakistan, and Indonesia (Figure 1.5).

Least Developed Countries and Africa

According to the United Nations' *World Population Prospects: 2015 Revision* report, the 48 LDCs as a whole still have a high total fertility (4.3 children per woman in 2010–2015) and fast growing populations, with an average growth rate of 2.4% per year. Although this rate of population increase is expected to slow significantly over the next decade, the population of the LDCs (954 million in 2015) is projected to increase by 39% between 2015 and 2030, and to double to 1.9 billion people by mid-century.

There are 54 countries in Africa, and six of them have a population of over 50 million (Nigeria: 182 million, Ethiopia: 100 million, Egypt: 92 million, Congo: 77 million, Tanzania: 53 million, South Africa: 54 million). The highest rates of fertility among LDCs can be found in Africa.

The fertility rates of selected countries in 2014 were as follows:

Angola: 6.1
Burundi: 5.9
Burkina Faso: 5.5
Chad: 6.2
Congo, Dem. Rep.: 6.0
Egypt: 3.3
Gambia: 5.7
Mali: 6.2
Malawi: 5.1
Mozambique: 5.4
Nigeria: 5.7
Niger: 7.6
Somalia: 6.5
Zambia: 5.4

The current total population in Africa represents only one-seventh of the world's population, but because of its very high fertility rate, the continent's population size and share of the world's population are growing exceptionally quickly. From 2010 to 2015, the population in Africa grew by 2.5% each year. From 2015 to 2050, Africa is expected to account for more than half of the world's population growth. During this period, the populations of 28 African countries are projected to more than double. By 2100 the population of many countries, including Nigeria, will be five times larger. At the same time, the population of Africa is the youngest in the world, with children under the age of 15 accounting for 41% of the population in 2015 and individuals aged 15 to 24 accounting for a further 19% of the population.

By 2050, Africa's population will make up 25% of the world's population (currently only 14%); by 2100, Africa's population will make up 40% of the world's population, amounting to over 4 billion people. However, not all countries in Africa have high fertility rates. The wealthier, more developed Southern African countries, including South Africa, have a fertility rate of 2.3, only slightly above the replacement level.

Other Developing Countries

After the end of the Second World War, the population in developing countries experienced a very high growth rate. Between the 1950s and the 1980s, the population in developing countries grew by 95% while in the same period the population in developed countries grew by only 36%. The rapid growth in this period for developing countries was the result of declining mortality rates and still-high fertility rates between the 1950s and the 1980s.

Following the end of the war, the mortality rate fell sharply as a result of improvements in health care, including access to medical technologies and particularly modern immunization technologies, which reduced the incidence of—or outright eliminated—many infectious diseases. By 1960, the mortality rate in developing countries dropped to 17‰, and by late 1970 to 12‰.

The birth rate, however, only started to decline later. During the mid-1960s, the birth rate in developing countries was very high at 40‰, and only started to decline in the late 1960s. Between 1970 and 1990, the birth rate dropped from 37‰ to 30‰, and continues to drop today. Most countries have a fertility rate between 2 and 3, and some countries such as Vietnam, Iran, and Thailand have a below-replacement-level fertility rate.

The following are the fertility rates of selected developing countries in 2014:

> Turkey: 2.1
> Argentina: 2.3
> Mexico: 2.2
> Iran: 1.7
> Pakistan: 3.6
> Bangladesh: 2.2
> Indonesia: 2.5
> Vietnam: 2.0
> Philippines: 3.0
> Thailand: 1.5

Emerging Countries

Emerging countries here refers to those countries that are significantly poorer than developed countries, but are catching up rapidly economically. In the past, the four "Asian Tigers"—Korea, Singapore, Hong Kong, and Taiwan—experienced very high growth rates. Today, these countries have gone on to join the club of developed countries; consequently, they currently all have an ultra-low fertility rate (lower than 1.5).

During the early 2000s, when commodity prices were high, many resource-rich countries, together with China and India, were considered to be emerging countries. The largest emerging countries—Brazil, Russia, India, and China—are referred to as the BRIC economies. The fertility rates of BRIC countries are as follows:

China: 1.3
Russia: 1.7
Brazil: 1.8
India: 2.5

The general negative relationship between income and fertility rate still holds true here. Of the four countries, India was the poorest with the highest fertility rate, but its fertility rate has already dropped sharply compared with the previous 10 years. China, which is much richer than India, has the lowest fertility rate. Recently, the Chinese government changed its "one-child policy" to a "two-child policy" in an effort to boost fertility. However, the natural fertility rate in China, given its cultural and economic environment, will be similar to that of Korea and Japan, and will likely remain at an ultra-low level (<1.5) without any further policy intervention. I will discuss this topic in detail in Chapter 7.

The BRIC countries are diverse. Russia and Brazil, though rich in resources, suffered greatly after commodity prices collapsed in the mid-2010s. Only India and China's economy experienced continued growth. India's economy grew by 9% in 2016; it is likely to remain the fastest growing major economy in the world. Because of this, it is projected that its fertility rate will continue to drop.

Developed Countries

After the Second World War, and perhaps in direct response to the trauma of it, most developed countries experienced a baby boom with rapid population growth. However, soon after, the fertility rates fell. The United States experienced the biggest and longest baby boom period, between 1945 and 1965. Europe had a smaller and shorter baby boom, while Japan had almost no baby boom period, with the fertility rate declining immediately after the end of the war. By 1980, all developed countries entered a period of slower population growth. Presently, several countries, such as Japan, have a shrinking population.

Currently, no major developed countries have a fertility rate higher than the 2.1 replacement level. The countries with the highest fertility rate are France, the United Kingdom, Australia, and the United States, where fertility rates are slightly below the replacement level. The following are the fertility rates of the selected major developed countries:

France: 2.01
United Kingdom: 1.92
Australia: 1.92

United States: 1.87
Canada: 1.61
Italy: 1.43
Japan: 1.43
Germany: 1.38
Korea: 1.19

Most developed countries have realized that low fertility is detrimental to economic development, and have implemented various pro-fertility policies with varying degrees of success. I will show in later chapters that Japan and Southern European countries seem to be in an ultra-low-fertility trap; as a result, their economies are likely to suffer in the near future.

Religion, Culture, and Fertility Rates

Culture and religion can also affect fertility rates. Figure 1.6 shows the relationship between fertility rate, income, and culture. From top to bottom, three regression lines show the relationship between fertility and income, respectively, for predominantly Muslim countries, for all countries, and for East Asian countries. (Predominantly Muslim countries are defined as those

FIGURE 1.6 Relationship between religion/culture and fertility rate

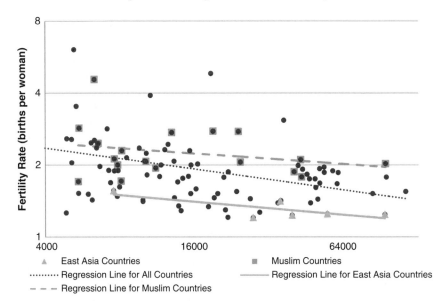

Data Source: World Bank, 2015.

countries with a Muslim population that is more than 50% of the total population.) The negative relationship between fertility and income is robust, as all three regression lines are downward sloping.

However, the regression line of predominantly Muslim countries is positioned higher than the regression line of all countries; in contrast, the regression line of East Asian countries such as Korea, Japan, China, and Vietnam is positioned lower than the regression line of all countries, and much lower than that of predominantly Muslim countries. In plain English, Muslim countries have higher fertility rates than other countries at the same level of income; countries in East Asia have lower fertility rates than other countries at the same level of income. The differences are quite striking. On average, at the same level of income, a Muslim woman produces 0.5 more babies than average, whereas an East Asian woman produces 0.5 fewer babies than average. This pattern, if it persists for several generations, will have huge implications for the long-term cultural and religious makeup of the world.

The West and Christian Countries

Predominantly Christian countries include most of the countries in Europe and the Americas, with populous countries such as the United States, Brazil, and Mexico. The West refers to European countries and affluent New World countries including the United States, Canada, and Australia. These Western nations were pioneers in industrialization and modernization; they are high-income countries whose population has expanded rapidly over the last 200 years, surpassing China around the turn of the last century. However, China overtook them when the country experienced a population explosion in the 1970s. Both the West and China are currently experiencing very low fertility rates, and they will be overtaken by India and the Islamic culture later in this century.

Predominantly Christian countries include the West and non-West Christian countries (mostly Latin America). According to a report issued in April 2015 by the Pew Research Center, as of 2010, Christianity had an estimated 2.2 billion adherents, nearly a third (31%) of the 6.9 billion people on earth. Islam was second, with 1.6 billion adherents, or 23% of the global population.

Muslim Countries

Predominantly Muslim countries comprise more than 50 countries around the world. Generally, they are poor countries, and have higher fertility rates than countries with the same level of economic development. The reason is that Islamic women have lower education levels and lower workforce participation rate when compared to other cultures. As a result, Muslim populations have grown much faster than the world average.

From 2010 to 2050, the world's total population is expected to rise to 9 billion, a 30% increase from today's level. During this same period, Muslims—a comparatively youthful population with high fertility rates—are projected to increase by 70%. In contrast, the number of Christians is projected to rise by 30%. If current demographic trends continue, the Muslim population will be as large as the Christian population by the late twenty-first century.

Though Islamic countries in general have a high fertility rate, Iran is an exception. Like many other developing countries, Iran's fertility rate was high between the 1950s and 1980s. But during the 1990s, as the country become richer, the fertility rate started to drop rapidly; by 2000, its fertility rate dropped below the replacement level. Recently, Iran started to implement a pro-fertility policy.

Recently, a growing number of Muslims have migrated to Europe. France, for example, has a significant number of Muslims from former French colonies, while Germany has many Muslim immigrants from Turkey. The Muslim population depending on various estimates currently accounts for 5–10% of the population in France and Germany. Muslim immigrants have a much higher fertility rate than non-Muslims. In France, for example, the fertility rate of Muslims (2.8) is 40% higher than non-Muslims (1.9). The difference in fertility rate means that the share of the Muslim population in France will double in two generations. This has generated many concerns about the Islamification of Europe. As discussed the higher fertility of Muslims is due to low level of education and workforce participation among women. The big question is whether Muslim women of Europe (and the world) will, given the opportunity, choose education and career over children and family in the future. We will elaborate on this topic in Chapter 9.

If we compare the major religions and cultures around the world, by 2100 Islam may possibly be the largest religion in terms of population as shown in Figure 1.7.

East Asian Countries

The countries in East Asia include Japan, Korea, China, Singapore, Taiwan, and Hong Kong. The people in these countries, either today or historically, were influenced by Confucian philosophy and Chinese written language. The ultra-low fertility rate in East Asia is closely connected with a culture that values education and the pouring of energy into offspring, which is consistent with the traditional Confucian teachings. Amy Chua, author of the popular book *Battle Hymn of the Tiger Mother* (Chua, 2011), is Chinese American and famous for raising her children in "the Chinese way." Like her, many Asian American parents spend a lot of time and effort on parenting, in order to push their children to enter top-ranking colleges. This style of intensive parenting prevents them from having sufficient resources or time to raise a large number of children. As a result, Asian Americans have the lowest fertility rates among

FIGURE 1.7 The relative population ratio of major world religions and cultures

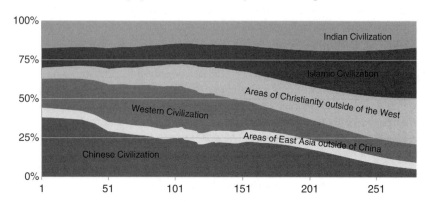

Data Source: 1820–1950 data for China from Zhao and Xie (1988). 1950–2100 data for China estimated from the 6th National Population Census. The rest of the data is from United Nations, Department of Economic and Social Affairs, Population Division (2008). World Population Prospects: The 2008 Revision.

minorities in the United States. Similarly, in East Asian countries such as South Korea, Japan, and China, where college entrance examinations are fiercely competitive, parents spend not only a lot of energy on their children's homework but also a lot of money on cram schools, which are big business in these countries. East Asian parents seem to care more about the quality of the upbringing of their children than their number. As a result, East Asian countries have the world's lowest fertility rates.

The fertility rates of several East Asian regions are as follows:

Mainland China: 1.24
Taiwan and China: 1.07
Hong Kong and China: 1.12
Japan: 1.43
Singapore: 1.19
Korea: 1.19

Notes: Data regarding mainland China is from the National Bureau of Statistics of China; data regarding Taiwan is from Taiwan's Ministry of the Interior; data pertaining to all other countries and regions is from the World Bank.

Out-of-Wedlock Births

In most East Asian countries, out-of-wedlock birth is still a social taboo. The percentage of out-of-wedlock births in Japan and South Korea is only 2% and

2.1%, respectively, while the percentage of out-of-wedlock births in European countries is above 20%. The percentage of out-of-wedlock births in Nordic countries is nearly 50%. A very low out-of-wedlock birth rate in Asian countries would not be a problem if almost every woman got married but, in recent decades, many women have chosen not to marry or enter into a stable partnership. For example, 60% of women under the age of 30 in Japan are unmarried, and 32% of women aged 30–34 are unmarried. Assuming that 20% of women remain unmarried and therefore childless for life, and each married woman has two children on average, the total fertility rate will be only (1 − 20%) × 2 = 1.6.

The low fertility rate in East Asian countries will result in a rapid decline of their share of the world's population. Although East Asia (primarily driven by China's huge population) was the most populous region throughout most of the last millennia, it will soon be surpassed by other regions in the next few decades.

Aging Trends

The population of the world is generally becoming older as a result of low fertility rates and higher life expectancy. According to the U.S. census report on aging, in 2015 the elderly (age > 60) accounted for 8.5% of the world's population. By 2030 it is projected that the number will grow by 50%, representing about 12% of the world's population. By 2050 the percentage will be over 15%, and will continue to increase (Figure 1.8). Japan and Korea

FIGURE 1.8 Median age forecast between 2010 and 2050

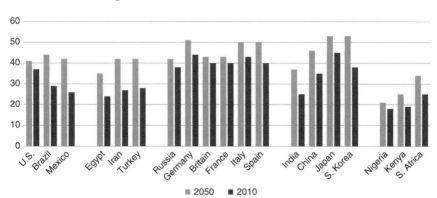

Data Source: United Nations, Department of Economic and Social Affairs, Population Division (2014). World Population Prospects: The 2012 Revision, Methodology of the United Nations Population Estimates and Projections, Working Paper No. ESA/P/WP.235.

FIGURE 1.9 Old-age dependency ratios between 2010 and 2050

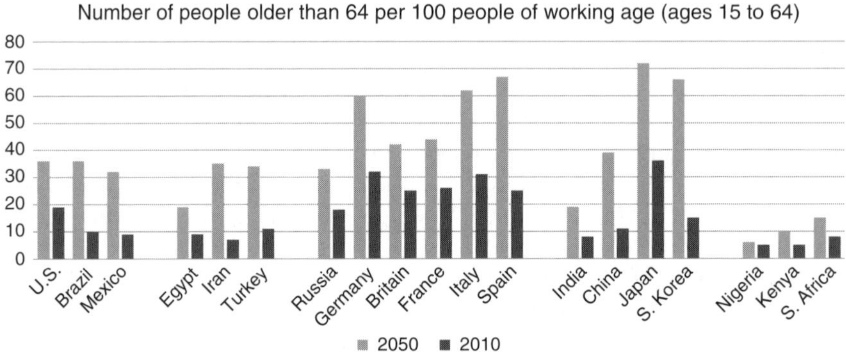

Number of people older than 64 per 100 people of working age (ages 15 to 64)

■ 2050 ■ 2010

Data Source: United Nations, Department of Economic and Social Affairs, Population Division (2014). World Population Prospects: The 2012 Revision, Methodology of the United Nations Population Estimates and Projections, Working Paper No. ESA/P/WP.235.

will be the "oldest" countries in the world, with a median age of 53 by 2050. Several countries in Europe with ultra-low fertility rates—such as Germany, Italy, and Spain—will also have a median age of over 50 by 2050, which is 7–10 years older than it was in 2010. By 2050 China will have a median age of 46, which is 9 years older than it is today.

The old-age dependency ratio measures the number of elderly people (age 65+) per working-age person (age 16–64). The old-age dependency ratio of Japan is expected to increase from 36% in 2010 to 72% in 2050, which will be the highest in the world (Figure 1.9). In 2050 Korea will have an old-age dependency ratio of 66%, four times larger than its 2010 ratio. Germany, Italy, and Spain will also have an old-age dependency ratio of over 60%, while China will have an old-age dependency ratio of over 40%, more than three times today's ratio.

Countries with an aging population and ultra-low fertility rates, such as Japan, Korea, China, Germany, Italy, and Spain, will face negative economic impacts. I will analyze the effects of an aging population in more detail in later chapters.

Urbanization

Another major trend in demographics is that with economic development, more people are living in cities (Figure 1.10). In 2008, more than 50% of the global population lived in a city. That number was only 30% in the 1950s. By

FIGURE 1.10 Percentage of the population living in urban areas by region between 1950 and 2050

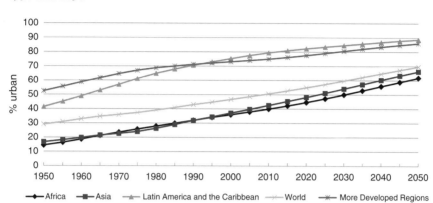

Data Source: United Nations, Department of Economic and Social Affairs, Population Division (2008). World Urbanization Prospects: The 2007 Revision.

2050, more than 70% of the world's population will live in a city. In developed countries, almost 90% of the population will live in a city. This is a direct result of the growth of the industrial and services sector, relative to agriculture.

People are not just moving to cities, they gravitate to large cities. The growth of large cities is much quicker than that of smaller ones. People, especially high-skill workers, are attracted to large cities for a variety of reasons. One reason is that large cities have the economies of scale to provide better public services. But, more importantly, bigger cities have advantages in terms of generating innovations. I will discuss the relationship between innovation and large cities in later chapters.

Table 1.1 lists the population of the 10 largest cities in the world as of 2016. The largest metropolitan area is Tokyo with 37 million people, which is about a third of the total population of Japan. Even though the Japanese population is shrinking, the population in Tokyo is still growing. The largest cities in China are Beijing and Shanghai; their populations have doubled over the last 30 years, despite the tough policies of the Chinese government that restrict people from moving to large cities. The population of Shanghai and Beijing would have been much larger without such anti-migration policies. In the United States, the growth rate of New York, Los Angeles, and San Francisco is much faster than that of smaller cities. As a result, over the last 20–30 years, real-estate prices have increased significantly in these cities due to increasing demand and limited supply. Despite this higher cost of living, large cities continue to attract many highly educated young people and immigrants, making them centers of innovation and entrepreneurship.

TABLE 1.1 Top 10 largest cities in 2016

Rank	City	Country	Population
1	Tokyo–Yokohama	Japan	37,750,000
2	Jakarta	Indonesia	31,320,000
3	Delhi	India	25,735,000
4	Manila	Philippines	22,930,000
5	New York	United States	20,685,000
6	Seoul–Gyeonggi–Incheon	South Korea	23,575,000
7	Shanghai	China	22,685,000
8	Karachi	Pakistan	22,825,000
9	Beijing	China	20,390,000
10	Guangzhou–Foshan (Guangfo)	China	18,760,000

Data Source: Demographia World Urban Areas (12th edn). Retrieved November 17, 2016.

The metropolization of the world will be another potential fertility killer, as people in large cities have fewer children due to the high cost of living, the high pressures and time required to succeed in city careers, as well as urban lifestyles not necessarily encouraging the prioritization of procreation. Large cities in Asia, such as Beijing, Shanghai, Hong Kong, and Taipei, have the lowest levels of fertility in the world. In addition to metropolization, other social and technological trends are likely to reduce fertility further than projected by earlier forecasts. Women, with better education and jobs, are more independent than ever. The advent of modern entertainment, particularly computer gaming, is capturing an increasing share of young people's leisure time. The great demographic shift is just beginning, and is likely to be more dramatic than anticipated.

CHAPTER 2

Demographics and Innovation

In this chapter, I will discuss the relationship between demographics and innovation. I will expound the three key demographic factors of innovation: the scale factor, the agglomeration factor, and the age factor.

Approximately 200 years ago, the English economist Thomas Malthus proposed the famous Malthusian theory of economic demography, which describes the following chain of logic:

> Technological progress can generate a short-term increase in income per capita. However, the increased income soon results in population growth and lower agricultural productivity, which, in turn, eventually wipes out any gain in per capita income.

The Malthusian theory was a good approximation of the world economy before the onset of the industrial age. In agricultural societies, the rate of technological progress was slow, and slow improvement in productivity leads to an increased population but does not result in significant increases in per capita income. Therefore, until the Industrial Revolution, the general pattern was that the world population grew gradually while the per capita income stagnated.

Three hundred years ago, China's agriculture was the most advanced in the world; as a result, it could sustain a much larger population than Europe, which had roughly the same landmass. However, income per capita was not much higher than that of the rest of the world, hovering just slightly above the subsistence level. During the reign of the Kangxi and Qianlong emperors in the 1700s, the population grew from 80 million to 300 million. Despite this growth in population, the per capita income barely increased as overpopulation dragged down productivity and living standards. The Malthusian theory characterizes the Chinese economy of this period accurately.

Although Malthus' theory is an accurate representation of historical realities, it is no longer applicable to modern economies. First, agriculture is no longer as important as it once was. In developed countries, agriculture contributes less than 5% to total GDP. In middle-income countries like China, agriculture only contributes about 10% to the total economy. Almost every modern economy is comprised primarily of industrial and service sectors. Technological progress in these sectors takes place more rapidly than it does in agriculture, and much more rapidly than the growth of population.

Second, the Malthusian logic that posited that increased population lowers productivity is no longer applicable to the industrial and service sectors. In theory, industrial sectors do require raw materials, energy, and other resources, hence a larger population will consume more of these resources and raise the cost of natural resources. Nevertheless, the intensity of usage of resources by the industrial sectors is much lower than the intensity of land usage in agriculture.

Moreover, unlike land, new materials as well as, surprisingly, energy sources are steadily being discovered by way of innovation. For instance, about 200 years ago we used wood and stone to build homes, whereas today we have many alternative building materials such as metal, glass, cement, and rubber. Historically, the main source of energy was wood and coal, but today many new energy sources are available and are becoming ever more efficient, for example solar, wind, and nuclear energy are all important sources of energy for many developed and developing nations. The cost of clean energy, such as solar power, is rapidly declining and approaching that of fossil fuels.

In the modern service and information technology sectors, the requirement for natural resources is even less significant, especially when we examine the Internet and entertainment industry, where products and services can be mass-replicated with almost no use of additional natural resources. For this reason, land and natural resource are no longer bottlenecks in the modern economy. Moreover, innovation becomes much more important for solving problems such as global warming. To keep innovation activity at a high level, a country needs to have a large, young, and highly educated workforce instead of a smaller, stable population as prescribed by the Malthusian theory.

Finally, in the post-industrial age, contrary to Malthus' prediction, the population explosion has not continued indefinitely, as people have had fewer offspring as they have become wealthier. All countries, without exception, have experienced a large decline in fertility rate as they have prospered. In almost all developed countries, the fertility rate has dropped below the replacement level of 2.1. In non-Muslim Asia, typically when a country reaches an average income level of US$4,000, the fertility rate drops below the replacement level of 2.1; when a country reaches a per capita income level of US$10,000, the fertility rate drops below 1.5, which is an unsustainably low level.

Today, most economists agree that the Malthusian theory of demographics and economics is applicable only to the pre-industrial economies or the poorest nations in the world. The world's demographic development has entered a new era, where most of the high- and middle-income countries have a stable or shrinking population; only the low-income countries have high population growth. We therefore need a new paradigm of economic demography.

In the history of modern economics, the most important economist is arguably Adam Smith, who discovered that specialization and trade is the primary source of economic efficiency (Smith, 1776). About 100 years ago, the Austrian economist Joseph Schumpeter developed the theory of "creative destruction," in which he argued that innovation and entrepreneurship is the main driver for long-term economic growth. Schumpeter did not develop a formal economic model, but his insights have been gaining influence in recent years (Schumpeter, 1942).

About 15 years ago, an American economist—Paul Romer—formalized the model of innovation and economic growth (Romer, 1990). I studied this model during my doctoral study in economics at Stanford, and noticed that one of the implications of Romer's model is that a larger population, under certain conditions, can engage more people in research and innovation, which drives faster technological progress as well as productivity growth. There are a few assumptions in the model. One of them is a free-market economy, where people can trade ideas and goods. The other is the enforcement of property rights for both goods and ideas, so that people are motivated by the potential reward of ideas to innovate and start new businesses. This relation of population and economic growth, implied by Romer's model, is opposite to the Malthusian theory. Through the channel of innovation, increased population will lead to faster economic growth and higher income.

Some people will question why China, which has consistently had the largest population in the world, has not become an advanced nation like those in Western Europe and North America. This can be attributed to long-term isolationism stemming from a specific historical event during the early part of the Ming dynasty, when China was the still the world's most advanced nation. Sea navigational technology used by the Chinese admiral and explorer Zheng He in his famous voyage was more advanced than that of comparable explorers from the West, but soon after Zheng He's voyage, for reasons that were mostly accidental, the Chinese emperor stopped all sea-exploring activity and closed the Chinese coast to trade. A few decades later, partly because geographically the Americas are much closer to Western Europe than to China, Western European countries were able to discover, exploit, and populate the new continents ahead of China, helping them expand trade and later initiate the period of innovation that led to the Industrial Revolution. Meanwhile, modern China (since the mid-1800s) suffered a series of wars, as well as failed experimentation with Soviet economic institutions; as a result, China's innovation capability remained underdeveloped and untapped until the Deng Xiaoping era.

In summary, over the last 500 years, China has implemented an autarky policy, which cut off the exchange of ideas with the rest of the world.

Consequently, gradually but steadily, China was left behind in terms of innovation and technological advancement. In contrast, Western countries, building on top of ancient Chinese inventions such as gunpowder and compasses, invented advanced weaponry and sea navigational technology. These inventions helped them to conquer the New World and create a trade economy spanning Africa, the Middle East, and India, a market much bigger than China could access. This is one of the key reasons why the Industrial and Technological Revolutions occurred in Western Europe instead of China.

If a country can stay abreast of the latest technology from the rest of the world, and engage in its own internal research and development to further innovation, then a large population becomes an advantage both in terms of innovation as well as economic development. The economic history of the United States over the last century is a manifestation of this population size advantage.

As far back as 1850, the United Kingdom and Germany were the world's industrial superpowers, whereas the United States was still a heavily agrarian economy. However, once the United States started to acquire technologies and absorb advancements from Western Europe, while at the same time attracting a large number of immigrants, it quickly became a competitor. Soon after its population exceeded that of all of Western Europe, the United States quickly evolved from a technology copycat into a trailblazer of innovation and technology in its own right. Inventors and entrepreneurs, such as Thomas Edison and Henry Ford, led the world in new technology and business organization. Key here was not only their ability to innovate, but also their ability to market and sell their products and methods to a large, unfragmented market. By the 1900s, the United States' income per capita caught up with that of Western European countries, and, soon after, the United States became the largest economy in the world. After 1900, the United States continued to bolster its population by way of immigration, creating economies of scale that far exceed those of other nations. In short, the United States leveraged the advantage of a large population to become the world's leading innovator and an economic superpower. I will elaborate and analyze the scale effect of innovation later in this chapter.

In the Industrial and Information Ages, a large population is an important advantage in terms of entrepreneurship and innovation. The experience of the Chinese economy over the last 40 years is another example. Once China opened its gates to the world in 1978, its huge market quickly attracted large foreign investment. At the same time, its large pool of highly educated workers was able to quickly absorb advanced technology and catch up with productivity. During the last few decades, entrepreneurs in China have been able to create successful indigenous firms to compete with multinationals not just in the domestic market, but also internationally. Huawei and Lenovo, for example, have gone on to become successful multinationals. By 2016, China's per capita GDP reached US$8,000. The size of its market and population will continue to be an advantage for China, not just in catching up with technological progress, but also in spearheading frontier innovation.

In this chapter, I will elaborate the population scale advantage and other demographic factors of innovation.

Economic Theory of Innovation

The most fundamental question in economics is how to make a nation wealthier and thus assure the happiness of as large a number of its citizens as possible. Besides innovation, there are a number of key elements that lead to a country becoming affluent. These elements include a stable government, property rights protection, good infrastructure, sound financial systems, good education, and trade openness. All these elements are important, but which ones are more difficult to implement from a policy point of view? Let us for now ignore LDCs such as those in Africa, since they are missing too many of these key elements; instead, we will focus on middle-income countries. Most middle-income countries do have many of these ingredients already. Thailand, for example, has a stable government, a reasonably good infrastructure, a high college enrollment rate, and a relatively open trade policy, and yet it has not been able to reach high-income status. The reason for this seems to be that the difference between high-income countries and middle-income countries is the capability to innovate.

Innovation is becoming more important. Why is this so? First, the globalized nature of trade has made the rewards that a country reaps from being innovative much greater, because it allows innovation to spread much faster and wider, therefore making more money faster in the process. Moreover, innovation is becoming more important, because innovations have been replacing routine jobs. One can think of innovation as creating new tools to replace humans. In the future, there will be more people creating tools, and fewer people operating them. Robots and artificial intelligence are hot topics today, but they are far from having the capacity to innovate. (Even if robots could innovate, humans would probably never allow it because it is just too dangerous.) Major countries, especially China, have increased their spending in research and development; in the foreseeable future, more capital and resources will be devoted to innovators rather than to operators. Innovation is critical for a middle-income country to transition to a high-income country.

Types of Innovation: Adaptive Innovation and Frontier Innovation

Adaptive innovation is prevalent in economies that are in the "catching up" phase of their development. Adaptive innovation is adjusting or fine-tuning an existing technology to fit the local market environment. For example, KFC in China tweaked their secret recipe by inserting Chinese spices into their fried chicken, while Indian smartphone makers designed a cheaper version to meet the needs of Indian consumers. For poor nations (per capita GDP < US$5,000), adaptive innovation is the primary form of innovation, because it is much easier to adapt existing technologies to local market conditions than to create technologies that are truly innovative, which I refer to as "frontier technology innovation." Frontier technology innovation is not as important at the early stage of economic development, but it is critical for a country that wishes to take the next step and attain high-income status. For the rest of the book, I will focus our analysis on frontier innovation.

Frontier innovation can include the following:

1. Academic theories.
2. Major improvements in processes and technology.
3. New technologies and products.
4. New business models and organization forms.
5. Creative content: music, films, games, etc.

Different types of innovation require different economic and incentive systems. For example, academic theories are discovered primarily by academics who are rewarded by way of faculty ranking and eminence. New business models are usually invented by new firms.

In terms of the degree of creativity, innovation can be either a disruptive innovation (that is, macro innovation) or a continuous (micro) innovation. Large, established firms tend to be very good at continuous innovations, but when it comes to disruptive innovations, typically new firms and entrepreneurs are better at turning them into a commercial success. For example, Japanese corporations today are very good at micro inventions; they continuously improve product quality via gradual enhancements in process and technology. However, they have not been very good at disruptive innovations in the last 20 years (I will analyze the reason for this later).

Historical Trends of Innovation

From a global standpoint, is the speed of innovation increasing or decreasing? To answer this question, let's first see how innovation is measured. There are many ways to measure innovation. One common way is to look at the number of patents. By most measures, the speed of innovation is becoming faster, although it is not accelerating rapidly. Even though most innovations are accidental, at a macro level, more investment in innovation generates more

FIGURE 2.1 Trend in age at "first innovation"

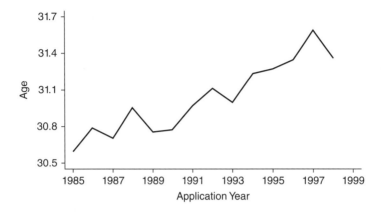

Source: Jones (2009).

innovation. As measured by research and development spending, the input in innovation globally has been increasing steadily.

On the other hand, the difficulty of innovating also seems to be increasing. Let us look at the patent data: Figures 2.1 and 2.2 show that the average age of patent applicants is increasing. Meanwhile, the probability that an inventor will switch fields is decreasing. This means that inventors are getting older and have become more specialized. Moreover, Figure 2.3 shows that the average number of co-inventors per patent has increased. During the 1970s, there were

FIGURE 2.2 Trend in field switch for innovators

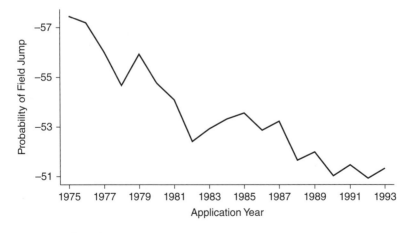

Source: Jones (2009).

FIGURE 2.3 Trend in number of inventors per patent

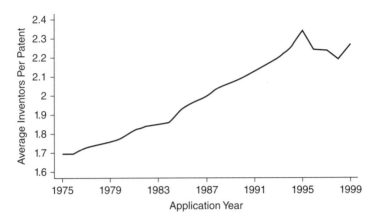

Source: Jones (2009).

only one or two inventors per patent; presently, there are two or three inventors per patent.

So, what does this information tell us? It suggests that innovating has become both more specialized and also more difficult. As Isaac Newton's famous quote that scientific discovery is "standing on the shoulders of giants," so the giant of human knowledge is growing taller, making it more difficult to stand on this giant's shoulders. Four hundred years ago, it was possible for geniuses such as Leonardo Da Vinci to become an inventor in many fields. Today's scientists and researchers tend to specialize in one field, and the classification of that field is becoming finer.

Innovation usually happens by accident. An epiphany moment occurs when combining knowledge from different fields; therefore, as the fields become more specialized, cross-disciplinary cooperation becomes more important. That is why the number of co-inventors per patent has been increasing, as illustrated in Figure 2.3. A good inventor not only needs to be an expert in his/her specialization, but also needs to have cross-disciplinary knowledge and be skilled at working with researchers from other fields. Similarly, successful entrepreneurs also need to have a broad range of diverse skills and job experience. Edward Lazear, a Stanford Economics Professor, analyzed the job history of Stanford MBAs and found that MBA students who take a variety of classes are more likely to become entrepreneurs (Lazear, 2005). In contrast, MBA students who take a more specialized business class— such as finance—are less likely to become entrepreneurs. Having a variety of interests and skills is a key trait of successful innovators and entrepreneurs.

Because innovation is harder, the average age of inventors is increasing. Disruptive innovation and entrepreneurship requires not only hard work, but also risk-taking behaviors that are more commonly found amongst the young. Consequently, the golden window of disruptive innovation and entrepreneurship is getting narrower. In certain fields, a PhD is an entry point to do research, and the number of years required to obtain a PhD is increasing. It is quite common for a student to complete their PhD at the age of 28. I will show later that the best age for entrepreneurship is roughly around 30. Hence, the golden window of opportunity for a PhD graduate to become an entrepreneur is very short.

In summary, the human knowledge base is becoming more extensive, and innovation is more difficult and requires cross-disciplinary cooperation. However, because more resources are invested in research and development, innovation has not slowed down, but actually accelerated in recent years. This is one of the most fundamental trends in human history. When innovations take place steadily, new technology solves resource bottlenecks of economic development, and per capita income continues to grow. If this trend continues, then human society could eventually reach a stage of general abundance.

Social Changes Driven by Innovation

Innovation and technology has driven many social changes throughout history. The rise of the factory is an excellent example. During the Industrial Revolution, production shifted from home production to mass production in large factories. Factories became necessary because the production technologies and processes became more complicated and required many specialized skills, such as machine maintenance, testing, and quality control; therefore, it was impossible for a single person or a few family members to master the whole production process. As the requirement for technical knowledge increased, society's economic activities needed to be divided and more cooperation was necessary; this created the need for factories and modern firms. This also led to the formation of modern labor unions, the so-called "proletariat," and, eventually, the Communist movement.

Second, modern transportation and telecommunication technology brought about globalization. Container shipping technology and freeways helped goods flow at a very low cost, while advancements in aviation technology brought almost the entire world within anybody's reach in a day. Further, the advances in telecommunication have allowed for an almost instantaneous flow of information around the world. With the globalization of goods, people, and information, innovation can spread much wider and faster than ever before. Just like the superstar effect, where a superstar artist can make much more money in a global market, any innovation can reap a much higher reward in a globalized world. Nevertheless, the globalization and innovation trend has increased the gap between innovative workers and routine manual workers. The silver lining of a large income gap is that more people are working hard to be innovative because the rewards are greater.

Third, we have the democratization of college education. To be innovative, one needs to have a comprehensive knowledge base; therefore, one needs more than just technical/vocational training, but rather a general-purpose college education. For example, to be a good game designer, one needs to know the basics of computer science, graphics, history, and so on. The skill requirements driven by innovation and globalization prompt the wider spreading of college education. The rate of college enrollment in developed countries increased from 20% to over 50% in just one generation. In China, the college enrollment rate grew from less than 10% in the 1980s to 30% in the late 2010s. Universities have become centers for knowledge creation and dissemination.

Despite more people than ever possessing a college education, the rewards for such an education have remained high. The wage premium earned by elite college graduates and PhDs is even higher because the reward for innovation is higher. For example, Silicon Valley has a high concentration of highly productive innovators, whose earnings have been growing much faster than those of the average American.

The other side effect of democratization of college education is that more women are attending college and entering the workforce. In many countries, women's college enrollment rate has caught up with men's, and in some instances even surpassed it. This contributes to the decline in fertility rate and family size around the world.

Lastly, the major metropolitan areas of the world have become the innovation centers of the world. As we discussed earlier, the process of innovation demands the participation of more people with different skills and fields of expertize. Large cities have the advantage of providing a large and diverse talent pool; therefore, the best innovative companies are concentrated in large cities. As a result, large cities are becoming larger, more expensive, and economically more important than ever.

Innovation Capabilities of Different Countries

Before we compare the innovation capabilities of different countries, let us first look at how to measure innovation. Figure 2.4 shows all the indicators for measuring innovation. From an input perspective, they include research and development spending and the number of researchers; from an output perspective, they include the number of patents, the export of high-tech products, and the number of academic publications. The Global Innovation Index is a measure (published by Cornell University, along with other organizations) that weighs and summarizes all of these indicators, and yields one number for each country to reflect its overall level of innovation.

Figure 2.5 shows the innovation index of major countries relative to their income. The vertical axis represents the innovation index of each country, and

FIGURE 2.4 Framework of the Global Innovation Index 2012

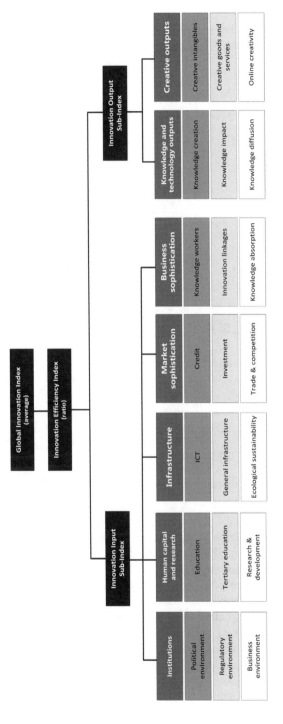

Data Source: Global Entrepreneurship Monitor, 2012.

FIGURE 2.5 Global Innovation Index vs. GDP per capita in PPP$ (bubbles sized by population)

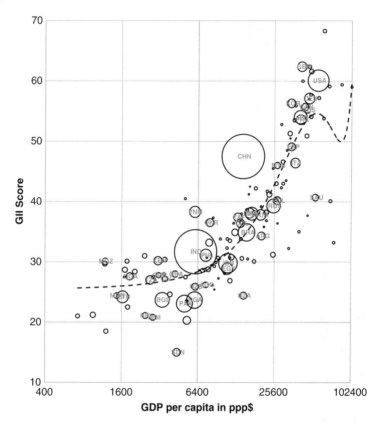

Data Source: Global Entrepreneurship Monitor, 2015; World Bank, 2015.

the horizontal axis represents the per capita GDP income of the country. Each circle on the graph represents a country, and the size of the circle is the population size of the country. The graph shows a clear positive relationship between the innovation index and per capita GDP income—that is, high-income countries tend to be more innovative. This is not surprising, as a high-income country has more resources and time devoted to research and development, and more innovation will create more wealth. We can predict the innovation index from per capita GDP income by drawing an upward regression line, as shown in Figure 2.5.

In Figure 2.5, three shaded regions broadly divide the countries into three categories. The top right regions are the developed countries and among them, the biggest circle is the United States. Underneath the top right region, there are two shaded regions; one is below the regression line and the other is above the regression line. Below the regression line are those countries that are not very innovative relative to their per capita GDP income. Above the regression line are those countries that are more innovative than their GDP income would tend to predict. In this region, two huge circles stand out. The largest circle is China, which is significantly more innovative than countries with a similar level of GDP per capita. India has a per capita GDP income of US $5,000 in purchasing power parity, but is also significantly more innovative than countries with a similar level of income.

In contrast with China and India, many countries' innovation indices lag behind what their per capita income levels predict. For example, many Latin American countries such as Brazil are not very innovative relative to their income. These countries typically have access to rich natural resources, but are low in human capital. If we analyze the recent growth rate of these economies, those countries with a high innovation index relative to their income tend to grow faster than countries with a low innovation index relative to their income. Innovation has become a key differentiator for economic growth for middle-income countries. Moreover, not very obvious from the graph is the "scale effect"; large circles tend to be above the regression line, which means that a country with a larger population tends to be more innovative relative to its income. I will analyze the "scale effect" in more detail later.

People's general perception is that firms in India and China are just low-cost producers or imitators, but relative to other developing countries at similar levels of income, by almost all measures of innovation, India and especially China are a lot more innovative than other developing countries. Let us look at some specific measures. Figure 2.6 shows the number of scientific researchers

FIGURE 2.6 Researchers in R&D (per million people)

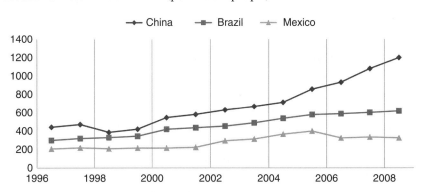

Data Source: World Bank, 2015.

per million people. Since 1996, China has had a lot more researchers per million people than Brazil and Mexico.

How to Promote Innovation?

I have shown that innovation is ever more important, so the next question is: What kind of government policy can promote innovation? Historically, the world's center of innovation has shifted quite a few times. First it was Egypt and other countries in the Middle East, then Greece and Rome, later it was China during the Tang and Song dynasties, and for the last 200–300 years it has been Europe and the United States. So, what are the factors behind these changes? What kind of environment can promote and foster innovation, and what government policy is required to promote innovation? These are the key questions this book aims to answer.

After a successful entrepreneurial career, I chose innovation as my field of specialization for my PhD study in economics at Stanford. I soon learned that even though the question "How to promote innovation?" seems to be the holy grail in the discipline of economics, the academic research on this topic has had limited success. Many years of research have yielded very few findings. Important questions like "Can more education promote innovation?" still remained unanswered. Many people say that the education style of rote learning in China is bad for innovation, because students are taught to conform rather than to be creative and independent. However, there is very little evidence that education style has an effect on innovation. Japan and Korea have a similar education approach to that of China, but their education institutions did not prevent them from becoming major nations of innovation. It seems that education provides the basic skills, and whether a person can be an innovator or an entrepreneur may simply be down to pure luck.

Of course, innovation prowess requires certain basic macro conditions, such as adequate property protection, trade openness, a functioning financial industry, and so on. Today, most middle- to high-income countries can provide these conditions for innovation. However, even though nations such as Malaysia and Argentina have similar macro policies to Korea and China, their innovation capacity and prospects of transitioning to a high-income country are much weaker. So the question once again is: What, besides these macro conditions, are the factors that drive innovation?

Economists have found a few things that seemingly do not work. For example, one thing that does not work is a government's industrial policy to promote innovation in certain "promising" sectors. In a market economy with access to a global market, the reward for innovation is so great that successful innovations have had access to plenty of capital in the last decade—the global venture capital industry has grown very large, so innovation opportunities are well funded by the private financial industry, even in the absence of government funding.

Second, the private financial industry does a better job of choosing the most "promising" technologies. The skills of government employees, hampered by bureaucratic decision-making processes, are usually outmatched by nimble venture capitalists. For example, the Chinese government in recent years has invested a substantial amount of money to support the solar energy industry. With technology advances being very fast, the government was not skilled at picking the right company or the right technology, and lost a large amount of money even though the overall industry is still healthy and growing.

It seems that the best strategy for a government is to provide a fair and stable environment for competition. Instead of investing government money to promote certain companies or technologies, it should simply provide an across-the-board tax cut for all companies. This is the policy recommendation of the so-called supply-side economists who advocate low tax, small government, little regulation, and allowing the market to dictate and reward the winners. Their basic conclusion is that government should "get out of the way" of innovation and entrepreneurship.

Of course, most governments are reluctant to accept this line of reasoning in its entirety, because it leaves them out of the most important of economic activities. It is not surprising that there is no easy fix or panacea for driving innovation. If there was one, many more countries in the world would be able to replicate the policy and become wealthy.

I will examine what governments can do to promote innovation from a demographic perspective.

To look at this problem from a different perspective, let us look at the key strategies to create a successful innovative company. Over the last 30 years, the churn rate of Fortune 500 companies has accelerated. The most valuable companies in the world—Apple, Google, Amazon, and Microsoft—are all successful innovators. If you ask the executives from these companies what the successful factors are, their answers could be quite different from each other, but they all mention one factor: the ability to attract top talent.

Michel Porter, a Business Strategy Professor famously known for his five-factor model of a successful business strategy, applied his theory of competitive strategy of companies to the competitive strategy of nations (Porter, 1990). In his model, there are four key elements for a nation to be successful in an industry: factor endowment, local demand, component industry, and local competition. My view on Porter's four-factor model is that all four factors are actually directly connected to population and demographics. A large population means a large talent pool (i.e. factor endowment) and a big local market (i.e. local demand). A large market also brings a more developed and complete component industry. Lastly, a large population and market can nurture more competitors. Therefore, a large population seems to be the most important source of advantage in innovation. Also, I will argue that not just size but also the age structure and the distribution of population are important factors in innovation.

There are three main channels through which demographics affects innovation:

1. The scale effect.
2. The agglomeration effect.
3. The aging effect.

The Scale Effect

Economies of scale are ubiquitous in the modern economy. The unit cost of producing 1,000,000 gadgets is usually much lower than the unit cost of producing 1,000 gadgets. In a typical service industry, the unit cost of providing a service (e.g. banking, postal, telecommunications) is also much lower in a large city than providing a similar service in a small village.

Economies of scale are an outcome of specialization and the division of labor. With specialization and the division of labor, each firm or individual can focus on a more specific task, and therefore become more efficient. The Ford Motor Company, in the early 1900s, leveraging the scale advantage of the U.S. auto market, was the first to popularize the assembly-line manufacturing process in which each worker specialized in just one task. China currently has the largest market in the world for most manufactured goods, which helps Chinese manufacturing companies become the most specialized and efficient in the world.

For innovation, the scale advantage of a large country is even bigger. For example, a movie (or a website) for a market of a billion people can have a budget 10 times larger than a movie (or a website) for a market of only 100 million people. For another example, the leading Internet travel brand in China, Ctrip.com (which I co-founded in 1999), leveraging the enormous size of the Chinese population, can afford to hire 5,000 software engineers. In contrast, a similar company in Japan, with only one-tenth of China's market, can only afford to hire a few hundred engineers, whereas a similar website in Taiwan can only afford to employ fewer than 100 engineers. This, of course, assumes that they are confined to the local market and unable to tap the global market. The ability to tap the global market almost always comes after local success and not before it. Even in a global access context, a larger local market can be an advantage as it is possible to outcompete other firms on a global stage when one's local market enables the support of more extensive resources.

It should be to no one's surprise that China has the best high-speed train technology, because the amount of research and development it can afford to invest in this area is so much bigger than that of smaller countries. Japan has the best high-end manufacturing technology; however, with a small domestic market, it is not able to compete with China in high-speed train technology, nor is it able to compete with the United States in the construction of commercial planes. Most new drugs are tested and approved in the United States first, because new drug research requires very expensive, large-scale clinical trials on thousands of subjects, and the United States has a market size advantage over other developed countries.

Some would argue that with globalization, even a small country has access to the global market. This is partially true, because shipping costs and trade barriers today are low. A company in a small country can export standardized manufacturing products around the world. For example, Nokia, a Finnish company, was able to capture a large global share of the mobile phone market. However, for service industries, a large domestic market is still a decisive advantage. Domestic companies have an advantage over foreign competitors because, in service industries, innovators need to interact deeply with the local culture, language, business, and legal environment, all of which are integral parts of the service product offering. A service company typically needs to experiment and tailor their innovation to the domestic market first, and only after it achieves volume production and good profitability can it adapt and export its innovation to other countries. Manufacturing industries in the United States, Japan, and Germany all have a large number of top manufacturing brands, but in service industries, U.S. companies, helped by the scale advantage of the U.S. market, have a disproportionately large share of the top service brands in chain restaurants, hotels, entertainment, and so on. Companies such as Starbucks, Disney, and McDonald's had all grown very big and profitable in the U.S. market before they went on to dominate the world market with their tried and tested business models.

This scale advantage is even more decisive in the Internet service industry. In an industry where network effect is huge, the winners will be those companies who can attract a critical mass of customers first. If, for example, 10 million customers represent a "critical mass," then to reach the critical mass, the required penetration rate for the U.S. market (with a population of 300 million) is 3%. For Japan (with a population of 100 million), the required penetration rate is 10%. For China, it is less than 1%. For this reason, innovations typically reach a critical mass in the U.S. market earlier than they do in the Japanese market. U.S. Internet companies such as Google, Apple, Facebook, Amazon, and Expedia, after successfully reaching critical mass in the domestic market, quickly expanded to other countries and dominated the world market. A head start for Internet/software companies in a large domestic market is often enough to differentiate a winner from a loser. Nokia was successful when the mobile phone was just a gadget and a simple communication device; when the mobile phone became a computer, software, and Internet product combined, Nokia was no match for Apple.

With a large market, there will be more competitors too, which will intensify the pressure to innovate and raise productivity levels. The U.S. and Chinese Internet markets are the most competitive, and venture capitalists are sometimes willing to support even the second- and third-place players in these markets, whereas in a small country, venture capitalists are usually only able to support the market leader.

The scale advantage of the United States in innovation has been growing, as innovation plays an ever-increasing role globally. In many high-tech and creative industries, the United States has become the global center of innovation. New York is the innovation center of the world for the financial industry; Los Angeles is the innovation center of the world for the film and entertainment industry; Silicon Valley is the innovation center of the world for the information technology industry. Universities in the United States have also become the centers of academic research in all of these areas. The U.S. dollar is the world reserve currency, and English is the international language. Indeed, the dominance of the U.S. economy has been growing in all areas, until the recent emergence of China.

At four times the size of the United States, China has surpassed the United States as the world's largest market for manufactured goods. Similar to U.S. companies, Chinese companies such as Huawei and Lenovo, after reaching critical mass and becoming successful in the domestic market, have also grown into global competitors for U.S. multinationals. China is also quickly catching up with the United States in terms of the size of the service industry. China's travel, logistics, banking, and health care industries are currently only second to those of the United States. In the future, we will see more global service brands from China. China's movie industry is quickly catching up with that of the United States in size. Although Chinese movies may never become as successful as Hollywood films (they might), they will certainly have budgets that will be the envy of the world.

China already has a larger Internet market than the United States. None of the U.S. Internet giants are able to dominate China in the same way as they have dominated much of the rest of the world. Some people think that this is partly due to the Chinese government's ban on certain foreign companies. However, the reality is that when Google exited the Chinese market, it had only 30% of the market share compared with its local rival, Baidu, which had 60% of the market share. Other examples, such as Amazon being soundly beaten by Jingdong.com, Expedia losing out to Ctrip.com, and eBay being outmatched by Alibaba.com, illustrate that Chinese indigenous Internet companies are strong, and U.S. Internet companies are not able to leverage their scale advantages in China in the same way as in the rest of the world. Again, this is the result of the size of the indigenous market. A highly successful local player may be able to leverage a sufficient amount of resources to outcompete a U.S. entrant, however successful they are in the United States and globally.

Innovations in the service and Internet sectors are new business models and practices, which are typically not patentable. Chinese Internet companies usually imitate successful U.S. innovations as they come out, and adapt these innovations quickly to the Chinese market, which is usually already large enough to have a critical mass. Typically, by the time U.S. innovators come to the Chinese market, it is often too late, as Chinese imitators have already built a formidable lead. A prominent venture capitalist commented that for a U.S. Internet company to be successful in China, they need to enter the Chinese market and the U.S. market at the same time. However, it is often too difficult a task for a new startup to try to capture the Chinese and U.S. markets at the same time.

Recently, breakthroughs in artificial intelligence (AI) technologies are transforming many industries. The most promising AI technologies are machine learning technologies, which require a huge amount of data. Chinese Internet companies, with a vast market, are endowed with a huge amount of data. According to a McKinsey report of 2016, China has become one of the leading global hubs for AI innovations, partly due to its data advantage.

In many lectures, when I have emphasized the importance of population in innovation, I have been asked about Israel, a tiny country with an exceptional entrepreneurial and innovation capability. I am not trying to say that population size is the only factor, other factors such as culture and ability are also important, but the ability to scale quickly is critically important.

Even Jewish people are not as successful in smaller countries as they are in larger countries. There are about 20 million Jewish people in the world, about one-third live in Israel, one-third live in the United States, and the final one-third live in the rest of the world. Of the 10 richest Jewish people in the world, eight of them live in the United States, two of them in Russia, but none in Israel. Among them are the founders of Google, Facebook, and Oracle. Because of the limited growth prospect in their small home market, many entrepreneurs in Israel sell their businesses to large international firms, and they are much less successful than Jewish entrepreneurs in the United States.

CAN THE UNITED STATES WIN THE HUMAN RESOURCE RACE? A large population also means a large talent pool. Even though the U.S. population is only one-quarter that of China, as shown in Figure 2.7, up until 2005, the number of U.S. college graduates still exceeded the number of Chinese graduates. College education is a basic requirement for research and development, and the number of college graduates reflects the size of human capital upon which innovation activities can draw. Throughout most of the 1900s, the United States has led the world in number of college graduates.

In recent years, with the expansion of college education, China has surpassed the United States in terms of number of college graduates. Many people doubt the quality of Chinese college education; it is often said, for

FIGURE 2.7 Population with a college education in China and the United States

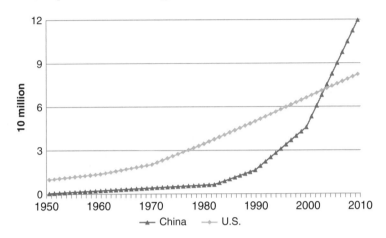

Data Source: The Census Report of China and the U.S. Census Bureau, 2010.

example, that the quality of higher learning must be poor because China has not produced many Nobel Prize winners. However, the lack of Nobel Laureates is not unusual in the early stages of a newly emerging innovation powerhouse. Usually, top-quality academic research lags behind commercial innovation, and Nobel Prize awards, which usually reward scientists for innovative research that took place decades earlier, come much later. While the U.S. economy was the largest and most innovative in the 1900s, it was only after the Second World War that the United States became a leader in academic research and produced a significant number of Nobel Prize winners.

Table 2.1 shows the top five countries by number of Nobel Prize winners in science, including physics, chemistry, and economics. The Japanese economy became one of the leading innovators of the world in the 1980s, but not until after 2000 did it rank high in the league of Nobel Prize winners. We know that Japan's innovation has actually declined since the 1990s; the Nobel Prize actually reflects its scientific research capabilities in the 1980s—as I have pointed out, the prize tends to be awarded to winners some decades after their innovation is first pioneered.

In Table 2.1, the numbers in parentheses are the number of native-born scientists. This shows that in the United States and the United Kingdom, there are a large number of foreign-born Nobel Prize winners. In contrast, almost all Japanese winners are native-born scientists; this shows the strength of the United States and the United Kingdom in attracting foreign talent. I will revisit the relationship between immigration and innovation in later chapters.

TABLE 2.1 The countries with the most Nobel Prize winners in science

	1949–1999	2000–2013
United States	169 (135)	64 (44)
United Kingdom	44 (33)	13 (10)
Japan	5 (5)	11 (10)
Germany	40 (37)	7 (6)
France	13 (12)	7 (4)
Korea	0 (1)	1 (1)

Note: The number in parentheses is the number of native-born scientists.
Data Source: The official website of the Nobel Prize, 2013.

In addition, academic research does not correlate perfectly with commercial innovation. The United Kingdom has a similar number of Nobel Prize winners as Germany, but in innovation (measured by number of patents) it has been much weaker. Korea thus far has had almost no Nobel Prize winners nor a world-class university, but still is able to foster innovative companies such as Samsung.

Over the next few decades, the college enrollment rate of many middle-income countries will increase to reach similar levels to that of developed countries; consequently, the number of college graduates will be a higher proportion of the total population in these countries. In China, the number of college students reached 33 million in 2012 compared with only 19 million in the United States. In India, the number of college students is expected to reach 26 million by 2020.

In the long run, India is likely to overtake China in having the largest number of college students. The low fertility rate in China will reduce the young cohort size significantly, and by 2040 the cohort size of 18- to 22-year-olds in China will be 40% smaller than that in India. By 2040, even if China's college enrollment reaches 60%, India will still have more college students than China, so long as India's enrollment rate exceeds 35%.

Of course, education quality also matters. Currently, U.S. universities are the best in the world. Moreover, although the United States has a smaller population, it has the advantage of attracting top talent from around the world. Consequently, the race for human capital among China, the United States, and India will be an interesting one to watch. I will discuss this in more detail in later chapters.

The Agglomeration Effect

In addition to population size, the geographic distribution of the population also matters. Modern industries tend to concentrate in the same region, with the necessary infrastructure in place, as well as ready access to supply chain and labor pool. The U.S. automobile industry concentrates in Detroit, while the Japanese automobile industry concentrates in Nagoya. The Chinese electronics industry has a high concentration in Southern Guangdong and Jiangsu regions. By being closer to upstream and downstream companies, a firm can reduce many costs, such as transportation costs, procurement costs, and other communication costs.

Thanks to its population size, China has the largest and most complete manufacturing industry cluster in the world, with a concentration of many manufacturing companies in densely populated Southern and Eastern regions. Anybody who invents a new product can find hundreds of suppliers capable of making the product quickly and cheaply.

China's cost of labor is no longer the lowest in the world. With a per capita GDP of US$7,500 in 2015, China's labor cost is already several times higher than that of Vietnam, Indonesia, and many other South East Asian countries. From a labor cost perspective, many multinational firms should have moved out of China by now. But many firms have found that for complicated products that require a non-trivial supply chain, smaller countries are no match for China, despite their much lower labor costs. That is the why most high-tech products are still manufactured in China today. In high-end manufacturing, many technologies, components, and manufacturing processes are interrelated, and advantages in one sector can be extended to related sectors. China is leveraging its agglomeration advantage in high-end manufacturing to dominate new manufacturing industries such as solar, wind, and high-end electronics, despite its rising labor costs. No doubt, China will continue to shift away from simple, low-value-added products, but for high-end manufacturing, its agglomeration advantage in the supply chain will continue to be important.

THE AGGLOMERATION OF TALENTS   The distribution of high-tech companies is even more uneven than that of manufacturing companies. In the United States, a large number of innovative companies concentrate in Silicon Valley. Six of the top 10 high-tech companies—Google, Cisco, HP, Apple, Oracle, and Facebook—are all in Silicon Valley, and almost half the venture capital in the United States is invested in Silicon Valley. Silicon Valley, a small area from San Francisco to San Jose, has attracted the best talents from around the world, which in turn has led to the creation of some of the most valuable companies in the world.

In manufacturing, the agglomeration effect is a result of the proximity of related firms. The agglomeration effect in high-tech industries is a result of the proximity of creative talents. When creative people get together, the effect is like a chemical reaction. In the evenings in Silicon Valley, restaurants and coffee shops are full of engineers discussing the next technological break-through and startup opportunities.

With many high-tech firms being so close to each other, it is easy for workers to move between the firms. Inter-firm mobility is very high in Silicon Valley. If an engineer has a creative idea but is unable to secure funding or support from his company, he can easily take the idea to a different company, or he can start a new company with venture capital funding. High mobility not only enhances the exchange of ideas and innovations, but also allows startup firms to find talent quickly in order to scale their ideas or build on their initial success. Moreover, high mobility fosters a strong culture of entrepreneurship and joining entrepreneurial firms. Critically, high mobility also lowers the cost of failed entrepreneurship, because it is easy for people in a failed startup to find a new job. The necessary condition for high mobility is the agglomeration of many high-tech firms in one region.

Secondly, large cities not only provide for more efficient matching of talent with firms, but also allow more talents from diverse disciplines to work together. The recent innovations in Internet and software technology often require multidisciplinary cooperation, which further strengthens the advantage of large cities. Large cities are particularly attractive to highly educated young singles and couples, because, in the former case, it is easier to find a partner and in the latter case, because both spouses have a greater chance of finding good careers—despite the relatively high cost of living. In recent years, as the agglomeration effect increases, large cities across the world have grown larger and more expensive, while smaller towns, in particular, have witnessed a reduction in population and competitiveness.

The agglomeration advantage is a network effect of a large pool of innovative human resources multiplied by the size of the network. If one geographic region becomes the center of innovation for one industry, then the agglomeration effect tends to self-reinforce, and the center grows larger and more dominant over time. Outside Silicon Valley, cities like Boston also have top universities such as Harvard and MIT, but the dominance of Silicon Valley as the center for innovation has lasted for over 40 years, despite the very high cost of housing. Once a place becomes the center for innovation, the network effect kicks in, and it is very hard for other places to catch up. If we extrapolate from this logic, there should only be one center for each industry in each country. With globalization, there may even be only one center for each industry in the world.

Given that these big cities are more efficient and innovative, what prevents everybody from living in one city? Let's hypothesize: if the earth is no longer habitable, and we all move to a different planet, are we going to spread out evenly on this planet? Such a result would be highly unlikely. We are more likely to live closely together in one giant city. The current distribution of the world's population can be explained in historical terms; when economies were based on agricultural production, the population needed to spread out to do farming; during the Industrial Revolution, the population needed to be close to minerals and ports. Today, high-tech and service firms are the main drivers of economic activity; as a result, more people concentrate in large cities that are the centers of innovation.

A similar pattern is emerging in China too. Large cities in China have grown much faster than other cities. Housing prices in the top 30 cities have soared, while housing prices in smaller cities have stalled or fallen. The difference in housing prices between first-tier cities and small cities in China is now over tenfold. The worry is that there is a real-estate bubble in the first-tier cities. In Shanghai, Beijing, and Shenzhen, the housing price to income ratios are among the highest in the world. In general, people can move more freely within a country but not internationally, so there is a positive relationship between the population of a country and the population of its largest city. Given China's population, it is to be expected that its housing price to income ratio will be the highest in the world for the city centers of its top-tier cities.

Let's look at a graph to confirm these findings. Figure 2.8 shows the relationship between a country's population and the population of its largest

FIGURE 2.8 Relationship between country population and the population of its largest city

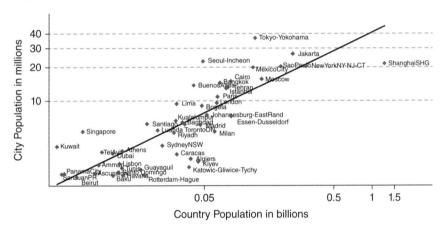

Note: I used data from Demographia (2013) to analyze the populations of major metropolitan clusters around the world. The definition of a metropolitan cluster here is a contiguous urban area, regardless of administrative city limit. Demographia applies a consistent classification rule to the satellite pictures to define a metropolitan area, and then uses the demographic data of the encompassing regions minus the agricultural population to reach the population of a metropolitan cluster. Of all the city population data sources, the data from Demographia is the closest to the economic definition of a metropolitan area, and is measured consistently across the world.

Data Source: Demographia and World Bank, 2013.

city. The horizontal axis is the population size (in log scale) of the country, while the vertical axis is the population size of the largest city in that country. As shown on this graph, there is an obvious positive relationship between the population size of a country and the population size of its largest city. Not surprisingly, the more people in a country, the more of them live in the largest city.

With the exception of the Chinese cities, Asia's mega cities are generally above the regression line, which means that their populations are larger than their country populations predict. Tokyo, Jakarta, and Seoul are the largest metropolitan areas of the world. New York, Paris, and London are right on the regression line, which means that their sizes are just as predicted by their country population sizes. The largest city of Germany, Berlin, is much smaller than it should be. The reason is that Berlin's population did not grow from the 1940s to the 1990s, because it was geographically surrounded by East Germany during the Cold War. Since the reunification of Germany, Berlin, as the largest city in Germany, is growing rapidly, something that is a reverse of the general trend for the German population as a whole.

Noticeably, Shanghai is significantly below the regression line. If we stick to our analytical logic, Shanghai (and Beijing) should have much larger populations than they currently do. The largest city in the world is Tokyo, with 37 million residents; Seoul has 23 million residents and is still growing. China's population is 10 times larger than Japan's and 25 times larger than Korea's; however, Shanghai and Beijing, its largest cities (due to the past policy of restricting migration), have only 23 million people, which is too small to fully take advantage of the agglomeration effect. Therefore, Shanghai and Beijing are likely to grow significantly in the future, and real-estate prices in central Shanghai and Beijing will likely be amongst the highest in the world, rivaling those of Manhattan and Central London.

Recently, the city governments of both Beijing and Shanghai have been concerned about overpopulation; they have made efforts to turn away new migrants. However, limiting the size of large cities will not only hurt innovation, but is also unnecessary because congestion and environmental problems can be solved by way of good city planning, regulations, and innovation itself. Building high-speed rail connections between different parts of the city is one way to solve the congestion problems of mega cities. Silicon Valley is currently very congested, and one way to enable more people to live there is to build an efficient high-speed public transportation system such as the one in Tokyo. With over 37 million residents, Tokyo has a very efficient public transportation system. I will examine the topic of demographics and urban planning in more detail in Chapter 4.

The Aging Effect

The third channel through which demographics affects innovation is the aging effect.

FIGURE 2.9 The age variation of different cognitive skills

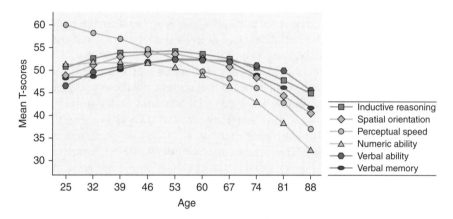

Source: Hedden and Gabrieli (2004). Reprinted by permission from Macmillan Publishers Ltd.

AGE AND COGNITIVE ABILITY   In general, a person's physical ability peaks in their 20s. In a modern economy, however, what drives productivity is cognitive skill. How do cognitive skills change as one ages? Different cognitive skills age at different rates, as shown in Figure 2.9.

As shown in Figure 2.9, some cognitive skills hold up very well in old age. Verbal skills, for example, peak in the 50s and hold up very well until the 70s. Most cognitive skills, such as numerical skills, peak around the 30s and 40s, but fall significantly after the 60s. Perceptual speed, which reflects the ability to absorb new information, drops quickly after the 20s, which is consistent with the general finding that learning ability usually peaks at a young age.

In general, a person in his/her 30s or 40s is the most creative, because they have already accumulated the necessary academic and business knowledge, yet are still energetic, and can think and learn quickly.

An American economist, Benjamin Jones, analyzed the 300 greatest inventions over the last 100 years (Figure 2.10), and found that 72% of the great inventions were made by inventors aged between 30 and 49, and 42% of the great inventions were made by inventors in their 30s (Jones, 2005).

The age distribution of Nobel Laureates in science (physics, chemistry, medicine, and economics) over the last 100 years also showed similar results; most of the scientists made their revolutionary breakthrough in their 30s (Einstein discovered the theory of relativity at the age of 26). Of course, Nobel Laureates are not your average scientist or inventor. So let's look at the age distribution of patent inventors.

Figure 2.11 shows the age distribution of U.S. patent holders. As shown, patent productivity declines after the mid-40s. Particularly in the information

FIGURE 2.10 Age and great invention

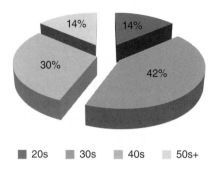

■ 20s ▨ 30s ▨ 40s ▨ 50s+

Data Source: Jones (2005).

technology field, the most productive and creative engineers and scientists are in their 30s and some even in their 20s.

INNOVATION AND ENTREPRENEURSHIP It is not enough to have just engineers and scientists; entrepreneurs are critical to making disruptive inventions commercially successful. In economics, the topic of entrepreneurship is a difficult subject to analyze. Even the definition of entrepreneurship is elusive. One definition is firm formation, where an entrepreneur is anybody who registers for a new legal entity. By this definition, however, not all entrepreneurs are innovative. Owners of coffee shops can be called entrepreneurs, but

FIGURE 2.11 Age distribution of U.S. patent holders

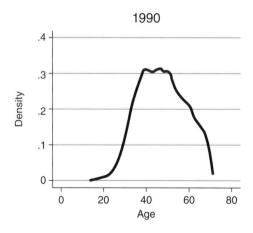

Data Source: National Bureau of Economic Research Patent Database, 2006.

they are just small business owners. Regardless of the definition, only innovative entrepreneurs are economically important. Innovative entrepreneurs may not be the sole owner of a startup, because the firm may have other financial investors like angel investors or venture capitalists, but what makes entrepreneurs different from researchers or professors is that they receive a big slice of the reward for their innovation.

Entrepreneurship is a critically important driver for innovation, especially disruptive innovations, which are, by definition, unpredictable. In contrast, micro innovation is usually a predictable improvement of existing technologies or processes. Large, established firms are good at micro innovations, whereas disruptive innovations usually come from new firms. For example, Amazon is an entrepreneurial firm that has disrupted the retail industry, and Uber is a new firm that has disrupted the taxi industry.

So why are incumbent firms not very good at disruptive innovation? The primary reason seems to be because incumbent firms tend to have a vested interest in the status quo (i.e. they benefit from the existing ecosystem and have little incentive to disrupt its functioning and risk their vested interest). For example, the executives at Barnes & Noble did not have the vision to create the best possible online book store. They created an online store only when they were forced to do so by competition from Amazon. Moreover, for disruptive innovation, the incumbent firms are slowed down by their bureaucracy. Lastly, the executives in large firms do not have the high power incentives of the entrepreneurs, who share a much bigger slice of the reward of success. Xerox invented many great technologies—such as the mouse, the local area network, and the graphical user interface—but the managers at Xerox did not have the incentive or flexibility to make risky investments to commercialize these great inventions. In contrast, entrepreneurs take more risks, have more decision power, and obtain a much bigger slice of the eventual reward.

Why is it important for innovative entrepreneurs to have a bigger slice of the reward? First, most innovators will work harder when there is a larger potential for reward. Moreover, only when the economic interest of the innovator is aligned with that of the business owner will the innovator be willing and able to take the right level of risk to make their innovation a commercial success. For micro innovations, where the outcome is reasonably predictable, large firms can design an effective bonus/reward system for innovation. But for disruptive innovation, which is inherently unpredictable, it will be impossible to design a bonus system that adequately rewards the innovator. The best bonus system is to offer a big slice of the profit, effectively making the innovator an entrepreneur. This is the reason why disruptive innovations can thrive only in a startup firm, but not in large incumbent firms, where the economic interest of the innovators is very different from that of the entrepreneurs.

Of the 10 largest high-tech companies, all but one company (the exception being IBM) were created over the last 40 years by young entrepreneurs before the age of 40; these firms quickly turned the latest technological inventions into a commercial success. After they grew very large, they invested heavily in research and development to retain a competitive advantage, which in turn sped up innovations in their industry.

AGE AND ENTREPRENEURSHIP   I co-founded Ctrip.com at age 29 with three other co-founders, two of whom were aged 33 and the third aged 36. I have many entrepreneurial friends, and most of them were in their 30s when they started their companies. It seems like 40 is an inflection point: people are much less entrepreneurial in their 40s than they are in their 30s.

My anecdotal observation is borne out by the Global Entrepreneur Monitor, a study by Babson College and London Business School, which surveyed hundreds of thousands of entrepreneurs in many countries. The study found that 25–34 is the most productive entrepreneurial age range, and entrepreneurship declines rapidly after age 45 (Figure 2.12).

The age distribution of entrepreneurship can be explained by way of economic logic. Entrepreneurship is a long-term, high-risk investment. An entrepreneur typically sacrifices a lot of personal savings and leisure time for years, and the probability of failure is high. Young people are more willing to take on such risky investment, because they will have more time to enjoy the fruits of success. A 55-year-old is not going to start a company and work hard for 15 years, because at age 70 a successful entrepreneur will not have many years ahead to enjoy the success—if any. In addition, people after the age of 35 usually have more responsibilities, such as children and family, and therefore are less tolerant of financial risk. Furthermore, as explained earlier, most cognitive skills peak in the 30s and 40s, and learning ability is at its best in the 20s, therefore young people are better at learning new skills and adapting to new

FIGURE 2.12 Age and entrepreneurship

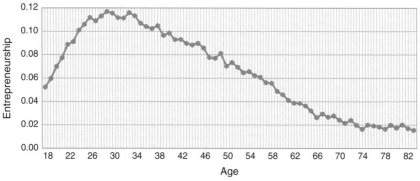

Data Source: Global Entrepreneurship Monitor, 2012.

environments. Lastly, coming up with creative business ideas and running a startup firm requires certain industry knowledge and business skills, which are typically acquired through experience. Consequently, the best entrepreneurs are aged between 25 and 35, having accumulated some knowledge and experience, but still being open minded, adventurous, and risk-taking.

ENTREPRENEURSHIP, AGING, AND THE BLOCKING EFFECT Because talented entrepreneurs tend to typically be in their 30s, having a large number of highly educated 30-year-olds in the population is good for innovation, especially for disruptive innovation. Conversely, if a country is aging rapidly, there will be fewer potential young inventors and entrepreneurs.

There is also a blocking effect in an aging society, where older people block the vitality of younger people. The probability of being in a senior and influential position depends on the age makeup of the workforce. If a firm has an older workforce, it is less likely that young workers will be given much in the way of management responsibility, because the senior positions are already occupied by older workers. It is also for this reason that the age structure of a country is potentially an important determinant of entrepreneurship. A young society provides more opportunities for the young to acquire the skills necessary for entrepreneurship. Conversely, in an aging country, where the cohort size is shrinking over time, young workers are promoted more slowly, are less influential, have fewer skills, and hence are less capable as potential entrepreneurs. Therefore, in an aging country, not only are there fewer young people, but these young people are not as entrepreneurial because their development is blocked by a larger, older cohort.

The link between entrepreneurship and aging has been examined by economists at Stanford and Beijing University (Liang et al., 2014). I first noticed this link when I studied data on Japanese innovation. Overall, the innovation performance of Japan is adequate. Large firms in Japan invest heavily in research and development and acquire many patents. However, these inventions are mostly micro inventions, not disruptive inventions. For example, Japanese firms are continuously improving digital cameras, making them smaller, enhancing their quality, and adding more functionality; nonetheless, they have failed to produce disruptive inventions, such as the iPhone. Since the 1990s, despite churning out many patents, these large Japanese firms have been unable to keep up with the innovations of U.S. firms, especially new high-tech firms.

It was not always like this for Japanese firms. Japanese firms were very creative in the 1970s and 1980s, and came up with revolutionary inventions such as the Walkman, the digital camera, and the video game console. The Japanese economy grew spectacularly in these years, and many economists predicted that it would soon overtake the United States in terms of GDP per capita. However, after the bursting of its real-estate bubble in 1991, the Japanese economy stagnated for the next 20 years, while the U.S. economy pulled ahead, benefiting from a vigorous high-tech industry. The cause of Japan's lost decades is still being hotly debated. Some economists attribute the stagnation to the extended financial crisis, which was triggered by the real-estate bubble bursting. However, the problem with this explanation is that no other financial crisis in history has lasted for more than 10 years, whereas Japan's economy has stagnated for more than 25 years. Many economists today are realizing that the real culprit may well be the aging population and lack of entrepreneurship.

The reason that Japan's economy has underperformed compared with the United States is a lack of entrepreneurship and the failure to develop a dynamic IT industry, as the United States has done over the last 30 years. As shown in Table 2.2, five of the top 10 high-tech companies in the United States were founded after 1985; the founders were very young when they established their companies, with an average age of only 28. In contrast, none of the top 10 high-tech companies in Japan was founded over the last 40 years.

The new firm entry rate in Japan dropped from a 6–7% range in the 1960s and 1970s to 3% in the 1990s (Acht *et al.*, 2004), which amounts to less than

TABLE 2.2 Top 10 high-tech companies and their founders in Japan and the United States as of 2015

United States	Age	Founded year	Founded age	Japan	Age	Founded year	Founded age
IBM	died	1911		Nintendo	died	1889	
HP	died	1939		Sony	died	1946	
Microsoft (Bill Gates)	61	1975	20	Panasonic	died	1918	
Apple	died	1976		Hitachi	died	1910	
Cisco (Leonard Bosack)	64	1984	33	Toshiba	died	1875	
Oracle (Larry Ellison)	72	1977	32	Kyocera (Inamori Kazuo)	84	1959	27
Google (Larry Page)	43	1998	24	Fujitsu	died	1935	
Intel (Gordon Moore)	87	1968	39	Sharp	died	1912	
Facebook (Mark Zuckerberg)	32	2004	20	NEC	died	1898	
Amazon (Jeff Bezos)	52	1995	31	Nikon	died	1917	
Average time of establishment: 43 years				Average time of establishment: 100 years			

TABLE 2.3 The age structure of the workforce

	Manager grade			Department head		
	Below 35	35–39	40 and above	Below 45	45–49	50 and above
1976	31.80%	31.90%	36.30%	24.50%	31.10%	41.40%
1984	18.30%	33.10%	48.60%	12.50%	37.30%	50.20%
1994	16.40%	23.50%	60.10%	7.60%	27.80%	64.60%

Data Source: Summary of Report, Basic Survey on Wage Structure (Ministry of Health, Labor and Welfare of Japan), various years.

one-third of that in the United States and trails behind all other OECD countries (Karlin, 2013). According to an entrepreneurship survey (Global Entrepreneurship Monitor, 2012), the entrepreneurial propensity in Japan is the lowest among all the developed countries. In the United States, 4.9% of adults between the ages of 18 and 64 are working actively to establish new businesses, compared with only 1.9% in Japan.

Japan is the first country in the world to experience a rapidly aging population, as it did not have a baby boom period like the United States or Europe. Almost immediately after the Second World War, Japan's fertility rate fell rapidly and dropped below the replacement level in the 1970s. As a result, the Japanese workforce aged rapidly during the 1990s.

When the workforce becomes older, the promotion speed of young workers slows down. As shown in Table 2.3, in the 1970s about 32% of managers were under the age of 35. This ratio had dropped by almost half to only 16% by the mid-1990s.

In the 1970s, about one-quarter of department heads were under the age of 45, and that ratio dropped by two-thirds to only 8% in the 1990s. This is a direct result of the aging workforce, because typically promotions are based on seniority. When the age structure is a top-heavy reverse pyramid, young workers have to wait much longer to be promoted to managerial and executive positions, and they have less responsibility and accumulate fewer of the skills required to be entrepreneurs. When they finally do get promoted and acquire the necessary skills or financial and social capital to be entrepreneurs, they are already in their 40s or 50s and have passed the golden age of entrepreneurship.

Let's compare the entrepreneurial potential of young people in different countries using the Global Entrepreneurship Monitor survey data (Figure 2.13). Japan has the oldest demographic and also the lowest rate of entrepreneurship. Particularly striking is that, in most countries, 30 is the most entrepreneurial age; however, this is not the case in Japan, as 30-year-olds in Japan are even less entrepreneurial than 50-year-olds. The blocking effect

FIGURE 2.13 Entrepreneurial rates by age group in selected countries

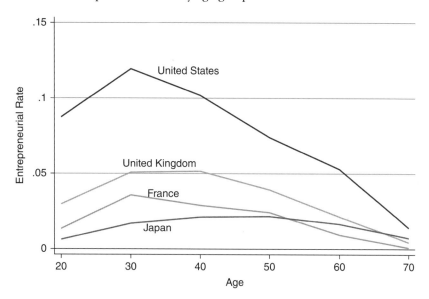

Data Source: Global Entrepreneurship Monitor, 2012.

magnifies the aging effect and damages the entrepreneurial vitality of the young disproportionately.

Over the last 30 years, not only has Japan failed to produce innovative new firms, but the existing large firms have also become very slow in creating disruptive innovations. The same blocking effect comes into play because an internal innovation project to create a breakthrough technology in a large firm resembles an "entrepreneurial project," and is best led by a young leader in their 30s. However, a typical 30-year-old in a Japanese firm has a low-ranking position and fewer skills and political power in the company, and therefore cannot be an effective leader of such projects. So in an aging country (or aging firm), not only are there fewer creative new firms, but the existing large firms also tend to be more conservative and less creative.

Now, let's look beyond Japan and examine the relationship between aging and entrepreneurship in other developed countries. In Figure 2.14, the horizontal axis is the young ratio (i.e. the share of young workers [20–39 years old] in the total working-age population [to age 59]), while the vertical axis is the probability of the adult population starting a business. As shown in the figure, there is a positive correlation between entrepreneurship and the youthfulness of the population. Of these countries, Japan has

FIGURE 2.14 Entrepreneurship and the age of the workforce (developed countries)

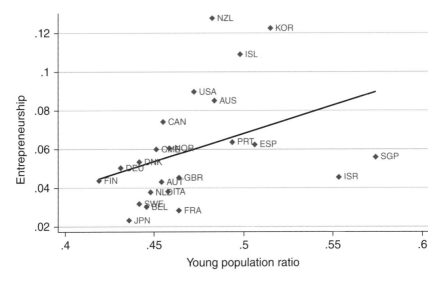

Data Source: Global Entrepreneurship Monitor, 2012.

the oldest population and the lowest entrepreneurial rate. In contrast, the populations in the United States and in Korea are younger and more entrepreneurial.

In Figure 2.14, if we compare the typical "youthful" country with 50% of the workforce under 40 to a relatively "older" country with just 45% of the workforce under the age of 40, we find that the entrepreneurial rate of the former is almost twice that of the latter. The effect is much larger than can be accounted for by simply having a larger number of young people, so the blocking effect (or other structural effects) must be at play to produce such a large difference in entrepreneurship rates.

If we look beyond the developed countries and include all the countries for which data is available, the positive relationship between a younger population and a higher level of entrepreneurship still holds (Figure 2.15). The age structure of China is currently still young, and Chinese workers are very entrepreneurial.

Finally, let's relate entrepreneurship to economic growth. Figure 2.16 shows the relationship between the GDP growth rate from 2000 to 2009 and the entrepreneurial rate. There is a clear positive relationship—higher levels of entrepreneurship correlate positively with higher economic growth.

See also Table 2.4, which relates the percentage of young people in a country's population to rates of entrepreneurship and GDP growth.

FIGURE 2.15 Entrepreneurship and the age of the workforce (all countries)

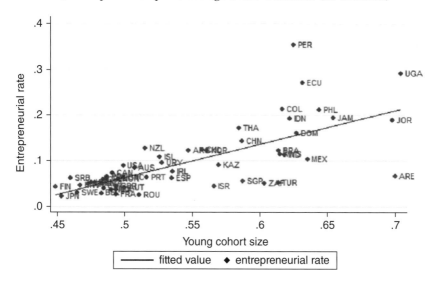

Data Source: Global Entrepreneurship Monitor, 2012.

FIGURE 2.16 Entrepreneurship and economic growth

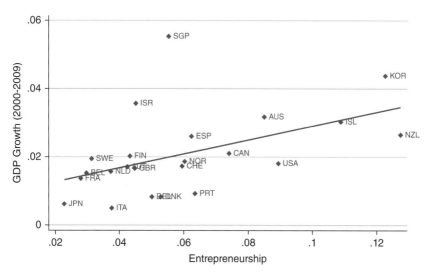

Data Source: Global Entrepreneurship Monitor, 2012.

TABLE 2.4 Relationship between young population percentage and
economic growth

Country	Young population ratio	Entrepreneurship	GDP growth
Australia (AUS)	0.483879	0.085025	1.36656
Austria (AUT)	0.454646	0.04269	1.183716
Belgium (BEL)	0.446187	0.030048	1.163809
Canada (CAN)	0.45516	0.07417	1.229318
Denmark (DNK)	0.441637	0.053032	1.084757
Finland (FIN)	0.419621	0.04343	1.221713
France (FRA)	0.464112	0.028216	1.143666
Germany (DEU)	0.4316	0.050248	1.085561
Iceland (ISL)	0.498158	0.109003	1.346107
Israel (ISR)	0.55341	0.045406	1.420429
Italy (ITA)	0.458004	0.037943	1.049537
Japan (JPN)	0.436312	0.022922	1.061634
Korea (KOR)	0.515015	0.122566	1.53309
Holland (NLD)	0.448252	0.037473	1.167373
New Zealand (NZL)	0.482228	0.127477	1.297626
Norway (NOR)	0.458784	0.06058	1.202318
Portugal (PRT)	0.493871	0.063642	1.095549
Spain (ESP)	0.506265	0.062538	1.290549
Sweden (SWE)	0.441733	0.031428	1.209297
Switzerland (CHE)	0.451311	0.059754	1.18662
United Kingdom (GBR)	0.463995	0.044866	1.17953
United States (USA)	0.472314	0.089531	1.1952

Source: Global Entrepreneurship Monitor, 2012.

Other Factors that Can Enhance Innovation

I have argued in this chapter that demographic factors such as population size,
geographic concentration of population, and age composition are important
factors for innovation. An interesting question to consider is whether, besides
these demographic factors, there are other important factors or policies that
can drive more innovation. My general observation is that other policies are
either obvious ones that many countries have already implemented, or they
are a consequence of demographics themselves. I will list the most important
policies for innovation as follows.

Trade Liberalization

Trade liberalization is a very important and well-understood condition for
innovation, because the international market can make up the scale

disadvantages of a smaller domestic market. Even large countries such as China and the United States cannot ignore the international market, which is still much larger than their domestic market. Large countries in the past were prone to hold a mistaken belief that their domestic market was sufficiently large and therefore that trade with other nations was redundant. The Chinese emperors in the Ming and Qing dynasties made this mistake by shutting off sea trade following the famous Zheng He voyages. The Chinese emperors failed to realize that trade is not simply an exchange of goods, but more importantly it facilitates the exchange of ideas, which is critical to innovation.

Throughout history, those economies that have pursued autarky policies have inevitably ended up trapped in a vicious cycle of technological backwardness and economic stagnation. Fortunately, policy and decision makers in almost all countries have now understood this point, and trade barriers today are much lower than during any other period in human history; globalization is likely to have staying power.

Anti-trust Policies to Encourage Competition

A certain level of consolidation is actually good for innovation, because consolidation allows firms to achieve an economy of scale, which is critical for innovation. On the other hand, monopoly or near monopoly reduces competition and the incentive for innovation. Therefore, the optimal industry structure for innovation is to have several large-scale firms competing fiercely with each other. In many industries, only big countries have the market size to allow multiple large-scale firms to thrive.

Competition is good for innovation. Governments sometimes use this excuse to stop mergers that would otherwise create a monopoly. However, anti-trust policies have become increasingly unnecessary because, in most industries today, technological innovation and disruption are so frequent and fast that it is increasingly difficult for any company to dominate for a very long time. The churn rate in Fortune 100 companies over the last few decades has been accelerating. Moreover, competition is global today, so anti-trust actions on the part of a single country are not only unnecessary, but also often irrelevant.

Government Investment in Basic Research

This strategy helps innovation, but is not essential. Although the United States did not invest in basic research in a meaningful way prior to the Second World War, by the early 1900s, helped by leveraging its scale advantage, it was already leading the world in innovation—especially in automobiles and electronics—making it the richest country in the world. The top universities in the United States also became the wealthiest in the world, giving them the opportunity to hire the best scientists from around the world; not long after, the U.S. universities became the best universities in the world. In a way, the Chinese universities, with their generous government funding, are attempting the same feat today.

Investment in Military Technology

Some economists argue that the U.S. leadership in technological innovation is partially helped by its unmatched military spending. For example, Internet and mobile communication technology was initially funded by way of government and military research. In my view, modern communication technology was indeed greatly helped by access to research derived from military projects, but there are also examples where military projects slowed down innovation in civilian technologies. For example, if it had not been for the atomic bomb, the public today would be less paranoid about the safety of nuclear energy, and it may have been used more widely. At the end of the day, government spending on military technology and research is proportional to the size of the population; only governments from large countries can afford large military research budgets. So, we are back to demographics once again.

Investment in Infrastructure

Good communication, transportation, and energy infrastructures are the basics for economic development and innovation. Most governments understand this; the issue is a question of affordability. Young countries with a high savings rate will have more money per capita to invest in infrastructure. Population agglomeration in large cities also helps, because the utilization and efficiency of infrastructure are higher in densely populated areas.

Good Financial Market and Adequate Venture Capital

Financial markets and venture capital are important for the development of high-tech startup firms. However, governments do not need to do much to bolster this driver of innovation, because the venture capital market is global; capital will move in to provide funding wherever there is a good opportunity, bypassing policy barriers if necessary. Fifteen years ago, China did not allow foreign investors to invest in Internet companies, and the local stock market was effectively closed to Internet companies. However, lured by the enormous size of the market, U.S. venture capitalists invented the "VIE" structure to work around these laws. In a typical "VIE" setup, venture capitalists used a consulting agreement to invest in Chinese Internet companies indirectly. Not long after, the Chinese Internet sector was flooded with U.S. venture capital money. That is why most successful Chinese Internet companies today were backed by U.S. venture capitals and are listed on the NASDAQ.

Innovation and Education

Can education spending boost innovation? If one looks at the data, innovation is positively related to education. However, is there a causal relationship between education and innovation? Probably not, because causality could run the other way (i.e. when a country is innovative, it will be richer and can afford to invest and raise the level of education). Actually, most middle-income countries have greatly expanded their college enrollment rate in recent years. Countries such as Thailand and Malaysia have a college enrollment rate of over 30%, a level not much lower than that of developed countries. However, in terms of innovation, these countries still lag far behind high-income countries. It seems that a high education level is a necessary precondition but not the deciding condition for innovation.

Having a high college enrollment rate is not sufficient because the quality of higher education is just as important. If we use GRE General Test results as a measure of the quality of college students, we find that East Asian students have very high math scores. For GRE verbal scores, Asian and European students have roughly the same scores, whereas students from other parts of the world score much lower in both categories.

In general, the quality of education—as manifested by GRE scores—is strongly related to the economic development level of a country (see Figure 2.17). The exceptions are India and China. According to the quantity and quality of college graduate students, China is predicted to be a high-income country and India is predicted to be a middle- to high-income country. I will analyze the economy and innovation capacity of China and India in later chapters.

Expanding college enrollment rates is easy, but enhancing the quality of college education is very difficult.

Moreover, we have not yet found a way to teach creativity. Creativity is a combination of both personality and a very complex skill set. So far, no organization can accurately measure or test creativity, let alone try to teach it. After a country expands its college enrollment rate to a certain level, the return on further investment is low. In my view, rather than increasing investment in education, raising the efficiency of learning and allowing talented students to graduate and start working earlier is a better way to promote innovation. If talented people can start their career earlier, they will have more time to do creative work, therefore having a larger window in which to engage in entrepreneurial efforts. For talented young women, graduating earlier will give them more time in life to have children and a successful career. Speeding up the learning process is certainly possible in the Internet age. I will revisit the

FIGURE 2.17 GRE score by country

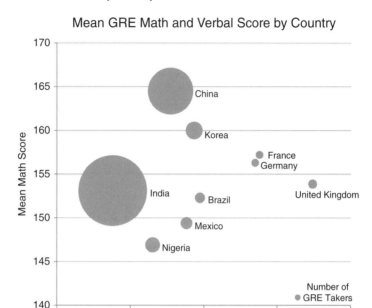

Data Source: Educational Testing Service, 2015.

topic of accelerated learning later in the book. Apart from getting talented students to finish school and start a career earlier, increasing investment in education is unlikely to significantly improve the creativity of young graduates.

Conversely, a poor education system does not seem to hurt creativity either. China, Korea, and Japan all possess an inefficient test-oriented, rote-learning high-school education system, where students spend one to two years memorizing and preparing for college entrance exams. However, this does not seem to hurt the high level of innovation capabilities in China and Korea (and Japan before it experienced a demographic shift to an older population).

Some would argue that the innovators are the cream of the crop; entrepreneurs, engineers, and scientists comprise no more than 5% of the world's population. So a country can concentrate its resources to provide the best possible education for these elites. This logic relies on the assumption that you know which 5% will become effective researchers and successful entrepreneurs. The reality is that nobody knows which 5% will be the next Steve

Jobs (of Apple) or Jack Ma (of Alibaba); to say that both of these men were not the best students is probably an understatement. The best innovators and entrepreneurs are largely random. It is not like picking a child to be a top basketball player; for that purpose one can use height as a strong predictor of future success. It is more like trying to select a kid to be a top football player. This is a much harder prediction to make, as no specific physical quality is determinative. Good football players tend to emerge from the bottom up in grass-roots organizations.

The Chinese government has been reasonably successful at building an effective basketball team, because it can concentrate its resources on training the few tall children who are selected for the team; however, the top-down approach will not work for football (as manifested by the abysmal performance of the Chinese football team). Similarly, to foster innovation and entrepreneurship, countries must provide high-quality basic college education to a large number of people, and allow talented people like Steve Jobs and Jack Ma to emerge.

The most talented entrepreneurs and scientists do not require much in terms of extra training or investment either. As long as there is an open and fair competitive environment, they will emerge. It is as if all those able to access a decent education have been dealt a lottery ticket in the game of talent. At the end of the day, the size of a country's talent pool will be proportional to the number of young people available who can access adequate education, and this ultimately is determined by the size and demographic makeup of the population.

The case of Japan tells a good story of the relationship between the quality and quantity of education vis-à-vis pure demographic and population numbers. In the 1960s and 1970s, Japan had a young and growing population. Despite most of its young people being from poor families, a large proportion of them turned into outstanding entrepreneurs and scientists. In the 1990s and 2000s, as young cohorts shrank, despite increased spending on education, their creativeness and entrepreneurship declined. During the 1960s and 1970s, many Japanese graduate students were attending top research universities in the United States; however, in recent years, the number of graduate students from China, India, and Korea has surpassed those from Japan by a wide margin. According to the *Washington Post*, over the past 10 years, the number of Japanese graduate students attending U.S. universities decreased by 27%, while the number of students from Korea, India, and China has more than doubled. The reason for this reduction in student quality could be another version of the blocking effect. When a country ages, young people's prospects of promotion are slight, and the reward for working hard is low; they therefore lose the motivation required to compete.

In Japan, both the quality and quantity of young talent has suffered as the country falls into the low-fertility trap with a shrinking and aging workforce.

Increasing investment in human capital cannot make up for the loss of quantity, and money should instead be spent on raising the fertility level to increase the number of young people in the talent pool.

In this chapter, I have showed that the fundamental factors that drive innovation are demographic factors. The three most important demographic factors are the size of the population, the age composition, and the geographic distribution of the population. To use a company analogy, this conclusion is not surprising because a company's competitiveness is ultimately determined by the number and quality of its human resources. Other factors—such as strategy and execution—are also important, but strategies are created and executed by employees. Similarly, for a country, the ultimate drivers of innovation are all connected to its population, primarily its size and distribution, and age makeup.

CHAPTER 3

Demographics and the Economy

In the previous chapter, I discussed the impact of demographic factors on innovation. In this chapter, I will analyze how demographics affect the many other aspects of an economy—including employment and old-age support.

Low Fertility and Old-Age Support

The demographic impact on old-age support is the most frequently mentioned effect of a low fertility rate. Holding the output of each worker constant, an increase in the number of the elderly or children relative to the number of workers will result in a decrease in output per capita and lower economic growth.

In traditional societies, children support their parents in their old age. In modern societies, private savings and public pensions are the main sources of support. A large portion of the fiscal revenue in developed countries is used to provide old-age support, including both direct pension payments as well as medical benefits. The public expenditure to support the elderly is financed via taxes collected from the younger, currently employed, generation. Therefore, in an aging society, as government expenditure to support the elderly increases, the tax burden and the fiscal deficit also rise. Figure 3.1 shows the relationship between aging and public expenditure as a percentage of GDP. As expected, the higher a country's dependency ratio is, the higher its public expenditure is as a share of GDP.

To meet the growing demand for old-age support, governments have several options:

1. Raise taxes.
2. Increase deficits.
3. Reduce benefits for the elderly.
4. Delay the retirement age.

FIGURE 3.1 Aging and public spending

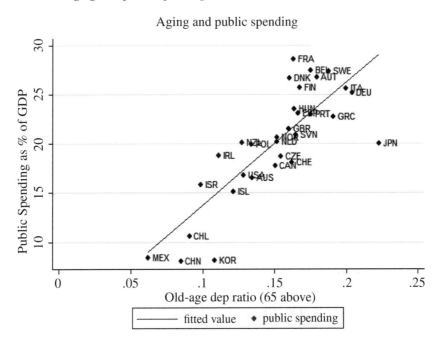

Aging and public spending

Data Source: World Bank, 2015.

Raising taxes reduces the vitality of the economy, especially the vitality of the young entrepreneurial class. Increasing the deficit simply delays the problem, because the deficit will eventually have to be paid back through higher taxes. Reducing benefits for the elderly is typically political suicidal in an aging society, because older voters exert strong political influence.

Extending the retirement age is a popular solution to reduce the burden of old-age support. For developing countries, such as China, the retirement age will have to be raised significantly from the current level. Over the last few decades, life expectancy in China has increased from 60 to 75 years; as a result, the current retirement age of 55 is unsustainable. In Japan, the retirement age has risen from 55 to 65 years, but this is still not enough as life expectancy (currently at 80) continues to increase. The Japanese government can barely afford the enormous expense of old-age support, and its debt level is among the highest of all the wealthy countries, having reached 240% of its GDP. Japan is likely to increase the retirement age again to 70 years in the near future.

Many people think that since the average lifespan has exceeded 80, and the elderly are healthier than ever before, working until 70 is not a serious problem and may well be beneficial. Certainly the fiscal problem of old-age support can largely be solved simply by raising the retirement age. However, there is a side effect of having an increasing number of older people in the workforce. When the political power and resources are shifted to older workers, the vitality of the younger generations is blocked, and the whole society becomes more conservative. Consequently, innovation and entrepreneurship inevitably suffer. I, and many other scholars, believe that this negative effect of an aging workforce was the main culprit for Japan's economic problems in "the lost decades," as explained in Chapter 2. I will examine this topic in detail in Chapter 6.

Low Fertility and Demographic Dividend/Deficit

Low fertility rates can generate a demographic dividend, but only in the short run. A demographic dividend is commonly measured by the dependency ratio, which is the number of dependents—including children and the elderly (age < 15 and age > 65)—per working-age person (age 16–64). The lower the dependency ratio is, the fewer children and older people need to be supported by each worker; hence, the higher is per capita income, resulting in a so-called demographic dividend.

China is a good case study, as its one-child policy caused an abrupt change in fertility and dependency ratio over the last 30 years. From 1985 to 2015, the number of children decreased rapidly as a result of the one-child policy, and the dependency ratio dropped from 44% to 37%. The Chinese economy has enjoyed a large demographic dividend in the last 20 years but this is beneficial only temporarily, as fewer children today will mean fewer workers 20 to 30 years later. By 2015, the number of workers peaked and the demographic dividend and dependency ratio reversed in China. From 2015 to 2040, the dependency ratio will rise from 37% to 60%. The rise in the dependency ratio, especially the old-age dependency ratio, will impose a heavy burden on public finances for pensions and medical expenditures, which will inevitably lead to higher taxes or a higher retirement age. Unless strong policy decisions are made, this could drain government funding and negatively impact economic prosperity in China.

Can High Fertility Lower the Per Capita Asset Level?

Another frequently mentioned issue is the per capita asset/capital level. A low per capita asset/capital level can lower the productivity and per capita income of a country. A number of factors can lower the per capita asset/capital level in the short run, such as immigration and high fertility. Here, assets refer to real estate, equipment, and infrastructure, such as roads and airports. During a recent visit to China, a friend from India commented that although the population density of the coastal region in China is similar to that of India, public places such as airports, train stations, and department stores are much less crowded than in India. This is because, although China is still a developing country, China's per capita asset level is much higher than that of other developing countries due to a very high investment level in assets and infrastructure over the last 20 years. If this visitor had come to China 30 years ago, he would have felt very differently, as the per capita level was much lower in China then. Airports and train stations in China in the 1980s were just as crowded as they are in India at present.

During public holidays, tourist attractions such as the Great Wall of China are very crowded. Some people attribute this to China's large population, but the real reason is the influx of visitors to these attractions during public holidays. For most workers in China, paid vacations are concentrated around the Chinese New Year and a few other national public holidays. Consequently, tourist attractions receive most of their visitors during these times, and are far less busy throughout the rest of the year. The tourist attractions have no financial incentive to expand facilities that would be underutilized for most of the year.

People often use a shoulder-to-shoulder image of the crowded Great Wall of China to illustrate the negative effect of a large population. In reality, a growing population is actually good for tourism development, because, in the long run, higher demand will lead to more investment to build more and better attractions. Historically, China was able to afford such magnificent projects— such as the Forbidden City and the Great Wall—because of its large population. Today, as travel demands increase, new sections of the Great Wall of China are being developed for tourism (Figure 3.2).

In that light, the negative relationship between population and per capita assets is short term. In the long run, more assets will ultimately be created by a larger number of people. The per capita asset level is not related to the size of the population, but is rather connected to the saving/investment rate. Moreover, there is an economy of scale in public investment in infrastructure. A common criticism of immigrants is that they make the roads more crowded, but with enough commuting demand, more roads and subways can be built. It is not a coincidence that the largest cities in the world often have the most efficient and densest public transportation systems.

I recently visited the island of Hawaii. Owing to its sparse population, the main roads of the island are four-lane roads along the coast. The average resident needs to drive 45 minutes to get to work. I asked a hotel worker why she did not live closer to the hotel. She said that the entire island only had one middle school, but the hotels were spread out. A few years ago, the government considered building an expressway, but could not afford to do so because of the low population density. The situation in Hainan Island, China,

FIGURE 3.2 The Great Wall of China

Source: A picture of the Great Wall during the May Day holiday in 2016, taken by Jiaojiao Liu.

is quite different. Hainan Island is a popular tropical beach resort, similar to Hawaii. Although only twice the size of Hawaii, its population is five times larger and the number of visitors it receives (mostly from China) is six times greater than that of Hawaii. Owing to a higher density of residents and tourists, Hainan Island can afford to build a highway network and, more recently, a high-speed railway around the island.

To sum up, the per capita asset level is not related to the population in the long run, because assets are created by investment that is funded by savings. In the long run, the saving/investment rate and productivity determines the per capita asset level. Typically, high-growth countries such as China also have a high savings rate; as a result, these countries will eventually match high-income countries in terms of per capita asset level.

The assets discussed here exclude natural resources. Obviously, a higher population will lower the per capita level of land and other natural resources.

In theory, this could lead to a decline in productivity. I will discuss the topic of natural resources in the next chapter. Today, one common argument against population increases (such as a greater number of immigrants being permitted to settle in a country) is that the additional population numbers will have a negative impact on the availability of public resources such as roads, hospitals, and so on. This argument is not defensible. Public resources are not natural resources, and particularly over the long term are created by the savings/investments of the population.

Can High Fertility Cause Unemployment?

There is a myth that a larger number of people in any given country will lead to higher unemployment figures. This is obviously based on the incorrect assumption that the number of jobs is fixed. Such an assumption could hold true in the context of a very short time span, because some jobs require some sort of capital investment. For example, waiters need to work in a restaurant, which cannot be built overnight. However, as more people demand restaurant services, restaurants will be built. Not only will there be more waiter/waitress jobs, but also more construction jobs, more maintenance jobs, and so on. Jobs are fueled by people, and jobs fuel other jobs. That is the basis of all economic growth.

Unless heavily regulated, the job market, particularly in countries with large populations, is very flexible and can adjust quickly to changes in wage levels. If there are temporarily more people who want restaurant jobs, the wages for waiters will go down, and restaurants will be able to hire more workers to expand or extend their business. Moreover, in a global market, low wages in one sector can often find an output market internationally. Following the reforms in China during the 1980s, there was a massive surplus of migrant workers. Instead of creating massive unemployment, the surplus workers kept wages low, and turned the Chinese manufacturing industry into an export powerhouse.

In sum, when more people enter the labor market, although it creates additional labor supply, it also creates more demand, and therefore more jobs. When an economy is open to international trade and has a flexible labor market, the presence of more people does not lead to higher unemployment. In fact, many low-fertility countries, such as Russia and Spain, have higher unemployment levels, as illustrated in Figure 3.3. Most economists agree that high unemployment is a result of inflexible labor markets and wage structures, not overpopulation. For example, high unemployment occurs when the minimum wage is too high, or when the unemployment benefits are too generous, or when firms are reluctant to hire permanent workers because labor laws make it difficult to let those who are unnecessary or unproductive go.

FIGURE 3.3 Unemployment rates of selected countries (2014)

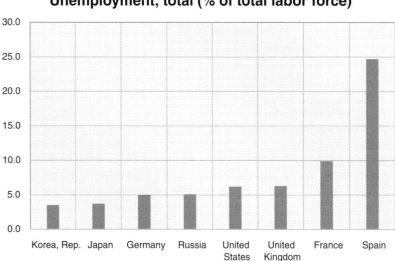

Unemployment, total (% of total labor force)

Data Source: International Labour Organization, Key Indicators of the Labour Market database, World Bank, 2014.

The effect of immigration on unemployment is similar to that of high fertility. There is no evidence that immigration causes unemployment. On the contrary, immigrants, not being part of the established society or economic networks and often with little to lose, tend to be more entrepreneurial on average than the native population. Cities and regions that attract large numbers of immigrants typically tend to be more vibrant and have low unemployment rates. Recently, public opinion in both Europe and the United States has turned against immigrants. U.S. President Donald Trump wants to reduce the number of immigrants. Immigration is a complicated demographic issue, which has implications for inequality and most importantly for innovation capacity. I will examine immigration policy in detail in Chapter 5.

Robots, Unemployment, and Innovation

As artificial intelligence (AI) and robotic technology advances, a common concern is that robots will take the jobs away from humans. Yet historically, progress in automation and technology has simply led to the replacement of old jobs with new jobs. Many agricultural and manufacturing jobs were rendered obsolete by machines, but many service jobs have been created in turn. This time, many experts say that things will be different, because even service jobs such as drivers are in danger, and so are some professional jobs such as lawyers and doctors.

Unemployment as a result of a totally automated economy is not an economic problem. Would it not be a good thing if only a small number of highly skilled, creative workers needed to work three days a week, while the rest of the population could play all day whilst maintaining the same level of consumption and enjoying a better quality of life? Rather, it could be a social problem, because some (perhaps many) people would feel unneeded, unable to derive their self-worth from contributing to something. It could also be a political problem, with most voters not being tax payers. We should really call the problem "too much leisure," instead of unemployment. But even this scenario is unlikely, because in the short run, a large number of service jobs would be generated in an economy. In the long run, even when most routine jobs are automated, there will still be many jobs connected to innovation.

First of all, service jobs are nowhere near replaceable by robot technology as it exists today. The computer may be able to beat humans at chess, but mechanical hands are still far away from the dexterity of human hands. In my estimate, it will be at least 30 years before a robot can do simple house cleaning jobs or replace airline stewards; even a driverless car is at least 10 years away from widespread use, because of legal and implementation issues. So, in the near future, service jobs will continue to grow rapidly, more than enough to offset the reduction in manufacturing jobs.

Second, even though computers can do some of the analytical work done by professional workers such as reporters, stock analysts, even lawyers and doctors, computers are more likely to make professional workers more productive rather than replacing them. Social interaction is and will remain an essential part of many professional jobs. It is hard to imagine a robot lawyer representing a defendant, because lawyers still need to make moral arguments and empathetic connections with human jurors (although, of course, AI can help with the analysis of cases).

Lastly, innovation-related jobs are likely to be reserved for humans. One reason for this is that it is probably too dangerous to allow non-sentient computers to innovate. Moreover, innovation frequently involves tastes, aesthetics, and moral judgments; for example, if the task is to evaluate a piece of music, a movie, or a new dish, we humans will probably always understand our needs better than robots.

To sum up, in the near future, there will be more service jobs. In the long run, there will be more innovation-related jobs. Some people say that innovation needs just a few smart people, not many people, but this clearly runs counter to the historical trend. As I have explained in Chapter 2, mankind has been devoting more human resources and capital to innovation, and there is no sign of this trend slowing down. Even though only a few successful innovations (including popular games and movies) make the vast majority of the profits, for every Google and blockbuster game, there are thousands of new startups trying to be next in line. All these new ideas are funded by personal savings and the massive venture capital industry. Moreover, in the future, more people will have the necessary skills and motivation to be involved in some kind of innovation activity, ranging from highly skilled jobs such as AI programming to less skilled jobs such as game testing and movie reviewing. More humans will have the necessary skills, partly because their analytical abilities will likely be enhanced by computers. More humans will have the motivation, because it is fun and rewarding to be involved in some kind of creative activity, even one as trivial as movie reviewing.

In the long run, innovation will not be just about solving a problem, but more about the exploring of the unknown. A person's taste for food and housing can be saturated, but humanity always has an appetite to explore new gadgets, new stories, new games, and new frontiers in space and elsewhere. The moment that human beings lose their appetite for exploration, human civilization will start to decline and eventually disappear. This, I am sure you will agree, would be a much bigger problem than "too much leisure."

A Little Bit of Economic Science Fiction

I will use a little science fiction story to show that even with the arrival of robots, so long as young people have higher productivity or creativity than older people, more young people will raise the overall living standard significantly.

In 2100, robots have taken over almost all the jobs, even highly interactive jobs such as looking after the elderly. People live much longer, with the average life expectancy hovering at over 100 years. All products are very inexpensive and accessible and the only good remaining a luxury is long-distance travel, which now includes space travel.

Let's build a simple economic model. Assume a person's daily consumption of goods and services requires the work of an average robot (unit), and each elderly person requires one extra robot to meet his/her health care needs. The main jobs for young people are managing robots, including developing, producing, and maintaining them. Assume that every worker can "manage" 10 robots. In addition to providing daily goods and services, robots also provide long-distance travel services (i.e. flying airplanes and space ships, managing space hotels, etc.).

Let's hypothetically compare two countries in the world, one called Greenstock and the other Whitestock. Whitestock has 1 billion elderly people, but due to a low fertility rate it has only 0.5 billion young people and 0.5 billion children; a total population of 2 billion. It needs 3 billion robots (2 + 1) to provide daily goods and services. These robots require 0.3 billion young people to manage them. The remaining 0.2 billion workers are managing 2 billion robots who are working in the travel industry, providing tourism services. On average, each person in Whitestock consumes one robot worth of travel services.

As for Greenstock, there are the same number of the elderly (1 billion) but, in contrast to Whitestock, Greenstock has a higher fertility rate; it has 1 billion young people and 1 billion children; a total population of 3 billion. The daily consumption of its citizens requires 4 billion robots (3 + 1), which require 0.4 billion workers to manage. That leaves 0.6 billion workers to manage 6 billion robots in the travel industry. On average, each person in Greenstock has two robots to provide long-distance travel services, compared with only one robot in Whitestock. Therefore, the per capita travel consumption is twice as high in Greenstock, and the overall market size of the travel industry is three times larger than Whitestock's.

The above model shows that, as long as older people require additional services from young workers, an aging country will have a lower consumption per capita in other goods and services, such as long-distance travel, thus lowering the standard of living. Moreover, there will be more deaths than births in Whitestock, and the demand for robots will shrink every year.

Most of the new demand for robots will come from Greenstock. Greenstock also has more workers devoted to the research and development of robots, and therefore has a much higher level of innovation and entrepreneurship than Whitestock. With a higher standard of living and vitality, Greenstock attracts talented young people from Whitestock who wish to migrate. This leads to Whitestock losing a significant portion of its already small young population, creating a vicious circle.

Impact of Aging on Different Industries

Entertainment and Tourism Industries

The entertainment and tourism industries are sunrise industries, because they address humanity's mental needs. Physical consumption, like the demand for food, clothing, or housing, is satiated after a certain point, but mental consumption is only limited by the availability of time. As people become wealthier, more and more time will be spent on entertainment and travel activities. Moreover, older people will have even more free time to pursue these activities. Therefore, even with an aging population, the travel and entertainment industries will have a growing share of the overall economy.

The travel industry will grow faster than the entertainment industry, because travel products are relatively more expensive. This is because productivity in the context of the travel industry is held back by the physical need to move a person from one place to another. In contrast, the digital entertainment industry can scale quickly, because digital products can be replicated at almost zero cost. The total size of the digital entertainment industry will grow at a slower pace, even though it will also take an increasing share of leisure time. As a whole, across all ages, people will have more time and money to spend on the entertainment and tourism industries.

Health Industry

The health care industry will also be a fast-growing industry in an aging society, because the elderly live longer and will spend more money in order to prolong their lives and try to maintain their quality of life as they age. The latest technological progress in gene technology has made health care one of the most vibrant industries for innovation. The U.S. health care industry is the most expensive among developed countries, and the least regulated. It is also the most dynamic and innovative, with the best quality of care available. The U.S. health care industry already accounts for 20% of total GDP in the United States, and that share is still growing.

For most countries, a large portion of health care expenditure comes from the government budget and from public pensions. As a country ages, the ever more costly medical benefit imposes a heavy burden on government budgets, and can be financed only by higher taxes or later retirement.

Financial Industry

The essence of the financial industry is the trading of labor outcomes across time. Children borrow wealth from their parents and society, and pay it back when they become adults in the form of taxes. Governments collect taxes from workers to provide a minimum guarantee for old-age support, as well as some level of medical care. In an aging society, old-age support is costly and governments are likely to reduce the pension benefits. As a result, more people increasingly rely on private savings/investments for old-age support, which leads to a more prosperous financial industry in an aging society.

As shown in Figure 3.4, during the early years of a career, people usually have negative savings because they need to borrow money to buy their first house and raise children. People typically start to save for their retirement when they reach middle age. The savings rate peaks between the ages of 40 and 60.

The sudden rise of China and its unique population size have exerted a significant influence on global capital markets. There is a bulge in the demographic pyramid of China. China's equivalent to the "baby boomer" generation of the West are those born between 1962 and 1991. The annual birth cohort size in China during this period was almost 40% larger than that in subsequent years, as a result of the strict enforcement of the one-child policy in

FIGURE 3.4 Relationship between income, consumption, and age

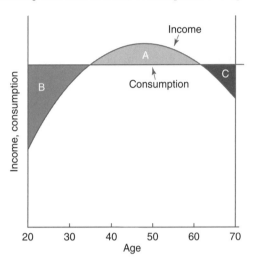

the 1990s. From 1962 to 1990, there were, on average, 22 million births in China every year. In contrast, from 1991 to 2015, the average birth rate dropped to only 16 million births per year (Figure 3.5). This absolute and relative change in the birth cohort size is unprecedented. Many economists have not fully appreciated the economic impact of the one-child policy.

FIGURE 3.5 Total births in China from 1950 to 2015

Data Source: State Statistics Bureau, 2015.

COMPARISON BETWEEN CHINESE BABY BOOMERS AND U.S. BABY BOOMERS   After 1991, when the one-child policy was strictly enforced, those Chinese born in the 1960s and 1970s typically had only one (or at most two) children and hence the economic burden of raising the young was not heavy. Moreover, with the rapid economic development of China during the last three decades, this generational cohort became affluent. Their rate of savings remained high as a result, which partly explains China's extraordinarily high savings rate over the last few decades. Let us do some simple calculations here. Typically, a person's savings peak around the age of 50. For the Chinese baby boomers born between 1961 and 1991, their peak savings years fall between 2012 and 2041. As shown in Figure 3.6, the household saving rate increased from 30% in 2002 to 40% in 2012; this is staggeringly high and very surprising, if one does not take into account the demographic factors.

The Chinese saving rate will remain high until 2041, which will bring abundant capital into the international markets. Consequently, the real-estate industry and stock markets will continue to be very liquid, as China exports its excess savings. The Chinese baby boomers will need to invest their savings internationally, which means that they will need to rely on children in other countries for support as they age. This is the reason why it is inevitable that China will need to export a huge amount of capital to the world, which will fuel the price of capital and depress the interest rate for years to come. In recent years, the United States sold US$1.2 trillion of government debt to China. Macroeconomic theory suggests that a large capital

FIGURE 3.6 Household saving rate in China

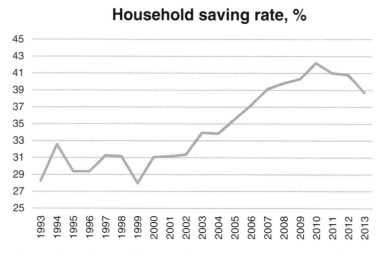

Data Source: China National Bureau of Statistics, People's Bank of China, Haver Analytics, Barclays Research, 2013.

outflow will inevitably lead to a large trade surplus. China's huge trade surplus can be partly explained by its unique demographics.

Real-Estate Industry

The real-estate sector is also heavily impacted by demographics. Although people from all age groups have housing demands, people generally buy homes between the ages of 30 and 45. People in most countries buy their first home around the age of 30, and switch to a larger home when they have children (Figure 3.7). By the age of 45, when their eldest child is about to go to college, they typically no longer require so much space and shy away from buying bigger homes. In fact, they tend to switch to a smaller home as their children leave the nest. Wealthy, older people may buy a second "vacation" home but generally, after the age of 45, people's housing demands tend to shrink.

The baby boom generation in the United States was born between 1945 and 1964. Let's suppose that they buy homes between the ages of 30 and 45. We could extrapolate from this that there should be a housing boom between 2001 and 2005, followed by a decline in housing demand after 2006. In hindsight, the housing bubble and decline could have been predicted by the demographics; the subprime crisis was partly due to Wall Street's failure to

FIGURE 3.7 Housing and non-housing expenditures, by age of reference person (2013)

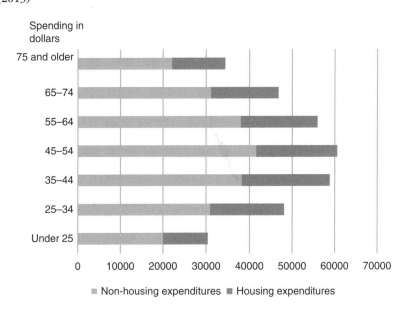

Data Source: U.S. Bureau of Labor Statistics, December 2015.

fully take into account the demographics in forecasting housing market demand.

Japan is a developed country with no baby boom generation. Its birth rate began to decline rapidly after the Second World War. Given that the peak age of real-estate consumption is 45, we could have made a forecast that the housing demand in Japan would peak in the 1990s, which is consistent with the timing of the real-estate bubble bursting. Houses tend to have long lifespans, so the demand for new houses only comes from incremental housing demand. As we know, the total population of Japan is on the decline, so the incremental demand is actually zero or negative. The only exception is Tokyo, which is still growing due to the agglomeration effect. In all other cities, negative housing demand will keep the real-estate prices in Japan depressed for the foreseeable future.

Again let us apply the home-buying patterns described above to forecast the housing demand of the Chinese baby boomers. Since the Chinese baby boomers are a generation born between 1962 and 1990, housing demand in large Chinese cities will remain strong until at least the mid to late 2020s (not taking into account further agglomeration effects). Large cities, with vigorous innovation and entrepreneurship activities, will continue to attract the baby boomers, even after this period of time. While the real-estate market in China's first- and second-tier cities (top 30 cities) will remain strong, overall housing demand will peak in the mid to late 2020s and stagnate once this generation's housing demands begin to wane.

Manufacturing Industry

Most manufacturing industries—such as automobiles, furniture, clothing, household appliances, steel, and cement—are closely connected to the real-estate industry. Therefore, just as the real-estate industry is influenced by demographics, so many manufacturing industries will be similarly affected. Of course, not every manufacturing sector is the same, because manufacturing is a very broad concept. For example, aircraft manufacturing should, in my view, actually be classified as part of the tourism industry, and medical equipment manufacturing should be classified as part of the health industry. Generally speaking, for most large, durable commodities, the consumption pattern by age is similar to that of real estate (i.e. people buy most of their durable goods between the ages of 25 and 45). Consequently, as a country ages, the demand for durable goods will decrease.

Energy and Commodities

For energy and bulk commodities, the peak age of consumption is also from 25 to 45. China, as the largest consumer of energy and commodities, hit a demand inflection point around 2010, as the demand from its baby boomers

FIGURE 3.8 Growth in young Chinese aged from 25 to 45

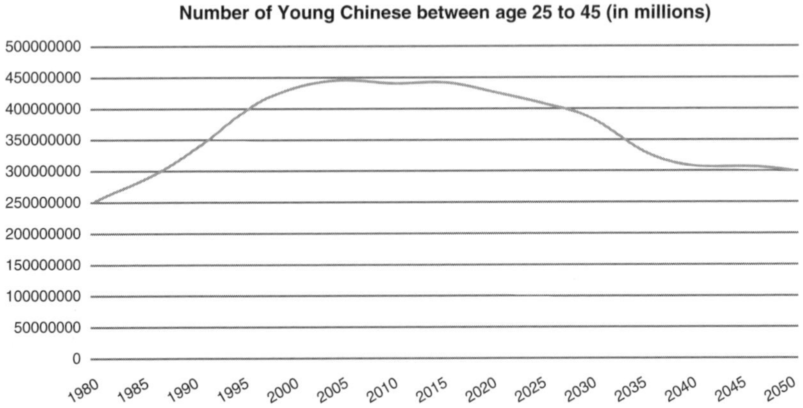

Number of Young Chinese between age 25 to 45 (in millions)

Data Source: World Bank, 2015.

reached the age of peak consumption (see Figure 3.8 for a graph depicting the trend in number of young Chinese aged between 25 and 45). Similarly, and connectedly, steel and iron ore demand in China peaked recently.

After China, the next country with a similar scale of demand is India. With the economic takeoff in India, global demand for energy and commodities will reach a peak between 2040 and 2070. After 2070, as the global population enters a period of stagnation and aging, the demand for commodities will decline, along with their price, as well as their economic significance. The competitiveness and wealth of each country will be increasingly dependent on innovation.

Demographics and Macroeconomy

For many sectors (health care being one very big exception), the peak age of demand is between the ages of 25 and 45. Young workers in their 20s are big consumers, and yet their productivity and wages are still low. So, in general, whenever there is a large cohort of 20-year-olds in the economy, the aggregate demand is robust relative to the production capability, thus causing inflation. The logic above accurately accounts for the high inflationary rates in the 1970s and 1980s in the United States, when the baby boomers were entering the workforce (Figure 3.9).

Conversely, when a young cohort shrinks as a result of low fertility, the economy will usually be in a slow growth and deflationary mode. Japan has a rapidly aging population and a shrinking young workforce; consequently, it has a zero-growth economy and a negative inflation rate (i.e. deflation).

FIGURE 3.9 U.S. inflation from 1960 to 2010

Data Source: World Bank, 2015.

Older workers tend to benefit from deflation at the expense of young workers. First, in a deflationary economy, the savings of the older generation increase in terms of purchasing power over time. Furthermore, because nominal wages rarely go down in a typical firm, when money increases in purchasing power, the effective wages of incumbent workers rise. To keep costs down, the firm has to lower the wages of incoming young workers. In Japan, this is exactly what has happened. Young workers suffer disproportionately from economic stagnation and deflation. There are a lot fewer high-paying full-time jobs than there were 30 years ago, and young people's income and career prospects are not nearly as good as those of their parents' generation. This is another example of "the blocking effect" that I have already described, and one that saps the vitality of the young in terms of innovation and entrepreneurship.

Demographics and Inequality

The French economist Thomas Piketty, in his best-selling book *Capital in the Twenty-First Century* (Piketty, 2014), paints a pessimistic outlook of the ever-increasing income gap between the rich and poor. Inequality seems to be the most challenging problem for the world economy. Let us first clarify some common misconceptions about inequality.

Is Greater Equality Always Better?

While equal opportunity is desirable, perfect equality in income is not only impossible (due to inherent differences in ability and effort) but also undesirable. In a perfectly equal world, people would lose the incentive to innovate, to take risks, and to work hard. This would lower the overall living standard. For an example of this type of stagnation, one needs only to look at the planned economies of the Soviet era, with their emphasis on equal pay and benefits for all, irrespective of their level of skill or productivity. As long as we want to have competitive and risk-taking behavior, there will always be winners and losers. Therefore, some degree of inequality is necessary.

Global Inequality

People tend to think that the problem of inequality has got worse in recent decades but if one looks at inequality globally, the very opposite is true. Global inequality has been increasing throughout most of human history. However, over the last 20 years it has declined due, to a large extent, to the rapid growth of China and India—two large, poor countries that are becoming wealthier far faster than the rest of the world. Regional growth in emerging countries is also a contributor, but China and India have contributed the most to lowering the levels of equality, due to their large populations. When we look at inequality within countries, it is clear that inequality has increased, as some segments of the population have disproportionately benefited from globalization, whilst others have lost out in a significant way. The Gini coefficient has remained relatively stable in most European countries and affluent Asian countries, but a significant increase in inequality is noticeable in the United States and China (Figure 3.10).

FIGURE 3.10 Global Gini inequality index

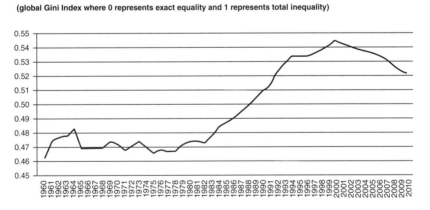

Word Inequality
(global Gini Index where 0 represents exact equality and 1 represents total inequality)

Source: The Conference Board of Canada, World Income Inequality—Is the world becoming more unequal? September, 2011.

Long-Term Inequality Trends

As communication and transportation technologies have improved over time, an innovator has a larger market to profit from. The overall historical trend is that technological advancement and globalization has resulted in more wealth concentration in the hands of innovators and entrepreneurs, and hence more inequality.

Inequality was minimal in primitive societies, where everybody was more or less equal, and increased in the pre-industrial world where a few large landowners were rich and everybody else was comparatively very poor (with an embryonic middle class confined to the few larger towns/cities). Globally, inequality increased further after the Second World War, when developed countries were far wealthier than developing countries. The reward for entrepreneurial success, as well as the demand for highly specialized skills, has been increasing throughout most of human history, but has accelerated since the 1980s.

As explained above, global inequality has actually decreased since the late 1990s, which is an amazing reversal of a centuries-old trend. However, once China reaches an average per capita income of US$20,000, which is almost certainly going to happen in the next few years, mathematically the future growth of China as a high-income country will actually contribute to increasing global inequality.

On the supply side, human capital and the number of highly skilled workers have been increasing too. During some periods when the supply of human capital (i.e. per capita education) grows faster than the demand for highly skilled workers, inequality can temporarily decrease, but will increase again when the supply of human capital levels off.

In the United States, from 1950 to 1980, when there was a huge increase in the supply of college graduates, the income inequality was reduced. But after 1980, the expansion of college education leveled off, and the U.S. college graduation level stagnated at 50%, lower than that of many other developed countries. Consequently, the income gap between high- and low-skilled workers in the United States continued to rise throughout the 1980s and 1990s. Why has the U.S. college graduation rate halted at this 50% level? The college enrollment rate continued to rise to almost 80%, but only about 60% of those who enrolled actually graduated. One of the reasons for the low college graduation rate is the low quality of K12 education for children from low-income families. This is a complicated subject, beyond the scope of this book. Although the United States has the most innovative high-skilled workers, it has a large population with a very low level of skills. As the skill premium increases globally, the income gap in the United States has widened as a result.

Besides education, there are many reasons for the bipolar distribution of skills in the United States; one of them is its immigration origin. Historically, the United States has attracted a very diverse population of immigrants from different cultures and diverse levels of human capital.

Immigration and Inequality

When a person moves from a poor country to a wealthy country, it almost always reduces inequality globally (from the combined perspective of both the source and the destination country), because when a poor person in a poor country moves to a wealthy country where he/she earns more money, world income is more equal. However, from the perspective of the destination country, it also matters whether the person is a highly skilled or an unskilled worker. If the immigrant is an unskilled worker, then he/she competes for jobs with native unskilled workers, which tends to lower wages for unskilled labor, thus increasing inequality in the receiving country. However, if the immigrant is a highly skilled worker, then he/she competes for jobs with native highly skilled workers, which also lowers their wages, thus decreasing inequality between highly skilled and unskilled in the receiving country. That is one of the reasons why countries always prefer highly skilled immigrants. Not only because their contribution to the economy may well be more valuable, but also because inequality within the country is incidentally reduced. Within a country, most governments allow free internal migration, because internal migration is always good for reducing overall inequality within the country.

The demographic impact of fertility on inequality is similar. If highly skilled families have more children, this will help reduce inequality, because highly skilled families tend to produce highly skilled children, thus increasing the supply of highly skilled workers and therefore lowering their wages and overall inequality. Conversely, if unskilled workers have more children, this tends to increase inequality by depressing the wages paid to unskilled workers. Throughout the history of the world until the Second World War, it was the wealthy who had more children surviving into adulthood, which acted as a decelerator of inequality.

Until the 1960s, the wealthier countries in the West—like the United Kingdom and the United States—experienced higher population growth than the rest of the world due to high fertility rates and better health care. The West's share of the world's population increased until the 1960s. However, a new demographic trend started to emerge after the 1970s in developed countries. Highly skilled workers began having fewer babies than unskilled workers, mostly because the highly skilled workers spent more of their time and effort on education and professional work. This reduced the supply of future highly skilled workers relative to future unskilled workers, causing increasing income inequality a generation later.

Policy Choices to Reduce Inequality

To sum it up, the overall increase in income inequality is primarily due to technological progress and globalization, about which little can be done. Moreover, the new demographic trend has partially contributed to this problem, which can only be addressed with demographic policies.

The desired demographic policy for the United States is basically a smart immigration policy to encourage more highly skilled immigrants and a pro-fertility policy to encourage highly skilled workers to have more children. I will discuss these policies in Chapter 5.

In contrast, China's inequality is mostly an urban–rural inequality problem. The human capital and skill level of the urban young are much higher than their rural counterparts. In recent years, not only has the gap between rural and urban been increasing, but also the gap between large cities and small cities, because most of the innovations are occurring in large cities. The best way to address this inequality is to allow more people to move to cities and to incentivize people in cities to have more babies. Unfortunately, the Chinese government continues to restrict internal migration and recently has imposed a limit on the population growth of large cities, based on misguided concerns regarding the effects of such growth on the environment and natural resources. The relationship between demographics and resource and environment is the topic of the next chapter.

CHAPTER 4

Resource and Environment

In 1968 an American biologist, Paul Ehrlich, published a popular book entitled *Population Bomb* (Ehrlich, 1968), in which he predicted that the earth would not be able to sustain an explosive growth in population. In 1972, in a report entitled "The Limit for Growth" (available online at en.wikipedia. org), several environmentalists predicted population growth would cause famine, pollution, and the depletion of natural resources. The report forecast that the world would run out of gold in 1981, oil in 1992, and copper in 1993. Of course, these predictions turned out to be very wrong, but many people still worry that overpopulation will eventually lead to resource depletion and damage the prospects of long-term economic growth.

I am often asked the question: What is the earth's carrying capacity? According to a meta-analysis of 69 past studies that have assessed the limit of world population (Van Den Burgh and Rietveld, 2004), the estimates range from 7 billion to 1,000 billion. Interestingly, the estimates kept rising with the growth in world population. Before 1950, the medium estimate was 6.1 billion; after 1950, the medium estimate was 160 billion. Malthus once predicted that the limit of the world's population was 1 billion. Earth is now home to 7 billion people. Owing to the great demographic shift currently occurring, the world's population will likely stop growing at around 10 billion. Almost all economists think that the earth can comfortably support a population of 10 billion. Moreover, it seems highly likely that in the next 100 years, humanity is going to colonize other planets or at least exploit them for their natural resources. And yet, every time there is a short-term energy or food price hike, the worry over resources and the environment comes back.

Natural Resources and Economic Growth

Let's look first at the relationship between natural resources and economic growth. The abundance of natural resources per capita is closely related to the population density. In general, low-density countries have high resource

85

endowment per capita. If we examine the relationship between population density and the per capita income level, we find that there are many high-density poor countries, such as India and Vietnam, and many low-density affluent countries, such as the United States and Canada; however, there are also many high-density affluent countries, such as Japan and the Western European countries, and many low-density poor countries, such as Brazil and most of the African countries. So, in general, there is no relationship between resource abundance and the potential for economic development. Over the last few decades, resource-poor Asian countries such as China and India have grown much faster than comparatively resource-rich Latin American and African countries. There actually seems to be a negative relationship between resource abundance and sustainable economic development.

In an economy based on agriculture, higher population density leads to lower per capita availability of farm land, and thus to lower per capita income. In industrial economies, a larger population allows for greater specialization and more opportunities for trade, and therefore higher productivity. On the other hand, more people tend to consume more resources and generate more pollution. For service and knowledge economies, a large population will lead to more innovation, hence higher productivity and faster economic growth. So, as the world economy progresses, higher density is increasingly becoming an advantage.

Figure 4.1 shows the relationship between population density and per capita level of income. There is no clear positive or negative relationship between wealth and population density. If one takes a look at the situation within each country, usually the higher-density regions are more affluent than more sparsely populated regions.

In modern economic history, no country has been economically constrained by resource bottlenecks. Countries with very poor resource endowment, such as Japan, Korea, and Israel, have done and are doing extremely well. In contrast, there are many examples of the "resource curse," a phenomenon sometimes called the "Dutch disease."

The "Dutch disease" describes the woes of the Dutch economy during the 1960s. After large gas reserves were discovered in 1959, Dutch exports soared. Gas exports resulted in an influx of foreign currency, and the local currency appreciated. That made other parts of the economy less competitive in international markets. Corporate investment was tumbling. That was not the only problem. Gas extraction was (and is) a relatively capital-intensive business, which generated few jobs. From 1970 to 1977, the unemployment rate increased and corporate investment tumbled.

Latin American countries are rich in mineral and oil resources, which generate high levels of export and income. However, these countries have low levels of economic development. Many economists have analyzed the "resource curse" phenomenon. The Nobel Laureate, Joseph Stiglitz, and his

FIGURE 4.1 Relationship between population density (# of people per km²) and income

Data Source: World Bank, 2015.

co-authors recently wrote a book on the subject of the "resource curse" (Humphreys et al., 2007). They argue that because these countries rely on the "oil dollar," or the resource dollar, they have fewer incentives to invest in strong institutions and in human capital. As a result, resource-rich countries tend to have corrupt governments, weak institutions, and poorly developed human capital. Moreover, because oil and commodity prices can fluctuate widely, the economies of resource-rich countries are at the mercy of the volatility of world commodity markets.

Many people still worry that with economic and population growth, natural resources will become increasingly scarce and therefore inaccessibly expensive. However, the data on resource prices and supply suggests the opposite.

It seems that the more resources we use, the more resources are discovered and can be extracted and exploited. As shown in Figure 4.2, if no more oil is discovered in the future, we will run out of oil in 2064 (beginning the countdown in 2010). However, in 1980, it was predicted that we would run out of oil in 32 years' time (i.e. 2012). This is because, even though oil consumption is growing, the amount of oil being discovered is growing even faster. Furthermore, there is still a lot of room for developing

FIGURE 4.2 Oil reserve/yearly oil consumption (1980–2014)

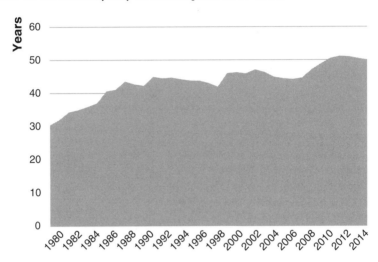

Data Source: BP plc, energy charting tool, 2015.

new alternative energy sources. Consequently, oil prices have remained quite stable in the long term. There was considerable concern regarding resource depletion in the 1960s and 1970s, and yet now that the world's population has doubled, the concern about resource depletion has subsided.

Similarly, there have been recent concerns that China's surging demand for energy would drive up global resource prices. China is the largest consumer of energy, even though its GDP is only 60% that of the United States. At a per capita level, the energy consumption levels of China are only 30% that of the United States, but already 70% that of Japan. As China grows wealthier, its consumption of energy will continue to grow. However, the growth of demand in China will slow down because its manufacturing industry, which is more energy intensive than its service industry, will slow down significantly. China could eventually be a more efficient energy user than the United States, because it is more densely populated and can, as a result, invest heavily in high-speed railways and subways, which are more energy efficient than airplanes and cars. The country's overall energy demand will grow at a much slower rate than its economy, at about 2–3% a year over the next 20 years, and this additional demand can be more than met by the global increase in energy supply.

In fact, if prices can reflect the supply and demand of a particular resource, then depletion of that resource will not be a big problem, because as the price of one resource rises, other alternative resources will be put to use. At one point, the price of oil was over US$100 a barrel. However, the high price stimulated innovation and, very soon after, solar power and the electric car industry took off in a big way for the first time as an alternative to oil. As a result, the price of oil came back down to about US$50 after a few years. Theoretically, there is virtually no limit to alternative energy sources. All the energy on earth ultimately comes from the sun. Only one hour of sunlight on earth is enough to support the entire annual energy consumption of the world today. The reason why we are still using a large amount of fossil fuel is because it is still relatively abundant and inexpensive. Shale-gas technology has further driven down the cost of energy, and the United States, with a rich shale-gas reserve, will be a net resource exporter in the near future. China also has rich shale-gas resources, which are more than enough to support its consumption if the price of oil rises.

Occasionally, there are periods of high energy prices. In the 1970s there was an oil crisis, caused by geopolitical events. But usually it takes just a few years for the world to adjust to alternative resource sources, so oil and energy crises are usually short-lived. In early 2000, the rapidly growing Chinese economy drove up the demand and oil prices soared. However, by 2015, the high price of oil accelerated the development of solar, wind, and shale-gas technology, which drove the oil price back down.

Figure 4.3 shows the added value of the oil, mineral, and agricultural industries as a percentage of the world's GDP since 1947. As shown, relative to the overall economy, the value of natural resources is on a long-term downward trend. This is a reflection of improved extraction and exploration technology, as well as the development of many new alternative resources.

FIGURE 4.3 Natural resources as a share of wealth (1947–2007)

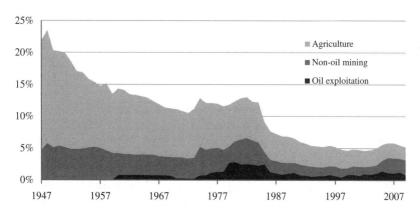

Note: Mineral = non-oil mining + oil exploitation industry. The value of the oil exploitation industry before 1960 is assumed to be zero, due to a lack of data.
Data Source: Madison, 2009 and World Bank.

Today, only 5% of the world economy is connected directly to natural resources. This is consistent with our everyday experience. Metal, plastic, and synthetic fibers in cars, computers, and houses are inexpensive relative to the value of the end-products. Moreover, service industries, which consume even fewer resources, are becoming more important economically; for this reason, one can extrapolate that the long-term downward trend of resource importance will continue.

Within a country, resource-rich regions in general tend to be comparatively poor, and densely populated regions are relatively affluent. In the United States, the vast majority of people live less than 50 miles from the coast, where most of the major corporations, universities, and research facilities are located. The United States is the most powerful country in the world, not because of its rich natural resources, but because of its rich human resources.

Clean Energy

Most scientists believe that global warming is caused by the emission of greenhouse gases such as CO_2. Industrialized nations have been the main source of emission historically, but in recent years, China has become the largest producer of greenhouse gases. As the Chinese economy continues to grow, its emissions will grow also. To curb this, China and other major countries have aggressive plans to invest in clean energy. Will clean energy be able to solve the problem of greenhouse emissions? Will clean energy technology be as abundant and cheap as fossil fuel energy?

If there was no progress in energy technology, we would still be using wood for heating and cooking. The world would be an even more polluted place. Relative to wood and coal, oil and gas are much cleaner and more efficient. In the last few decades, we have realized the potential risk of global warming from burning fossil fuels; this has created a need for cleaner, alternative energy sources. In recent years, a lot of money has gone into clean technology research and development, and a significant amount of progress has been made.

The widespread utilization of clean technology has only just begun. On the demand side, the world's population will grow slowly and peak in this century, and on the supply side, advances in clean technology will progress steadily. So, in the long run, clean technology will almost certainly be able to meet most of the energy requirements of the world.

There are many promising clean energy technologies (e.g. nuclear—including fusion in the future—wind, and solar). I will focus on a few of these energy technologies.

First, solar power is the ultimate energy source, and is an almost unlimited supply source. One hour of solar energy on earth is enough to supply the annual electricity consumption of the world. In order to build a solar power plant to supply electricity for the entire population in the United States, only 1% of the U.S. landmass is needed. The main raw material for solar panels is silicon, which is one of the most abundant resources on earth. With the current technology, solar panels have a useful lifespan of 20–30 years, but the energy required to produce a solar panel is equivalent to only about 2–3 years of electricity generated by that solar panel.

Moreover, the technology behind solar power is rapidly improving. Currently, the cost of solar-powered energy is still twice that of a coal-powered energy source. Figure 4.4 shows the cost forecasts for electricity generated by solar power vs. coal power.

The two downward-sloping lines are forecasts of the cost of solar electricity; one is a more optimistic forecast, the other is a more conservative forecast. The two upward-sloping lines are the forecast of the cost of electricity from coal. One represents the direct cost, while the other includes the environmental cost. As shown, the cost of solar power is declining rapidly, at about 7–10% each year, while the cost of coal power is increasing as

FIGURE 4.4 Cost trends of electricity from solar and coal

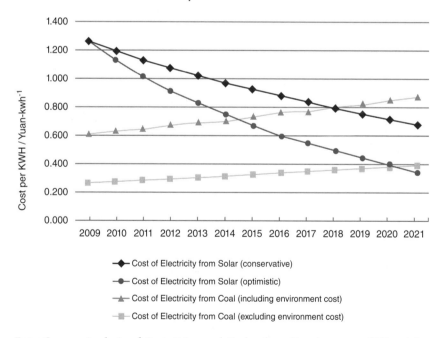

Data Source: Analysis of Cost, Price and Technology Development of Electricity from Solar in China, Institute of Electrical Engineering, Chinese Academy of Sciences, 2009.

transportation and environmental costs increase. Currently, if we include environmental costs, the cost of solar power is already on a par with that of coal power, and in 10–15 years it will be on a par with coal power in terms of direct costs as well.

The other promising clean technology is nuclear power. Although nuclear power is theoretically limited in supply, it is also very abundant; the world's current known reserves of uranium alone are estimated to be able to provide all the energy consumption of the world for 200 years. The cost of nuclear-generated electricity is already cheaper than that of coal. The main concern regarding nuclear power is safety; however, in fact, the number of people who have died from nuclear power generation is far smaller than the number of people who have died in coal-mining accidents, never mind those deaths connected to the polluting effects of coal usage. The early nuclear accidents were caused by the use of an immature technology. France has been able to generate most of its electricity from nuclear power, and has never had a major accident. Of course, like solar power plants, a nuclear plant requires considerable investment, and also takes time to build.

Besides solar and nuclear energy, there are quite a few other promising energy sources, such as wind and thermal power. Currently, their costs are higher than those of traditional sources, but declining steadily. In the future, mankind will have many sources of energy as alternatives to fossil fuel. Of course, all of these new technologies require substantial investment and take time to develop and scale safely.

Given the speed with which the cost of clean energy is declining, fossil fuel will be replaced by clean energy sources within a few decades. The only scenario that could prevent this from happening is the cost of fossil fuel also dropping rapidly with improved technology. The recent discovery of shale-gas technology has dramatically lowered the cost of natural gas and oil, and the subsequent drop in prices is slowing down the adoption of clean energy. In sum, mankind does not need to worry about the depletion of energy or resources, which are not scarce; and neither is human ingenuity.

World Food Production

Similarly to energy, world food prices have been stable or declining over the last three decades, despite a steady increase in both population and consumption.

As shown in Figure 4.5, there was a spike in food prices in the 1970s. However, after the 1980s, advancements in agricultural technology gradually caught up with the increasing demand. This was particularly the case in the 1980s when the Green Revolution spread to India, turning it from a food importer to a food exporter, despite its rapid population growth throughout

FIGURE 4.5 World food commodity prices

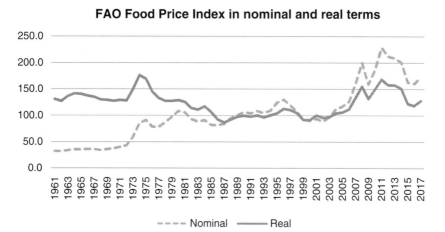

Data Source: Food and Agriculture Organization of the United Nations, 2017.

this period. China's agricultural technology and output also improved greatly in the 1980s, especially after farming was re-privatized by Deng Xiao Ping's reforms.

Figure 4.6 shows the grain output per hectare of selected countries. As we can see, production per hectare has increased steadily at an annual rate of 2–3%, much faster than the overall growth in the global population. Also, the increase has been across all countries, including high-income countries such as France and Germany, as well as poor countries such as India. Even given all

FIGURE 4.6 Grain output per hectare in selected countries

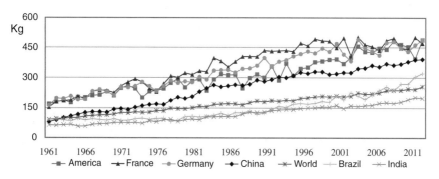

Data Source: Food and Agriculture Organization of the United Nations, 2013.

of these improvements, the efficiency gap between rich and poor countries is still large, and there is still ample room for improvement for countries such as India and Brazil.

China has shown the largest improvement in production efficiency. Its food production per hectare is approaching the level of high-income countries. China is the largest consumer of food, and is roughly 95% self-sufficient. It is also important to recognize that with advancements in agricultural technology, China is able to support nearly 20% of the world's population with only 7% of the world's arable land, which implies that the world has more than enough land to feed the world's population. China will import more food in the future, not because it cannot produce enough food itself, but because of the lower food prices from other producing countries. With lower prices of imported food, China will no longer have the comparative advantage of producing all the food it needs.

On the demand side, the growth of food consumption will slow down significantly. First of all, the growth of the world's population has slowed down significantly. Moreover, food consumption per capita for major countries, including China, has already leveled out (Figure 4.7). China's per capita calorie intake is already at 3,000 per day, almost the same as Korea's, and higher than that of Japan (2,800 per day). So, it can be predicted that with reduced demand and continued progress in agricultural technology, food prices will be stable in the foreseeable future. The overall share of agriculture in the world economy will continue to decrease. In summary, food will likely be both abundant and cheap in the future.

FIGURE 4.7 Calorie intake and food self-sufficiency ratio of China, Korea, and Japan

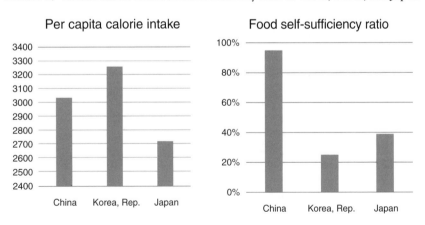

Data Source: Food and Agriculture Organization of the United Nations, 2014.

Will Water Become Scarce?

Water is a renewable resource, and the total quantity of water on earth is fixed. There is plenty of water for everybody on earth; however, the distribution of fresh water is uneven. Typically, in densely populated areas, water infrastructure projects need to be built to produce, recycle, or transport water from other areas. Water scarcity is not a resource problem but an economic problem of investment in water production, distribution, and conservation.

For example, water usage in agriculture is far more efficient in developed countries than in developing countries, because of investment in water-conserving technology and facilities. Israel, a country with one of the lowest levels of water resource per capita in the world, pioneered the use of drip irrigation systems, which use 50% less water than conventional irrigation. Moreover, the technology of seawater desalination has improved to a point where costs of desalination are under US$1 per cubic meter, just slightly higher than those of conventional water plants. Israel produces a lot of water with desalination technology. With most of the world's population living near the coast, there is no limit to how much water can be supplied, and the price of water should never exceed US$1 per cubic meter.

When a government sets the water price below its cost, this will invariably lead to shortages of water. Setting the price below cost is economically inefficient, but for many reasons that is exactly what many governments are doing right now. Whenever something is priced below cost, there is a need to either subsidize or ration, which gives the impression of a physical water shortage.

For example, in Beijing, there is a constant concern that water is going to "run out." In fact, the problem is that the water price is too low; it is set at US $0.3 per cubic meter when the actual cost is US$0.7 per cubic meter. Beijing is surrounded by farmland, which uses a lot of water inefficiently. Because of the low price, Beijingers do not have an incentive to conserve water. For example, one of the major uses of water in Beijing is for the washing of cars! Moreover, due to the low price having been set, the government needs to provide huge subsidies to water plants. The government's message to the public is that water is scarce and that everyone should save water; this creates the wrong impression, that water is scarce. Beijing is very close to the coast and in theory can produce an unlimited amount of desalinated water at a cost of under US$1 per cubic meter, a price certainly affordable by the now wealthy city. However, no private company will engage in such a project because the water price is artificially capped at only US$0.3 per cubic meter. The example of Beijing is typical of most cities around the world, where water shortages are a byproduct of government-regulated pricing of something considered a necessity, rather than actual water shortages. As these cities grow wealthier, there will be more water available as a result of either continuing government subsidy or private investment.

Demographics and the Environment

With rapid industrialization, major cities in China and India have become the most polluted places in the world. Will population growth and industrialization inevitably lead to environmental disaster?

Air Pollution

For the last few years, the eastern and northern parts of China have been frequently affected by heavy smog. In the fall of 2014, PM2.5 (a measure of the air pollution index) hit a historical record of 500, making headline news across the world.

Undoubtedly the smog was caused by modern industry trying to meet the consumption needs of a large population. Based on this reasoning, environmentalists generally believe that there are too many people in the world, and population control will be good for the environment.

There are even extreme environmentalists who openly advocate a human extinction movement, in which they ask volunteers to stop having children. They believe that this is the only way to protect the environment. However, nothing could be further from the truth! Population size is only a minor factor in environmental pollution. The choices of technology and lifestyle have far greater impacts on the environment than population size. For example, using automobiles for commuting consumes 10–20 times more energy and resources compared with the use of public transportation or clean-energy vehicles. Furthermore, the most aggressive population estimate is that the peak world population will only double from today's level of 7 billion to 14 billion. So, the demographic factor will have a much smaller impact than changes in lifestyle and technology, for example transportation technology.

From 1980 to 2012, energy consumption in China grew by 400%, but China's population only grew by about 10%. In the future, when the population of China stabilizes, whether or not China can solve its environment problems depends almost entirely on the speed of adoption of clean technologies.

Historically, humans have been able to successfully solve severe environmental problems by investing in technology specifically intended to address it. For example, London was once called "the city of fog." Interestingly, the heavy fog in London early in its industrial history was considered a sign of progress, and was believed to generally be good for health. Its negative effects were not understood, and nothing was done about it. However, as the smog or "fog" became heavier and a more frequent occurrence, it became obvious that it was harmful to the health of the city's inhabitants. After a five-day heavy fog in 1952, which caused many deaths, the U.K. government decided to take a series of measures to solve its pollution problem. Today, London has many more residents living in the city, but its air quality is greatly improved and ranked 38th out of 143 large cities (WHO, 2011).

In another example, between 1943 and 1980, Los Angeles experienced heavy smog. Under the joint efforts of government, businesses, and residents, especially after the enactment of the Clean Air Act in 1970, air quality in the city gradually improved, despite its still notoriously heavy traffic. The number of pollution days dropped from 121 in 1977 to only 54 in 1989, and to zero in 1999. At the same time, over the last 50 years, the city's population has increased from 4.3 million to over 14 million. With better emission technology, air quality has continued to improve, despite oil consumption in and around the city increasing many times over.

The experience of London and Los Angeles shows that air quality can be improved in the context of rapid population growth. Figures 4.8(A) and (B) show the relationship between pollution, country population density, and per capita GDP for the largest cities in the world (>2 million population). In both graphs, the vertical axis is the air population index, which is PM10. Figure 4.8(A) shows that there is no strong positive correlation between population density and air pollution. In contrast, Figure 4.8(B) shows a clear negative relationship between air pollution and per capita income. Therefore, it is evident that as a country becomes wealthier, its air quality improves regardless of its population density.

For example, Japan and Korea have a much higher population density than China; however, Tokyo and Seoul have much better air quality than Beijing. Mongolia is one of the most sparsely populated countries in the world,

FIGURE 4.8(A) Relationship between air pollution index and country population density

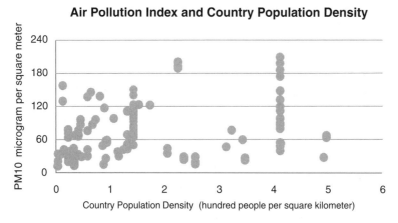

Air Pollution Index and Country Population Density

Data Source: WHO, 2011 and World Bank, 2011.

FIGURE 4.8(B) Relationship between air pollution index and per capita income

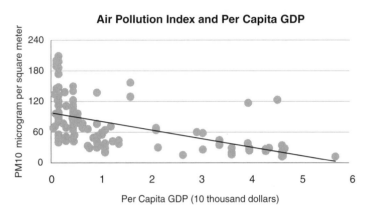

Air Pollution Index and Per Capita GDP

Data Source: WHO, 2011 and World Bank, 2011.

but the air quality in its capital, Ulaanbaatar, is among the worst in the world. Densely populated Europe has better air-quality results than sparsely populated Africa. According to a 2013 ranking by the Blacksmith Institute Green Cross, five of the 10 most polluted cities in the world are low-density countries such as Russia, Ukraine, Argentina, and Zambia.

Air quality is just one of the measures of environmental protection. Grossman and Krueger (1995) analyzed the relationship between economic development and various kinds of pollution. They found a common pattern. During the early stages of industrialization, all pollution indexes deteriorate rapidly; however, most of the measures hit a turning point when a country's per capita GDP level reaches US$8,000 to US$10,000. The reason is that when a country becomes wealthier, it will have access to (and be able to afford) better technologies, and will also be able to invest more in environmental protection.

In 2016, China's per capita GDP stood at US$7,500, and it was one of the most polluted countries in the world. But over the next decade, as the per capita GDP exceeds US$10,000, China's environmental conditions will start to improve. A few rich cities located along the coastal regions have already adopted very high environmental standards, and have seen environmental improvement in recent years.

Urban Congestion

In Chapter 3 I discussed the agglomeration effect of the urban population. Not only do large cities have more job opportunities, they also have better health and education facilities. Moreover, innovation occurs disproportionately in

FIGURE 4.9(A) Relationship between city density and country population density

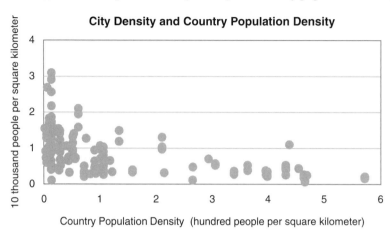

Data Source: WHO, 2011 and World Bank, 2011.

large cities. As a result, metropolitan areas of the world keep attracting new residents, and those that are most successful have grown into mega cities with over 10 million in population.

As they have grown, the major cities in populous countries such as India and China have become very congested. People mistakenly believe that city density is related to country density. Does country population density relate to city density? Our analysis of city density uses data from Demographia (2011), which collects information from the major metropolitan areas of the world to calculate the city density of each metropolitan area. Figure 4.9(A) shows the relationship between city density and country population density. In the figure, the vertical axis is the city density and the horizontal axis is the country population density.

It is evident from Figure 4.9(A) that city density has no clear relationship with country density. In Argentina, a very low-density country, one-third of its 40 million residents live in Buenos Aires, which has a density higher than that of Beijing. The largest city in Brazil also has a higher population density than Shanghai and Beijing.

Figure 4.9(B) shows the relationship between city density and per capita GDP. The vertical axis is the city density, and the horizontal axis is the per capita GDP income of the country.

It is evident from Figure 4.9(B) that city density is negatively correlated with per capita income. As a country becomes wealthier, its cities will cover a larger surface area and have a lower density. This is because, with increased wealth, the cities are able to invest in better roads and public transportation, enabling people to comfortably commute longer distances to work. Los

FIGURE 4.9(B) Relationship between city density and per capita GDP

City Density and Per Capita GDP

Per Capita GDP (10 thousand dollars)

Data Source: WHO, 2011 and World Bank, 2011.

Angeles has a very low population density, because it has a very extensive system of satellite towns and suburbs, all connected with an extensive highway system. Tokyo has 37 million residents, but it has the largest public transportation system in the world, with over 3,000 km of subways and train lines. Poor cities do not have adequate highways or public transportation systems, so residents have to live close to city centers, which become very densely populated and overcrowded as a result.

Let's look at the top 10 most congested cities in the world.

As we can see in Figure 4.10, many congested cities are in Russia and Brazil, which are low-density countries. On the other hand, mega cities such as Tokyo or Seoul are not on the list. So, it is clear that the largest cities are prone to congestion only when countries are relatively poor, regardless of the population density of the country.

Country Population and City Population

As discussed in Chapter 2, in the recent past, large cities across the world are growing disproportionately larger due to the agglomeration effect (Lu, 2016). In Japan, low fertility has caused a decline in the overall population; nevertheless, the population of Tokyo, its largest city, is still growing. In fact, it is the only place where the population is growing in Japan. In Russia, a low fertility rate has caused many small cities to decline in population; however, the population of Moscow has grown significantly in recent years. Even though the overall population is nearly stable in China, the population of Beijing and

FIGURE 4.10 The world's worst cities for gridlock

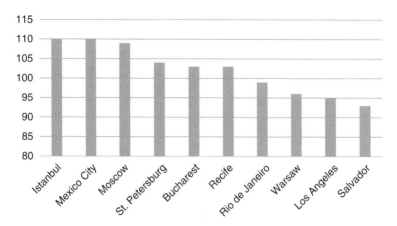

Data Source: Niall McCarthy and Statista, These Are the World's Worst Cities for Gridlock, 2015 (available online at www.forbes.com).

Shanghai has grown to over 23 million and counting. How large can these cities grow? Are Chinese mega cities too big?

There are two basic competing forces that determine how large a city can become. On the one hand, people are attracted to large cities, which have more jobs and better public services; on the other hand, they are deterred by high housing prices and a potentially long commute. The balance of these two forces will determine the size of a city. Because major cities attract people from rural areas and other small cities in the same country, the population in the largest city is positively related to the country's population size.

By this logic, Shanghai and Beijing should be the most populous cities in the world. However, their populations hover around just 23 million, which is much smaller than the populations of other mega cities in Asia. This is primarily due to the Chinese government's restriction on internal migration. Japan, with only one-tenth of the population of China, is home to the largest city in the world (Tokyo), with 37 million residents. Korea's largest city, Seoul, is also larger, with a population of 26 million. Optimally, therefore, Shanghai and Beijing should both be metropolises of around 40–50 million people.

Too Many People in Beijing?

This may come as a surprise to many people who have lived in or visited Beijing. Beijing is notoriously polluted and congested, but it is also too small in

TABLE 4.1 Car ownership in selected major cities of the world

| | Car ownership statistics | | | | Demographia agglomeration | |
	Scope	Car ownership	Landmass	Population	Landmass	Population
Beijing	Subdistrict	502	16,808	2,019	3,479	1,731
New York	New York's 5th district	196	850	780	11,642	2,046
	New York and suburban areas	1,037	30,670	2,209		
Tokyo	Tokyo City	385	2,188	1,319	8,547	3,713
	Tokyo City and 3 other suburban areas	1,379	13,556	3,562		
LA	Los Angeles district	580	10,518	989	6,299	1,490
	2nd district	832	12,520	1,283		
	5th district	1,052	87,490	1,808		
London	Greater London	269	1,572	817	1,623	859
Paris	Greater Paris	489	12,012	1,179	2,844	1,076
San Paulo	San Paulo city district	697	7,944	1,989	3,173	2,019

Note: Landmass, population, and car ownership units of quantity, respectively, are the square kilometer, 10,000 people, and 10,000 vehicles. Greater London and Paris car ownership shown only accounts for private and light vehicles.

Data Source: Related government websites and media sources.

terms of population size in relation to the size of the country. Poor urban planning rather than population size is the main culprit for its pollution and congestion problems.

The density of Beijing is similar to that of other large cities in the world. Table 4.1 compares the number of cars, city population, and area of the major cities of the world. Beijing has fewer vehicles than New York and Los Angeles, and a lower population density than Tokyo.

So, why is Beijing so congested? The two photos in Figure 4.11 reveal the reasons. Comparing the two satellite photos, we can see that the road density in New York is much higher than that in Beijing. In New York, 25% of the total landmass is covered with roads (New York City Bureau of Transportation), whereas in Beijing, only 7% of the total landmass is covered with roads (Beijing Statistical Year Book, 2012).

Moreover, the subway/railway density in Beijing is not very high compared with other cities around the world. In 2015, the total subway length was 600 km; only 30 km per million residents. However, in Tokyo and London, the length of subway/railway per million residents in 2015 was

FIGURE 4.11 Comparison of city road density between Beijing and New York

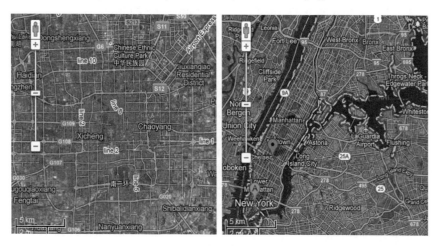

Source: Google Maps, 2016.

69 km and 192 km, respectively. Consequently, Tokyo is much less congested, even though it has over 37 million residents, a population that is 90% larger than that of Beijing.

Obviously, Beijing's congestion is caused by underinvestment and poor planning of roads and public transportation. As a wealthy city, Beijing has the resources to invest heavily in infrastructure. And, of course, as India grows wealthier, the same pattern will need to be repeated in its large cities.

Planning for a Mega City Comprised of 30 Million People

I have argued that large cities are good for innovation, and cities such as Shanghai and New York should be larger. But both Shanghai and New York already have over 15 million people; does this mean there is no more room for growth? Population growth in a city is not limited by space but by commute time, which could become intolerable for residents.

Mega cities like Shanghai and New York can learn from Tokyo, which uses high-speed railway to connect satellite cities. Yokohoma is a satellite city 28 km away from Tokyo's city center, and a non-stop high-speed railway connects Yokohoma to the city center in less than 20 minutes. High-speed train technology in Japan has been around for almost 40 years. China's high-speed railway is even faster, with a speed of 350 km/h. The Chinese high-speed railway can connect a satellite city center 40 km away to the metropolitan city center in less than 10 minutes non-stop, and in less than 20 minutes with three to four stops. If fast metro lines were to be built on top of existing metro lines, the commute time could be reduced significantly.

For mass transit systems to work efficiently, the population density of a city needs to be high. The population densities of most cities in the United States are too low. Singapore has a density of 10,000 people per square kilometer, while Tokyo has a density of 5,000 people per square kilometer. New York and Los Angeles have a population density of only about 2,000 people per square kilometer (although the population density in Manhattan is much higher). If high-speed railways can connect satellite cities 40 km away to city centers in less than 20 minutes, the city can be enlarged to have a diameter of 80 km, which will be roughly 5,000 km^2 in landmass. With a density of 10,000 people per square kilometer, a city can have over 50 million people, and residents can still travel from any location to the city center in under 40 minutes.

To further reduce commute times, current zoning laws need to be revised. It is clearly necessary to separate industrial areas and residential areas, but the separation of commercial and residential areas is unnecessary and contributes to longer commute times. Today, even the concentration of banks and financial firms in central business districts is unnecessary, because (unlike in the past) financial transactions no longer require face-to-face meetings. Still, creative workers need face-to-face interaction with other team members; however, the typical team size is just a few dozen to a few hundred. Moreover, high-tech firms do not create nearly as much traffic in the neighborhood as other businesses such as banks, and do not need to be located close to other businesses or in a central business district. Therefore, most high-tech firms can be located near residential areas, thus reducing commute time. Of course, some employees still may not be able to move to a residential area close to the office for a variety of reasons, for example their spouse may need to work for a far-away firm. But for many people, and overall by mixing commercial and residential areas, commute times can be reduced.

Lastly, with the emergence of Uber-like bike rental services, the last-mile connection to the metro railway is made easier. In China, a new startup is providing on-demand bike rental services by which anybody can locate a nearby bike using a smartphone. People are using bicycles to ride to and from subways to reduce their commute time. Further down the line, as automated driving technology becomes legal and commercially available, driving will be less tiring and parking will be easier as well. In sum, the combination of high-speed rail, Uber-like services, and automatic driving technologies will likely solve the commuting problems of the mega cities of the future.

I would like to conclude this chapter by discussing the view of the prominent American economist, Nobel Laureate, Gary Becker. I was fortunate to have the opportunity to carry out postdoctoral research under his guidance

FIGURE 4.12 Author's photo with Gary Becker in 2011

Photo Credit: James Liang.

from 2011 to 2012 at the University of Chicago (Figure 4.12). He was a pioneer in the field of human capital and labor economics, and wrote extensively on public policy in many areas, including environment and population. In commenting on the 2011 United Nations' forecast of 10 billion people by the end of the century, he wrote a blog entitled "Yes, the world will have ample resources for 10 billion people." First, he thinks that the UN forecast of 10 billion people by the end of the century may be an overestimate—if the GDP per capita in many developing countries continues to rise, their fertility rates will drop and it is likely that the peak world population will be significantly smaller than 10 billion. Then he explains why the growing demand for food, water, and other resources can be met by adopting improved technology and innovations. At the end of the article, he concludes:

If world population grew to 10 billion by the end of the century—an unlikely outcome—that would present considerable challenges. However, greater population would add real benefits as well, and I am inclined toward the view that the benefits will exceed the harm.

CHAPTER 5

Public Policy

In Chapter 2, I argued that the most important factors for economic growth and innovation are demographic factors. These include the size of the population, the geographic concentration, and the aging makeup of the population. In this chapter, I will discuss policy issues related to each of these demographic factors.

After the Second World War, most developed countries experienced a baby boom, and most developing countries improved their healthcare systems and significantly reduced their infant mortality rate. Consequently, the population of the world experienced unprecedented growth during the 1960s and 1970s, and a widespread global concern was that overpopulation would be disastrous for the environment and the economy.

Against this background, many developing countries started to adopt fertility reduction policies. For example, Vietnam implemented a two-child-only policy. India tried to impose forced sterilization after a woman had given birth to two children, but had to abandon this policy after strong opposition from voters. China implemented the extreme policy of only allowing one child for most of its urban residents.

About a generation later, the fertility rate dropped sharply globally, as many of these countries became wealthier and more urbanized. During the 1980s and 1990s, the fertility rate in many countries—including Japan, Korea, and Singapore—dropped below the replacement level; consequently, they started to reverse their fertility reduction policies.

Today, the majority of high-income and middle-income countries face the opposite problem of overpopulation—low fertility and aging. In 2002, the Center for Strategic and International Studies organized a study of the problem of low fertility and aging. This committee reached the conclusion that aging will present five challenges:

1. Rising old-age support will challenge the financial health of government budgets and public pensions for many aging countries.

2. An aging workforce not only leads to a shortage of workers, but also reduces productivity.
3. Reduced demand will hurt many industries, especially real estate and its related industries.
4. Reduced savings and declining asset values in aging countries, as in Japan.
5. Aging will lead to the realignment of world power, as the aging developed countries become weaker.

The recent financial crisis in Southern European countries, including Portugal, Italy, Greece, and Spain (PIGS), can be at least partly attributed to demographic factors. All PIGS countries have a severe aging and low fertility problem. Their fertility rates are respectively 1.2, 1.4, 1.3, and 1.3, which are amongst the lowest in Europe and the world. Of all the large affluent countries, Japan has the lowest fertility rate and the oldest workforce; it is not a coincidence that its economy has experienced nearly two decades of stagnation. The only way to escape the low-fertility trap is to encourage people to have more children (or to open borders to immigrants, thus increasing the population). And, indeed, most low-fertility countries have implemented pro-fertility policies.

Recent Pro-fertility Policies in Developed Countries

In Europe, with fertility falling below replacement levels, most countries have adopted generous pro-fertility policies. Recently, in France, a family could receive 177 euros per month per child. For families with three or more children, the cash bonus is increased to 600–800 euros per child, per month until the age of 19. The cash bonus in France is very generous, even by European standards.

In the United Kingdom, the welfare system provides many benefits to families with children. In 2014, they include: for most families, a bonus of £20.50 per week for the first child, and £13.55 per week for every additional child, up to the age of 20; for low-income families, £122.50 per week for the first child, and up to £210 per week for families with more than two children. Also, under certain conditions, when both parents are working, most of the daycare expenses can be reimbursed.

In Germany, regardless of citizenship, a child cash bonus is paid to parents until their child reaches the age of 25. The amount of the bonus is adjusted every year. In 2012, the bonus was 184 euros per month for the first two children, 190 euros for the third child, and 215 euros for the fourth child. Mandated maternity leave benefits include two-thirds of the mother's previous monthly salary, up to 1,800 euros, paid for 14 months.

In Russia, since 2007, for every child after the first two children, the government gives a one-time bonus of about 250,000 rubles (three times the average annual income); this is a very generous bonus relative to Russia's per capita income level.

Reversal of Fertility Policy in Asia

In East Asia, the fertility policy has experienced a reversal over the last 30–40 years. In the 1960s and 1970s, East Asian countries were still relatively poor, and like the rest of the world, their governments were deeply concerned that a fast-growing population would hurt their ability to sustain their economic development. Accordingly, they implemented various policies to reduce the fertility rate. However, when their economies developed rapidly during the 1980s and 1990s, their fertility rates dropped precipitously. Today, most of these countries have various pro-fertility policies in place.

Japan was the first country in the world to experience an ultra-low fertility rate. Its fertility rate dropped right after the Second World War, with almost no post-war baby boom. Its fertility rate dropped below the replacement level in the 1970s, and by 2010 had dropped below 1.5, becoming the first ultra-low-fertility country. Currently, the fertility level is only 1.4, one of the lowest among high-income countries. The Japanese government has realized the damaging effect of low fertility in recent years, and started to implement pro-fertility policies.

In Japan, a one-time bonus of 1 million yen (about US$10,000), which represents approximately one-quarter of the average annual income, is given for every new child. In 2013, the government raised the budget for enhancing fertility from 9.4 billion yen to 14 billion yen (roughly US$0.14 billion), which represents only a small portion of the overall GDP. Compared with European countries, Japan's spending to raise fertility is quite low.

The situation in Korea is similar to that of Japan, albeit with a 20-year time lag. The population grew rapidly between the 1950s and the 1980s. In the 1970s and 1980s, wary of overpopulation, the government implemented policies to reduce the fertility rate; for example, they gave housing priority to sterilized couples with fewer children. But in the 1990s, when the country grew much more affluent, with GDP of around US$6,000 per capita, the fertility rate had already dropped below 2. Moreover, in the 2000s, as the country grew even wealthier, the fertility rate continued to drop steeply, reaching an ultra-low level of 1.4 and currently sitting at 1.3, below even the level of Japan. The Korean government had to completely reverse its policies, and implement many measures to raise the fertility rate. In 2010, Korean President Li announced the allocation of 3.7 trillion won (US$3.7 billion) to raise the fertility rate. This amount represents less than 0.5% of Korea's GDP, which is still relatively stingy compared with European countries.

Taiwan followed a similar trajectory to Korea. In 1945, Taiwan had a population of 6 million, and in 2014 its population stood at 23 million. In 1964,

Taiwan established the Family Health Committee, which was responsible for implementing policies to reduce fertility. In 1967, the committee advocated that families should only have two children; it stated that they should wait three years after marriage to have their first child, and another three years to have their second child. In 1971, it used the slogan: "Two children are perfect, boys and girls are equally as good." Similar to Korea, the fertility rate in Taiwan started to drop below the replacement level in the 1990s, and below 1.5 in the new century. In response, the Taiwan government reversed its fertility policy and rolled out measures to encourage people to have more children. In 2012, it allocated 3.2 billion Taiwan dollars (about US$100 million) to raise the fertility rate; however, the fertility rate of Taiwan remains very low at only around 1.3, one of the lowest in the world.

Singapore's reversal of its fertility policy was the quickest and most dramatic. Singapore has a land area of only 683 km^2. Its population grew from 1.7 million in 1960 to 5.5 million in 2014; it is one of the most densely populated countries. Singapore has almost no natural resources, and imports most of its water from Malaysia. In 1960, Singapore had a high fertility rate of 5.4 and a fast-growing population. In the 1970s, like many other Asian governments, the government of Singapore started to implement policies to reduce the fertility rate. These policies included an advertising campaign of "two is enough," the legalizing of abortion and sterilization, and the cancellation of maternity leave and childcare benefits for women with more than two children. These policies had a disproportionately significant effect on low-income families. As a result, the fertility rate declined rapidly from 3.0 in 1971 to 1.6 in 1985. In 1986, Singapore's first Prime Minister, Lee Kuan Yew, quickly realized that the fertility rate was too low, and decided on a 180-degree reversal of the fertility policy. On June 30th, 1986, the government of Singapore eliminated its Family Planning and Population Committee and in the following year, introduced a new advertising campaign to convey the benefits of marriage and raising children. Its slogan was: "Have Three or More (if you can afford to)." In the meantime, it changed its immigration policies to attract more immigrants. With a reversal of its fertility policy in 1986 and 1987, the fertility rate rebounded to 1.92 in 1987 and 1.87, 1.77, and 1.76 in the following three years. The next Prime Minister of Singapore, Goh Chok Tong, was optimistic that the fertility rate would soon recover to the replacement level, but to his dismay the fertility rate started to drop again in 1992. In the new century, the fertility rate has dropped to 1.4, an ultra-low level. However, being a very small country, Singapore has another way of very quickly boosting its population, which is to attract immigration. I will analyze immigration policies later in this chapter.

China, with a much larger population and a very different political regime, actually followed a similar narrative to that of other Asian countries. From 1949 to 1980, the population of China grew from 430 million to over a billion. In

1980, the government started advocating its one-child policy. In the cities, anybody who had more than one child was faced with a steep fine and the loss of jobs, which effectively forced everybody to have only one child. However, in the countryside, where most people live, due to strong opposition to the one-child policy, the government effectively implemented a 1.5 child policy (i.e. allowing people to have a second child only when the first child was a girl). This one-child policy represents the most drastic policy implemented in the world to reduce fertility. China's fertility rate dropped like a rock in the 1990s. By 2000, the fertility rate was around 1.6 and by 2015 it was below 1.3, one of the lowest in the world. But unlike other Asian countries, the Chinese government was very slow to reverse its fertility policy. Only in 2015 did the government officially relax the one-child policy, allowing people to have two children (two-child policy). In later chapters, I will discuss future demographic trends in China and their significant impact for the world.

In the long run, China will have to completely reverse its fertility policy in order to raise its fertility rate to a near replacement level. An increasing number of countries are joining the low-fertility-rate club. Iran, an Islamic country, which surprisingly has a below-replacement fertility rate, has recently reversed its fertility policy to encourage people to have more children. How to raise fertility to the replacement level will be a common problem for most developed and middle-income countries, irrespective of their cultural specificity.

Analysis of Pro-fertility Policy

The following are the common pro-fertility policies:

1. Financial support (i.e. cash transfer or tax relief to families with children).
2. Daycare and education support.
3. Benefit to mothers, such as paid maternity leave.

Financial Support

Cash transfers or tax reliefs essentially transfer tax money collected from all taxpayers to only those families with children. Is such a transfer fair? In pre-industrial societies, old-age support was provided by children, whereas in modern societies, old-age support is partially provided by a public pension benefit, which is available to everybody irrespective of whether they have had any children. In other words, tax paid by the younger generations supports the older generations, including those who chose not to have any children. This way, people with children (who are future taxpayers) are actually subsidizing those without any children. To use the United States as an example, the pension and medical benefits to support the elderly account for about 15% of

GDP, so it should therefore be fair to offer subsidies to families worth 15% of the average annual income for every extra child raised. Education is one way for such subsidization; typically, public education spending is about 5% of GDP. So, it is fair to give an extra 15% − 5% = 10% income a year to child-raising families for every extra child raised. In the United States, 10% of per capita GDP is around US$5,000 a year, which is about what it costs to raise an extra child. In China, 10% of per capita GDP is only US$800 a year, which is nowhere near enough to raise a child in a typical urban family.

Many low-fertility developed countries give various levels of child-raising bonuses to families, ranging from 1% to 5% of GDP. How effective are the bonuses in raising fertility? Figure 5.1 shows the relationship between the level of child-raising subsidy and the fertility rate. The vertical axis is the fertility rate, and the horizontal axis is the level of financial subsidies provided to families with children as a percentage of GDP. Apparently, there is a positive relationship: higher subsidies are associated with higher levels of fertility. Increasing the bonus by an extra 1% of GDP will raise the fertility rate by about 0.1 children, which implies that financial support works, although it is very costly.

FIGURE 5.1 The relationship between child-raising subsidies and the fertility rate

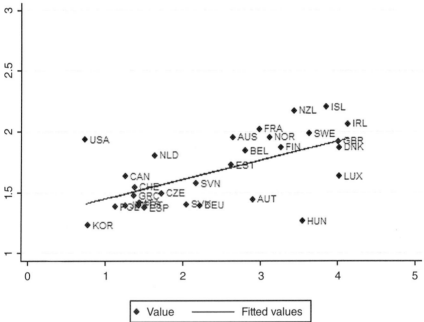

Data Source: World Bank, 2015.

Scandinavian countries—such as Norway, Sweden, and the Netherlands—all have high levels of subsidies and relatively high fertility rates. East Asian countries—such as Korea and Japan—are ungenerous in child-raising subsidies and therefore have low fertility rates. Some countries, like Southern European countries, which may be constrained financially, also have low subsidies and low fertility rates. These countries may have fallen into the "low-fertility trap." Because of their low fertility rates and aging societies, their economies have weakened to a point where they can no longer afford large subsidies to raise the fertility rate.

The United States is one of the very few developed countries in the world that has a near replacement fertility level of around 2. Although the U.S. government does not directly give cash to child-raising families, it does allow families to claim about US$3,000 worth of tax deductions per dependent. The United States is exceptional in that even without a large cash bonus, it still has a relatively high fertility rate. Economists and sociologists still debate the cause of this high fertility in the United States. In my view, it is probably due to a high level of religiosity and a large immigrant population, who have a greater number of children.

Daycare and Education Support

Besides direct financial support, education subsidies are an important measure in order to raise the fertility rate. Most countries already provide 12 years of free education. Some Western and Northern European countries also provide generous pre-school benefits, including subsidies for kindergarten and day-care services.

France is famous for its excellent government support for pre-school children. Not only does the government provide free kindergartens, but also crèches (daycare centers) throughout the country. From the age of two-and-a-half months to three years, a child can be placed in a crèche. Crèches are funded by local and state governments, and are free for most people (except those with high incomes). They are open 11 hours a day, and closed on public holidays and for a month in the summer. All cities, towns, and some villages have a local crèche. Some employers offer a crèche for the children of their employees, which is usually located in or near the workplace. For those who hire a nanny at home, a part of this expense is tax-deductible. With a generous cash bonus and excellent daycare support, France has a fertility rate of 2, which is much higher than the average European fertility rate of 1.6.

Parents in other countries are far less fortunate than the French. In recent years, low-fertility countries in Asia have been trying to catch up with European countries in daycare-center benefits. Until recently, Korean parents typically had a hard time finding government-funded daycare centers. In 2013, the Korean government decided to vastly expand its free daycare and kindergarten benefits in order to raise the fertility rate. Pre-school vouchers are issued to most families (the bottom 70% of the income distribution) to pay for daycare centers and kindergarten.

Japan does not have enough daycare centers either. In 2016, President Abe pledged to create and fund 400,000 new daycare slots by 2018. Despite these efforts, Japan still has a long way to go before it matches the kind of daycare benefits offered by Western and Northern European nations.

The situation in China is even worse. Daycare centers and kindergartens are mostly privately run and expensive. Government-supported daycare centers and kindergartens are in such short supply that children of migrant workers in cities are generally not qualified to enroll. In large cities, there are not even enough primary schools and middle schools to meet the demands of their growing populations. Many children of migrant workers in large cities have to return to their home towns to attend school, and are consequently separated from their parents. This has exacerbated an already ultra-low fertility rate in large cities in China. Cities such as Shanghai and Beijing have a fertility rate of below 1.0, the lowest fertility level of any city in the world.

Maternity Leave

In the United Kingdom, paid maternity leave is 39 weeks at 90% of full pay. In addition, employers have to keep each mother's job open for a year. If the employer cannot afford these maternity benefits, then the government can step in to provide funding. Fathers are also entitled to some limited paid leave too.

In France, mothers can obtain 16 weeks of full paid maternity leave, and a partial paid leave until the child is three years old. The government even provides free pelvis correction and weight-loss training.

In Germany, employers are required to keep mothers' jobs open for up to three years while they are on leave. Fully paid maternity leave is 140 days in length, after which 40% of pay is offered until the child is one-and-a-half years old.

The maternity benefits in Europe are typically very generous. In many Asian countries, such as Singapore, paid maternity leave is 16 weeks. Figure 5.2 shows the length of maternity leave (in weeks) for many countries, ranging from just a few weeks to three years.

Building a Pro-fertility Culture

In addition to providing pro-fertility benefits, governments have also tried to build a pro-fertility culture. On the streets and subways of Russia, there are many poster adverts encouraging women to have more children. One poster

FIGURE 5.2 Length of maternity leave in selected countries

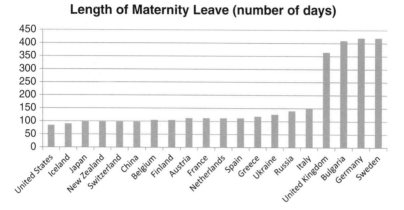

Length of Maternity Leave (number of days)

Data Source: Working Conditions Laws Report (2010). ILO Working Conditions Laws Database, ILO, Geneva.

in the Moscow subway shows a woman with three babies with the slogan "Patriotism begins with family." Russia officially advocates that it is a woman's patriotic duty to have three babies. The government issues a medal of honor to women with more than three babies, and a "Heroic Mother" medal and cash reward to women with more than 10 babies. Some cities have even set up "pregnancy holidays," where couples can have a day off from work to try to conceive babies.

The French government gives a medal of honor to mothers with four or more children. A bronze medal is awarded to mothers with four or five children, a silver medal to mothers with six or seven children, and a gold medal to mothers with eight or more children.

In Korea, the government has developed many interesting marketing slogans, such as: "Daddy, I am lonely, I want a brother or sister"; "Many candles are brighter than one candle"; "The best gift to give your baby is a sister or brother"; and "We can make beautiful people."

Marriage Ratio and Out-of-Wedlock Births

It is a global trend that the marriage ratio is declining. The map in Figure 5.3 shows the percentage of people who are married in the population. In India and China, the marriage ratio (the percentage of the population that is married) is roughly 70%, which means that almost everybody over age 25 is married. The marriage ratios differ in developed countries. The ratio for

FIGURE 5.3 Marriage ratio map

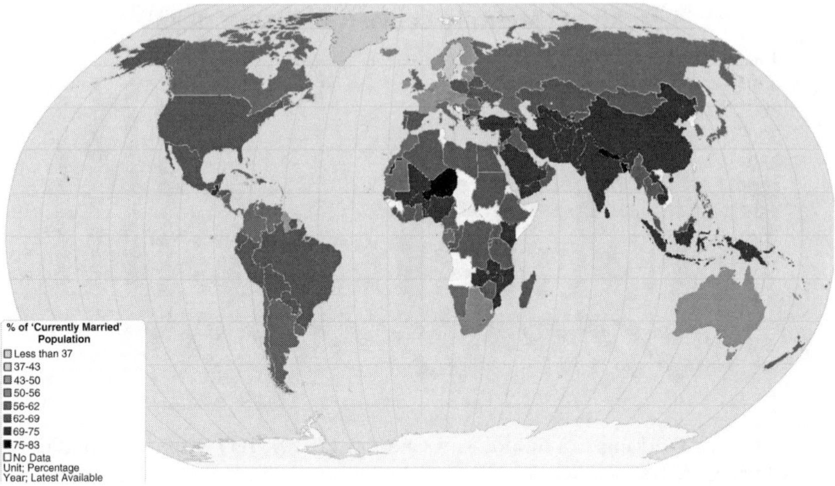

Data Source: United Nations, Department of Economic and Social Affairs, Population Division (2013). World Marriage Data 2012 (POP/DB/Marr/Rev2012); World Bank, 2015.

Americans shows that 60% of the population is married, while in Europe less than 50% of the population is married.

Surprisingly, in Japan, approximately 50% of the population is married. A 50% marriage ratio of the overall population implies an approximate 75% marriage ratio for people over age 25. One generation ago, in the 1970s and 1980s, Japan was like China and India, where almost every adult was married. But today, nearly 20% of women and men will remain unmarried for life.

The reason for the declining marriage ratio is that as an economy develops, women become more educated and economically independent. They have the option of staying single. Moreover, in Asian countries, women are reluctant to marry down (i.e. marry somebody with lower social and economic status). An adult unmarried ratio of 20% is a major contributor to the low fertility rate in Japan. Assuming that only married women have children, even if the fertility level of married women is 2, then the overall fertility rate is only $2 \times (1 - 20\%) = 1.6$. But actually, married Japanese women on average are having 1.87 children. And with only 80% of women married, the overall fertility is only 1.4. The situation in Japan is quite typical in other Asian countries, such as Korea, Taiwan, and Singapore. Wealthy cities in China are also experiencing a declining marriage ratio.

The low marriage ratio is a major problem for fertility in Asian countries, because out-of-wedlock birth continues to be culturally unacceptable. For

FIGURE 5.4 Percentage of births to unmarried women, selected countries, 1980 and 2007

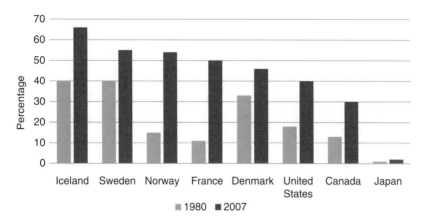

Data Source: CDC/NCHS; National Vital Statistics System; Stat Canada; Population Statistics of Japan; European Commission; Eurostat.

China, India, Korea, and Japan, the unmarried birth rate is nearly zero. In contrast, this is not a problem for European and North American countries, because unmarried births have become socially acceptable and thus a lot more common. Figure 5.4 shows births to unmarried women as a percentage of overall births in different countries in 2007 compared with 1980. Evidently, births to unmarried mothers have increased rapidly over the last 30 years, especially in Western and Northern European countries such as Sweden, Norway, Iceland, France, and Denmark. In these countries, children from non-traditional families are culturally accepted and receive as good-quality education as other children. President Obama was from a single-parent family, and so was the late Steve Jobs. Families where parents are unmarried but live together are common and effectively function as traditional families.

Births outside of marriage are quite common in Europe, partly because governments in these countries do not discriminate against single mothers when providing child-raising benefits and education subsidies, making it much easier for single women to raise children. The high unmarried birth rate contributes significantly to the high fertility rates in Northern Europe, for example. Asian countries need to somehow either raise the marriage ratio or change their culture to be more tolerant of births outside of marriage, both of which are very difficult to do. At the very least, governments of East Asian countries need to fix the discriminatory benefit regulations to provide the same level of benefit to single mothers as they do to traditional families.

The Future of Pro-fertility Policies

It is increasingly difficult and expensive to persuade couples or single women to have more children. Women today have many competing demands, such as education, career, leisure, and entertainment. The availability of public pension plans has also reduced the incentive for bearing children. Many governments have provided increasingly generous benefits to help families raise children, although they are still significantly lower than what could be considered a fair level (i.e. 10% of GDP). For wealthy East Asian countries, the level of benefits is still ungenerous, and not nearly enough to raise the fertility rate close to the necessary replacement level. The prospects for East Asian countries in the near term are quite grim.

In the long run, reproductive technologies, such as in vitro fertilization (IVF), may help address some of these problems. A woman can freeze her eggs and delay pregnancy, or even outsource pregnancy to other women. With the IVF technology available today, twins can also be implanted. In the long run, with breakthroughs in artificial womb technology, babies may be produced in laboratories, but they will still need to be raised by human parents. Today, many governments restrict the use of these technologies, as the legal and moral implications are complicated, but in the long run, this may be the only way to reduce the burden of pregnancy imposed on women and to keep the fertility rate from falling further.

Immigration

From a global perspective, immigration will not solve the problem of aging populations, but for any single country or region, immigration seems to be an easier and faster solution than persuading people to have more children. For example, a college graduate is a very attractive immigrant, because this individual can immediately work and pay tax, and the receiving country effectively gets a free ride on the educational investment made by the sending country. In recent years, most developed countries have turned toward immigration to deal with the problem of labor shortages and aging populations.

The issue of immigration varies considerably among countries. High-income countries are generally destinations and developing countries are the source of immigrants. Figure 5.5 shows the net migration for major countries in 2012. The United States was the largest net immigrant country. Among the largest emigrant countries, India is ranked first, China is ranked second, and Pakistan is ranked third.

Immigration not only helps to solve the problem of labor shortages, but it can potentially also enhance entrepreneurship and innovation. In the United

FIGURE 5.5 The net migration for major countries in 2012

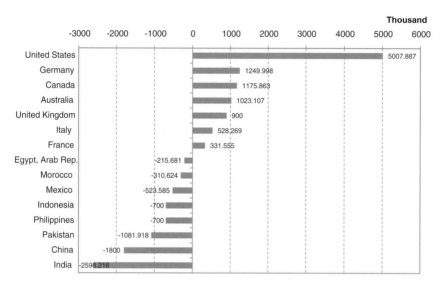

Data Source: World Bank, 2015.

States, immigrants are on average more entrepreneurial and innovative than the natives, as I will show in Chapter 8.

However, voters in the destination country usually have many concerns regarding immigrants. The common concerns regarding immigration are quite similar to the concerns connected with overpopulation. People worry that an influx of immigrants will cause shortages of jobs and schools, lead to congestion on the roads, and so on. I have argued previously that these are short-term problems. Although immigrants will consume public resources in the short term, in the long run, immigrants, especially young immigrants, will work, save, and pay taxes, leading to more public resources becoming available. Immigrants will not raise unemployment either, because they not only take jobs but also create jobs by way of their own demand for goods and services. The cultural concerns are also blown out of proportion. Although first-generation immigrants might have a hard time assimilating completely, second-generation immigrants usually become native speakers and fully functioning members of society. Some people are worried about Muslim immigrants in Europe; I will discuss this in detail in Chapter 9. For a country like the United States, there are many more people who want to enter than can be accepted. Therefore, there has to be an immigration policy to choose a certain number and a certain mix of immigrants. Not all immigrants can be welcome.

Welfare Immigrants

Welfare immigrants are those who enter a country in order simply to access government benefits. This is obviously a burden for the receiving country. For example, a retired person may enter a country to receive public old-age support and medical benefits. However, it is likely that such a person will be a relative of another native citizen, and it is morally unacceptable to refuse entry to such immigrants. Obviously, welfare immigrants will choose the country with the best welfare, which will put pressure on the governments of countries with generous welfare. For these countries, if they wish to benefit from immigration and yet keep their welfare benefits generous, they may need to discriminatorily deny some benefits (including voting rights) to recent immigrants.

Unskilled Immigrants

Unskilled immigrants are those who work in manual labor positions, such as maids, construction workers, gardeners, and so on. These immigrants will benefit their employers because of their lower wages, but will hurt native unskilled workers. Usually, the overall benefit outweighs the cost, but the benefit tends to accrue to the affluent, and the cost is borne by the poor—thus increasing the level of inequality in the country. This is one of the main reasons why many countries do not seek unskilled immigrants.

Highly Skilled Immigrants

Highly skilled immigrants, especially young high-tech workers, will benefit their employers. They will also create more demand for unskilled services, such as maids and gardeners, raising the level of unskilled wages and hence reducing inequality in the receiving country. Their arrival could hurt the wages of the native highly skilled workers, but this may not be true, especially for globalized high-tech industries. In the global race for innovation, a talented Chinese engineer hired by a Silicon Valley firm is unlikely to replace an American engineer, but will possibly replace a job in a competing firm in China. Conversely, a talented Indian scientist, not hired by the U.S. firm, will still be a competitor to the American highly skilled workers, albeit working from a different country, such as Canada or the United Kingdom. Moreover, there is a strong agglomeration effect in innovation. A higher concentration of innovation in one region breeds even more innovation. More immigrants working in the high-tech industry will probably create more complementary high-skilled jobs rather than simply fill them. Kerr and Lincoln (2010) have found that a larger number of incoming highly skilled immigrants have no negative effect on native highly skilled workers.

I had a Singaporean friend who complained that children from recent immigrant families became the top students in his son's high-school class. His son, who used to be at the top of the class, now ranked only fourth best in the class. My friend worried that his son's chances of getting into a top U.S. college would be reduced. I told him that these talented immigrant kids would be competitors for college slots, regardless of where they go to school in the world. Moreover, top colleges around the world will soon realize that the quality of this Singaporean school is much better than before, and his son's prospects for college will not be negatively affected. Lastly, by being in the same class with more talented classmates, his son will probably study harder and learn more. The reason I tell this story is that competition among high-school students for college admission to the world-leading universities is analogous to competition among high-tech workers, because both competitions are global. The impact of highly skilled immigrants on skilled wages in the high-tech industry may well be neutral or even positive.

Most countries have policies in place to attract highly skilled immigrants. The United States, having already established itself as a center of innovation, enjoys a huge advantage in attracting them. According to a recent placement report for college graduates in the top engineering programs in China and India, about 10–30% of graduating classes go abroad to pursue a postgraduate degree, and a vast majority of them (more than 60–70%) go to a university in the United States—more than all other countries combined.

However, the United States is squandering its advantage somewhat by setting a quota for the H1-B employment visa. Actually, the best policy choice for the U.S. government would be to take anybody with a recent college degree in engineering or science. What a bargain! It is the sending country that should complain, as it has already paid for the education of this highly skilled person and is not getting any return on its investment.

After graduation with a computer science degree from Georgia Tech, I worked as a software engineer at Oracle headquarters in Silicon Valley in 1991 on an H1-B visa, until I returned to China and co-founded Ctrip.com in 1999. I was fortunate, because the H1-B visa was relatively easy to obtain in the early 1990s. Later cohorts at Oracle were not so lucky, and by the late 1990s, as the high-tech industry grew rapidly, the H1-B visa quota was not nearly high enough to meet the growing demand for foreign talent. The queue for an H1-B visa lengthened to several years. Consequently, many Silicon Valley companies were forced to establish research and development centers outside the United States, mostly in China and India. When I was at Oracle in the late 1990s, Oracle established many such centers in India, hiring thousands of engineers. Later, these Indian engineers helped India to jump start their IT outsourcing industry, which has become the most competitive in the world.

Internal Migration

Much like every country that seeks to attract highly skilled immigrants, every city within a country would also like to attract highly skilled workers from other parts of the country. Following a similar logic, cities would want to turn away unskilled migrant workers, because they would hurt the earning potential of native unskilled residents. However, a country as a whole should consider not just the welfare of the native residents of a specific city, but also the welfare of the migrant workers (and everybody else in the country). For a migrant worker in a developing country, moving to a large city is far better than staying in the village, as it is probably the only way to escape poverty. Moreover, when one farmer leaves for the city, the other farmers remaining in the village will also benefit because there will be more farmland available per farmer. Internal migration in a developing country is an important mechanism in reducing poverty and income inequality. So, for the overall welfare of all the citizens in a country, the government should remove all restriction on internal movement. Following the same logic transnationally, the best program for the relief of poverty globally would be for the United Nations to require every country to open their borders. Of course, this is impossible, because nation states are committed to the welfare of, primarily, their citizens only.

The War for Talent

More countries have come to realize the benefits of highly skilled immigration, and that the race of innovation will be won by the country or region that can attract the most talent. The strong agglomeration effect suggests that only a handful of innovation centers can prosper globally. The stakes are high and the competition for talent is fierce. So which places can, and are most likely to, attract the brightest and the best? Economists have ranked the most attractive cities in which to live. The criteria include: transportation, environment, education, diversity, and economy. Clearly, in today's world, the winning centers of innovation appear to be mostly in the United States. Silicon Valley is the center of IT innovation, Los Angeles is the center of the entertainment industry, and New York is the center of financial innovation. This is not surprising, since the United States has the largest market and the largest talent pool among all the developed countries. The only countries that can realistically compete with the United States are China and India, as both have a much larger population than that of the United States. Chinese cities like Shanghai, Shenzhen, and Beijing, with their mega-sized populations, are thus becoming new centers for innovation.

The first-tier cities in China—Beijing, Shanghai, Guangzhou, and Shenzhen—have populations of 20, 23, 18, and 17 million residents, respectively. They have the potential to become global innovation centers. However, they are congested and polluted, and also have some of the most expensive real estate in the world. In short, they are not great places to live. All of this is due to inadequate urban planning. It is crucial not just for China but also for any country around the world to plan adequately for the development and growth of large cities. With more innovation activities concentrated in large cities, the importance of these metropolises increases. A country will lose the global race of attracting talent if its largest cities are congested and expensive. Moreover, a country is likely to fall into the "low fertility trap" if its largest cities cannot provide adequate housing or schools, as residents will find it difficult to raise children and hence will have fewer of them.

Competition among Countries: Large Countries vs. Small Countries

In the global race of innovation, large countries have many advantages. They have bigger markets, more talent, and larger cities. The scale advantage of a large country is overwhelming. Small nations can use free trade agreements to form large, free-trading blocs to take advantage of the benefits of a large market. The European Union (EU) is just such a free-trading bloc, where all restrictions connected to the movement of goods and labor have been removed. However, due to differences in culture, language, local laws, and regulations, non-tariff frictions still prevent small nations from enjoying the full benefit of one large homogeneous market, like that of the United States, China, or India. Culture and language barriers also prevent the movement of labor without friction, even in a theoretically single labor market like the EU. As long as large countries do not make colossal economic mistakes, they are endowed with significant advantages in the race of innovation.

Is there a downside to a country possessing a large population? Would a population increase ever create a shortage of natural resources? I have argued in previous chapters that natural resources are no longer an important factor in the development and growth of a modern economy. In developed countries and middle-income countries, including China, the value of natural resources accounts for less than 10% of the economy.

A Tale of Ctrip.com: An Analogy between Company Size and Country Size

In one of the classes that I taught at Beijing University, I was once asked by one of the students: "Professor Liang, you have been telling us that a large population is good for innovation, but in the business world, why are small companies more innovative than large companies?"

I quickly dealt with the question by asking the student to examine patent filing patterns; by this measure, large companies are much more innovative than smaller companies. But in the next few days, I was intrigued by this question. Although large companies are better innovators on average, there are indeed many very creative small companies, and some of them have managed to beat the large companies in the race of innovation. There are also many examples of failures of large companies to effectively harness the latest technology trends as a growth driver.

My company Ctrip.com is an interesting case study for innovation. I co-founded Ctrip.com in 1999, and ran the company until 2006. Through a series of innovations, Ctrip.com quickly grew to be the leader in the Chinese online travel market, with more than 50% of the online travel market share. Ctrip.com became a very profitable public company, with a multi-billion-dollar market cap. I was so confident that Ctrip.com's dominance would continue that I resigned from my CEO post and went to Stanford to pursue a PhD in Economics between 2007 and 2012. After graduation, I became a professor at Beijing University and continue to do research on demographics and innovation. However, during my absence, Ctrip.com lost its innovative edge, and was out-innovated and out-maneuvered by smaller rivals. Beginning in 2009, Ctrip.com started to lose market share and its profitability suffered. By 2012, its market capitalization was as low as US$2 billion (it is currently over US$20 billion). The situation became so bad that I was asked by the board to return from my deeply enjoyable academic foray to run the company again.

So, in 2014, I was back at Ctrip.com trying to turn around a large company. The problem at Ctrip.com is actually not an unusual one for large companies. Like many large and successful companies, it became complacent and conservative. Moreover, Ctrip.com became overcentralized, and innovative ideas were blocked by a stifling bureaucracy. To boost innovation and speed of execution, I decentralized the company into a number of autonomous business units. Each business unit has its own research and development, product, service, and distribution function. They became much quicker to experiment with new product ideas and technologies. In order to make the leaders of business units more like entrepreneurs, they were allowed to purchase a significant chunk of virtual stock, and they were also granted virtual stock options in the business units themselves. Cooperation between the business units was handled by free-market negotiation between the parties, instead of being coordinated by headquarters. Headquarters was no longer a bottleneck, and became only responsible for unified branding, financing, investment, and strategic relationships with external partners. These functions were still centralized, because these are areas where economies of scale are key. With most of the function decentralized, speed, flexibility, and innovation greatly improved. Between 2014 and 2015, Ctrip.com quickly reinvented itself as a one-stop mobile travel platform, and was faster than its smaller rivals in building innovative mobile functionality, including new products such as train and bus ticketing. In less than three years, Ctrip.com regained its leadership position in innovation, and is now once again one of the most successful Internet companies in China, with a market capitalization of over US$20 billion.

Policy Pitfall of a Large Country

The rise and fall of Ctrip.com's innovation capabilities in a very short period of time is a lesson analogous to the innovation capabilities of a large country. Complacency and overcentralization are the most common policy pitfalls of a large country.

Only a country as large as China could ever consider autarky out of complacency and overconfidence. When asked about the rationale of China's closed-border policy, Chinese Emperor Qianlong commented that China was so vast that it had everything it needed within its territory. But he was wrong, because the outside world is much larger and has many more people too. The autarky policy that grew out of Chinese emperors' complacency effectively squandered its size advantage in innovation, and was the main reason for it being the loser in the race of innovation against the West over the last 500 years.

The other policy pitfall is overcentralization. Large countries tend to implement uniform laws and regulations nationwide that are applied in a top-down fashion. This is clearly an advantage in terms of efficiency. For example, if the EU were a single nation, a pan-Europe business would not need to worry about different tax laws that exist in the different EU countries. But there is also a downside to uniformity. First, one size may not fit all, as optimal policy for each region might be different. Second, an extreme form of uniformity does not allow for enough experimentation with different policies or for competition between different regions. Even homogeneous countries like China should allow for experimentation with different policies in different regions. Successful policy reforms will be imitated by other regions, or residents will move to regions with a successful set of economic policies. In some areas, a free market of competing policies is beneficial and worth the cost of not having absolute uniformity in a nation.

The absurd anti-fertility policies pursued to date in China are an example of overcentralization. Some poor, remote agricultural provinces in China may still be at a Malthusian economic stage of development, but most of the coastal regions like Shanghai and Guangdong are developed economies with very low fertility and are not so much different from Korea and Japan. If China left the fertility policy to its provinces, many of the wealthy provinces would have ended the "one-child policy" many years ago. But the overcentralized political system in China prevented such policy experimentation by different regions.

When I advocated revoking the "one-child policy" in 2011, I was surprised to learn that the anti-fertility policy was enshrined in a constitutional amendment. The optimal policy arrangement is one that balances the high efficiency of a uniform policy and the benefits of having some regional differences. Large countries should allow for different regions to have some differences in economic policies and to experiment with new controversial technologies, while maintaining some level of uniformity to reduce transaction costs across regions. In general, for anything that is of little economic significance but more of a convention, uniformity is preferred (e.g. language, unit of measure, etc.). Other things are much trickier, so it is a delicate balancing act for any large nation or transnational policy bodies like the EU or World Trade Organization (WTO).

Policy Strategies of Small Countries

The pitfalls of a large country are the opportunities for smaller countries to outperform their larger rivals. When a large country has high trade barriers, a small country can act as a gateway to that large country. For example, when China had just opened its doors in the 1980s, there were significant practical barriers to connecting it with the world. Hong Kong thrived, being a gateway to China and effectively connecting it with the rest of the world. In recent years, as the barrier lowered, the role of Hong Kong as a gateway diminished.

Large countries tend to have uniform policies and are usually slow to adopt new policies related to innovation. For example, when large countries are slow to permit the introduction of controversial new technologies, such as reproductive assistance, self-driving, and genetic engineering technology, small countries can experiment by introducing these new technologies, potentially surpassing larger countries in terms of innovation in the related industries.

The policy strategy for a small nation should be that of a free-trading economy with a progressive and flexible policy toward new technologies. However, it is an uphill battle, because smaller nations—even with a high fertility rate—face the constant pressure of emigration. Large nations with vibrant and innovative large cities, such as the United States, are constantly cherry-picking the best talent from smaller nations, simply because they can offer both more opportunities and greater rewards. Eastern European countries have a high-quality workforce, but they are still losing many talented citizens to the United States, as well as to Western European nations—the United Kingdom in particular. To make up for a loss of talent to bigger nations, it is critical for small nations to have a successful immigration policy to attract talent from around the world, capitalizing on talent that is not captured by the larger countries.

In my economic PhD class at Stanford, most of the foreign-born students stayed in the United States after graduation; only those students from large countries such as China and India would even consider returning home. Almost all the Southern and Eastern European students stayed in the United States. However, there were quite a few international PhD students who went to work at universities in small English-speaking countries such as Australia and Singapore.

Language Barrier and the English Advantage

There is an interesting tale in the Bible. God wanted the people to spread out and populate the earth. Instead, they congregated and started making Babel, a tower to heaven. God was displeased at their disobedience and changed their languages, which forced them to disperse away from each other over the earth. One of the major barriers in the exchange of ideas and goods is language. China historically was the largest unified country throughout most of its history, partly because Qin Shi Huang unified the Chinese writing system about 2,000 years ago. Unlike the phonetic Latin language, which has morphed into many different languages over the years, Chinese written language uses glyphs, making it immune to dialectal change over the years. The unified written language is a key factor behind China's uniform culture.

Today, English is the world language of commerce and academics, and English-speaking countries have an advantage. The small English-speaking nations such as Singapore, Hong Kong, Canada, and Australia are much more integrated with larger English-speaking countries such as the United States and the United Kingdom. It is easier for these English-speaking countries to attract global talent, because immigrants can more easily collaborate with the native population. In small Northern European and West European countries, English is also the lingua franca in high-tech companies and universities, because the natives are proficient English speakers. It is more important for smaller countries to adopt English as their first or second language. Even large countries like China or Japan should consider introducing English as the second language in their universities. Otherwise, these countries will, in the future, be at a great disadvantage in attracting global talent.

Trade vs. Immigration

One can argue that a country need not rely on immigration to realize the benefits of a large population. Instead of importing people, a country can trade with larger nations to realize the necessary economies of scale. Indeed, trade openness is an essential ingredient for innovation and economic efficiency. That's why more and more countries are joining the WTO and forming free-trading blocs such as the EU. However, importing goods is still quite different from importing the people who make the goods. Immigrants can work together with the local population to generate creative ideas, start up a local new business, pay taxes, and vote to ensure that free trade and open border policies prevail.

Brexit and Donald Trump's Presidency

The benefits of immigration and trade on innovation are long term, but its distribution and disruptive effect on the native populace are often short term. Sometimes voters can be swung by taking a shortsighted view, like those who voted for Brexit and those who voted for Donald Trump. To everybody's surprise, Donald Trump won the 2016 election on the platform of anti-globalization and anti-immigration. It was the elderly and the less educated who voted for Donald Trump and for Brexit; they understandably are not the immediate beneficiaries of innovation.

The country that needs immigrants most is Japan, which has a rapidly shrinking young workforce. However, the older Japanese voters, who significantly outnumber the young voters, would reject any policy allowing large-scale immigration, because they care much more about the short-term disruption stemming from the arrival of immigrants rather than the long-term economic vitality of the country or a vague concept such as innovation. For this reason, it is important to have young and highly skilled immigrants enter the economy as future voters, so that the political interest is aligned with the long-term interest of the country. Otherwise, a country will fall into the "demographic trap," as the country's economic policy is trapped in the short-term populism of anti-immigration and trade.

Even with Brexit and Donald Trump's presidency, the United States and the United Kingdom are still the most open and attractive places for talent in the world. I believe that the setbacks for these two countries are temporary. The United States and the United Kingdom both have large and growing young, highly skilled populations, continuously fueled by the large number of highly skill immigrants and a relatively high fertility rate as well. The United States will remain the most attractive place for immigrants, compared with most of Europe, Japan, and other Asian countries, whose political policies will likely be even more handicapped by their much older populations.

Education Reform

My son recently transferred to a private high school in Boston. Observing his progress, I have been surprised that it compared to my high-school experience 30 years ago. Despite all the productivity improvements everywhere else, the education sector is no more efficient than it was 30 years ago. Actually, primary and secondary education is arguably less efficient than it was 30 years ago. Despite the fact that students are working harder and the facilities and access to technology are much improved, at the age of 18 students still only manage to acquire approximately the same amount of knowledge as in the past.

On the other hand, as argued in Chapter 2, the knowledge required for innovation keeps increasing. Today, most research fields require a PhD as a minimal starting point; some fields even require postdoctoral study or years of work experience. Moreover, people are graduating with a PhD much later; it is now common for students to complete their PhD at the age of 27 or 28. Meanwhile, as we have discussed in previous chapters, the best age for entrepreneurship is around 30, and the most creative age for innovation is between 30 and 40. That leaves only a short window after graduation to create the best innovation (for women it is even shorter, because of their biological clock). So, the dilemma for policy makers and educators is that we need people to speed up their learning in order to fuel innovation, but the education sector is effectively standing still or, at best, advancing very slowly. And this is primarily due to onerous regulations and a lack of pressure to improve.

In China and other Asian countries, the national college entrance exam dictates what students learn in high school; these exams still cover the same material as they did 30 years ago. In China, students are estimated to waste two years in high school just studying for the tests. Cram schools have prospered in China, which further saps the energy of young high-school students, who become unmotivated and exhausted when they enter college.

In the United States, even the most talented students are discouraged from skipping grades, and almost everybody has to wait till they are 18 years old to attend college. Private high schools and some public schools do offer college-level classes to talented high-school students. For example, Philips Academy, a prestigious boarding school in Boston, offers computer science and calculus classes even to 15-year-olds. Bill Gates and Mark Zuckerberg attended such private schools, which allowed them to finish college-level classes earlier than their peers. While clearly exceptional, they were able to start their companies before they graduated from college. But such high schools are the exception, as most high schools do not give students an option for graduating early. In recent years, with the "No Child Left Behind" initiative in the United States, the average standard of public high schools has actually decreased.

In my opinion, Internet technology can help speed up the learning process. First of all, a lot of material can be learned outside of class, or later in life. For example, it is possible to reduce the length of history classes, given that all the facts and materials are available online. Social issues can be taught later in life, as students will have a better understanding of social issues later on. English classes can be shortened for native speakers, partly because writing in the Internet age will be quite different; for one thing, perfect spelling is not that important any more with spell-checkers. Furthermore, subjects such as history, economics, and physics today are repeated multiple times in middle schools, high schools, colleges (and graduate schools), and there can be quite a lot of overlap in learning between different levels of the same subject. On the other hand, subjects like computer science or basic finance should become part of the standard curriculum, either in high school or college. The availability of good teachers for these subjects should not be a bottleneck, because all the best lectures and exercises are online, and teachers just need to monitor progress.

I am not advocating speeding up education for everybody, but for the most talented students it is my opinion that a significant speedup is achievable with the latest technology and a redesign of high-school and college curricula. (A one- to two-year speedup is certainly possible in many East Asian countries, as the high-school students there waste at least one to two years in preparing for the college entrance exam.) If we can allow a portion of students to graduate a few years earlier, this will benefit not only those students over their lifetime, but also society overall in terms of vitality of innovation and entrepreneurship in the long run. Of course, such a reform would still require a lot of research and innovation. But, unfortunately, because the education sector is heavily regulated, the incentive for innovation and reform is weak compared with other sectors.

At the core of the problem is the fact that high schools and elementary schools (and even parents) do not have any incentive to shorten the number of school years. If college admission is based on test scores regardless of age, then it is in the high school's interest to keep every student until he/she is 18. However, students suffer because they waste precious prime years studying for tests rather than working or innovating. Major education reforms are required to change the status quo, and the first thing to do is to encourage colleges to admit talented students younger than 18.

Graduating from college and starting to work one year earlier could have a huge lifetime benefit. It is not just one extra year of salary, but also, much more importantly, one extra prime-age year of getting promotions and raises. If, on average, one gets a 10% raise in the 20s, then one extra working year in the 20s means a 10% overall increase in terms of lifetime earnings, which is huge. Moreover, during the mid to late career stage (age > 50), a person who is a few years younger than another candidate has a significant advantage in getting promotion to senior executive positions. Therefore, the benefit of graduating earlier, although small initially, could be very big later in life.

A handful of Chinese universities offer young genius programs for talented students before the age of 15; I was one of the lucky few to attend Fu Dan University at the age of 15. For me, the advantage of graduating from college three years earlier was not obvious at the beginning, but later on in my career, being three years younger than my peers was a distinct advantage. I co-founded Ctrip.com in 1999, and turned it into a successful Internet company in China. By 2007, at age 37, I decided to apply to the economics PhD program at Stanford. The Stanford economics program usually admits students in their 20s, and occasionally students in their 30s, but almost never anybody in their 40s. If I had been 40 instead of 37, I would not have had the chance to pursue a second career as an economist. Now, at 47, I am still considered young as the executive chairman of a major Internet company in China. The advantage of attending and finishing college a few years earlier means a few more productive years over one's lifetime, which is hugely beneficial. A speedup in education not only increases labor supply, but also boosts the potential for innovation, simply because there is more time to take risks and change tack if early ventures fail.

Recently, Stanford has announced that it will accept applications from talented students younger than 18, and offer more flexibility in the number of years required in order to graduate. I hope other colleges will follow suit. Learning is a lifelong journey; graduating earlier can offer a lot more flexibility later in life.

There is another benefit of shortening the number of school years. If women can finish college earlier, they will have a few more years to start a family and have children. In the United States, on average, the fertility rate of a high-school graduate is about 40% higher than that of a woman with a bachelor's degree, and about 50% higher than that of a woman with a graduate degree. If school years can be reduced by two years, I estimate that it will boost the fertility rate by 10–20% (i.e. a 0.2 to 0.4 increase in fertility). If a government uses cash bonuses instead, based on our analysis earlier in this chapter, it would require an annual spend of 1% of GDP to achieve the same level of increase in fertility. The education reform suggested here is a rare policy reform that can simultaneously boost the fertility rate, reduce education expenditure, increase the tax base, and enhance innovation.

PART II

The Race of Innovation

The race of innovation will be played out between the countries with the largest stock of human capital. These are naturally China, India, and the United States. I will discuss the demographics and economy of these three countries in detail. China and the United States will imminently compete head-to-head in the race to be the global leader of innovation, while India is still a generation away from becoming a major economic force. I will also discuss Japan, because it was the first country in the world to be significantly impacted by an aging society. I will also talk about the EU, given the fact that it is still a large single market for goods and labor.

The competition I refer to here is economic competition. It is quite different from competition among countries historically. In the past, competition was usually a zero-sum game. Countries used to compete fiercely for land and resources, which often led to conflict and wars. Today, major countries compete for innovation and human resources, which is not a zero-sum game, because innovation benefits not only the innovator, but also the rest of the world. Moreover, fierce competition for talent will raise the return on investment in education, and prompt more investment in human capital; consequently, there will be more talent to go around. But the stakes of the game are still very high, as there can only be a few centers of innovation in the world. When a city or a region becomes the center of innovation in an industry, it will be much more vibrant and wealthier than other cities. Land and resources are no longer important; rather, economic competition is a race of innovation and a war for talent.

CHAPTER 6

Japan

Japan is the best case study of an aging society, because Japan was the first large economy to experience the structural issues that an aging society causes. Some small European countries are also experiencing the effects of an aging population; however, because labor is more mobile in the EU and some countries have a large immigrant population, the effect of aging is much milder than that in Japan. Despite recent policy changes, Japan still fails to attract a large number of immigrants (immigrants make up less than 2% of the total population), which makes it an excellent case study for the effects of aging and low fertility. The negative effect of aging on innovation and entrepreneurship in Japan is something that we have discussed previously, and is a particularly alarming and unexpected outcome.

The Aging of the Japanese Economy

Over the last few years, I have often traveled to Japan to study its demographic problems. One day, I learned that one of the country's prominent Internet entrepreneurs, Takafumi Horie, was arrested for violating security laws. I did not pay a lot of attention to this piece of news at first, because his company was not very large. But when I discussed the topic of innovation and entrepreneurship in Japan with other economists, Takafumi Horie was constantly mentioned. One economist commented: "You want to know why Japan has so few young entrepreneurs? Just look at what we did to Takafumi." Later, I found out that Takafumi was one of the rare breed of entrepreneurs under the age of 40. He founded a popular Internet portal called livedoor.com and challenged the dominance of traditional media. He is independent, conspicuous, and sometimes eccentric. He wears t-shirts instead of business suits to work. He dates models, drives expensive sports cars, and openly challenges and criticizes the status quo. These behaviors are not accepted by the Japanese business community, so he was demonized by the media. When he tried to acquire a TV station, he was sued and later arrested for accounting and security violations. Interestingly, the Japanese economist said "his down-fall discourages any non-conformist to challenge the status quo."

Takafumi may well be guilty of breaking the law, but what is striking is the sympathy for him among the academic community following his conviction. I have now come to understand that the reason is that many scholars believe that Japan really needs more people like Takafumi. Many economists think that the long stagnation of the Japanese economy is a result of a lack of entrepreneurs, especially young high-tech entrepreneurs. Compared with the United States, Japan has far fewer new high-tech companies. Even China and Korea have a larger number of new high-tech companies than Japan.

Japan was not always short of entrepreneurs. In the first half of the twentieth century, young Japanese entrepreneurs started high-tech companies such as Sony and Panasonic; however, over the last 30 years, there have been almost no successful new high-tech companies. Is it any wonder that the Japanese people place their hopes on young entrepreneurs like Takafumi? But the older-generation business community controls all the power and resources, and young entrepreneurs, especially non-conformists, are mistrusted, often marginalized, and sometimes oppressed.

The Lost Decades

The Japanese economy was the most vibrant among the developed countries from the 1950s to the 1980s. The GDP growth rate exceeded 8% per annum for over 30 years. Japanese firms grew rapidly to become leading innovators in many industries, such as electronics, automobiles, and industrial equipment. In the competitive country rankings of the world in 1990, Japan was ranked number one, and it looked like its per capita GDP would soon surpass that of the United States.

However, as its population started to age rapidly during the 1990s, and its economic fortunes reversed completely, the engine of innovation quickly lost steam, and even the most innovative Japanese firms became sluggish and conservative. First in semiconductors, then in software and communication, and lastly in genetics, Japanese firms were leapfrogged by entrepreneurial firms from the United States and emerging countries such as China and Korea. In 2008, the competitive ranking of Japan dropped out of the top 20 for the first time since the 1980s, and the growth rate of the Japanese economy was near zero. In recent years, the country's per capita GDP has been far lower than that of the United States.

Economists used to refer to Japan's economic stagnation, which began in the 1990s, as "the lost decade." However, it should be "the lost decades," because the economic recession has lasted almost three decades now. In the first few years of "the lost decades," many economists attributed the problem to the financial crisis triggered by the crash of real-estate prices; they believed that after the financial crisis passed, the Japanese economy and Japanese firms would regain competitiveness. Today, many economists have begun to realize that the financial crisis was not the problem, although it may have been an important inflection point. A financial crisis usually lasts between two and four years, and the longest and deepest financial crisis—the Great Depression—lasted 12 years. Japan's economic recession has now lasted for more than 25 years. Other economists have attributed the problem to the sharp rise of the yen against the dollar, which affected the competitiveness of its export industry; however, Japan maintained a large trade surplus throughout "the lost decades." Japanese companies lost out to U.S. and Korean firms not because of high costs, but because of the loss of leadership in technology and innovation, both directly related to the aging of the Japanese workforce.

Figure 6.1 shows the economic growth rate and the aging index (old-age dependency ratio) over the last 60 years in Japan. The aging index went up sharply in the 1990s, and at the same time economic growth slowed to 1% a year.

The population of Japan became the oldest in the world after the 1990s because, unlike the United States or other developed countries, Japan did not have a post-war baby boom and its fertility rate dropped rapidly in the 1950s and 1960s (Figure 6.2). Meanwhile, the Japanese became wealthy very quickly. When the country reached a per capita income of US$5,000 in the 1970s, its fertility rate dropped below the replacement level. When it reached a

FIGURE 6.1 GDP growth and the aging index of Japan

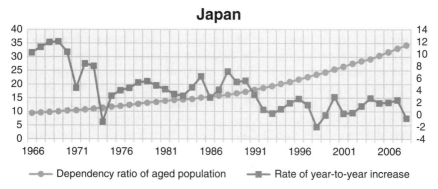

Note: Old-age population index = (population above 65 years of age/population aged 15–64) × 100%.

Data Source: Statistical Survey Department, Statistics Bureau, Ministry of Internal Affairs and Communications, 2008.

FIGURE 6.2 Post-war fertility rate in Japan

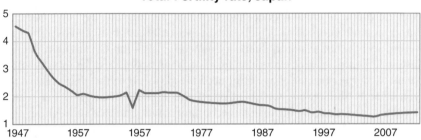

Total Fertility rate, Japan

Data Source: Statistical Survey Department, Statistics Bureau, Ministry of Internal Affairs and Communications, 2011.

per capita income of US$10,000 in the 1980s, its fertility rate dropped to below 1.6. In the 1990s, the fertility rate dropped to 1.5, and currently stands at 1.4.

The low fertility rate in Japan since the 1970s has caused severe aging in the population structure. The number of people over age 65 has increased from 7% in the 1970s to 22% in 2016. People between the ages of 20 and 39, as a total share of the population, dropped from 35% in the 1970s to only 27% in 2016. Figure 6.3 compares the population structure of Japan and that of the United States in 2016 and China in 2040. As we can see, the U.S. population is much younger than that of Japan today, and although China has a much younger population today, by 2040 it will have almost as old a population as Japan does today.

Currently, in Japan, every worker needs to support 0.8 elderly people; in addition, many people in Japan continue to work after the age of 65. Japan's annual government revenue is 8.3 trillion yen (about US$83 billion), but the size of the public pension fund is over 100 trillion yen. The huge expense required to support the elderly has made the Japanese government the most indebted among all high-income nations, with over 600 trillion yen in debt. In the future, to deal with the budget-deficit problem, Japan will either have to increase the retirement age further or raise taxes, which will put a break on entrepreneurship.

With an aging workforce, a typical Japanese company has more 40- and 50-year-old employees than 20- and 30-year-old employees. Usually, Japanese companies put a lot of weight on seniority when evaluating employees for promotion. When there are more middle-aged and older workers in companies, the promotion of young workers slows down. Table 6.1 shows the ages of managers in Japanese firms.

In the 1970s, 32% of Japanese team managers were under the age of 35, but by the 1990s, only 16% of team managers were under 35. Let's look at the age composition of the executives. In 1970, 25% of department heads were

FIGURE 6.3 Age structure of Japan vs. the United States in 2016 and China vs. Japan in 2040

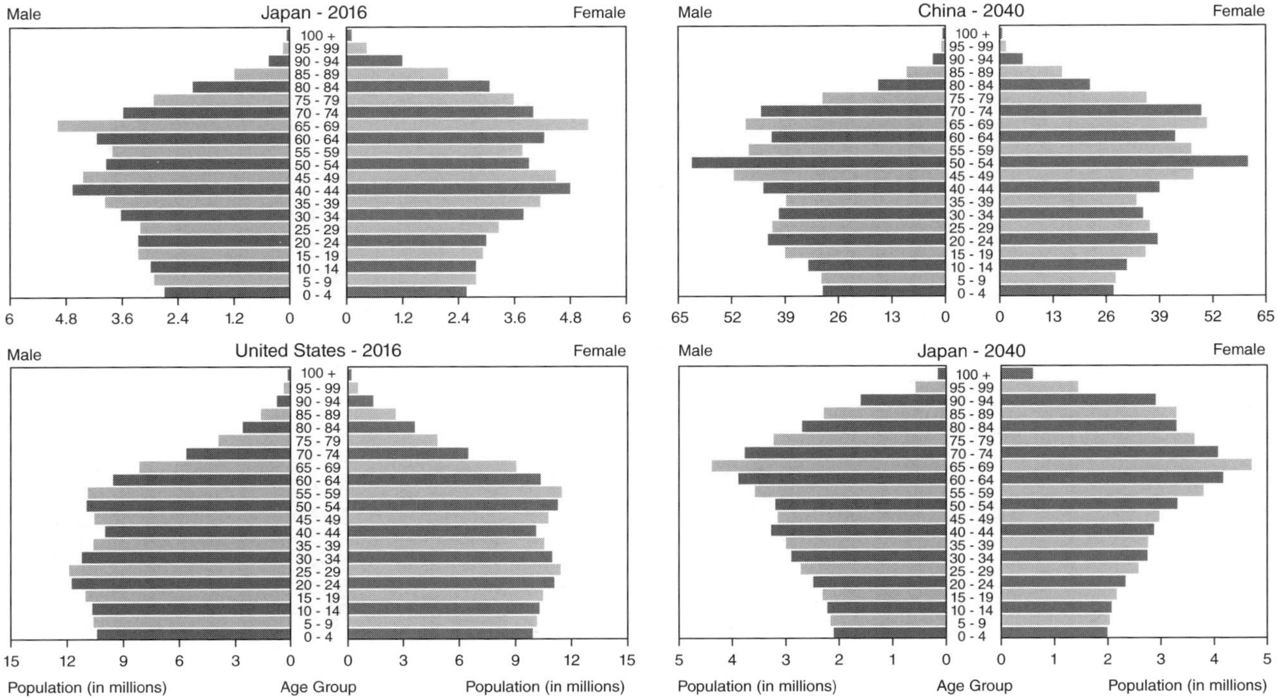

Data Source: U.S. Census Bureau, 2015.

TABLE 6.1 Age composition of Japanese managers

	Team managers			Department heads		
Year	<35	35–39	>40	<45	45–49	>50
1976	31.8%	31.9%	36.3%	24.5%	31.1%	41.4%
1984	18.3%	33.1%	48.6%	12.5%	37.3%	50.2%
1994	16.4%	23.5%	60.1%	7.6%	27.8%	64.6%

Data Source: Summary of Report, Basic Survey on Wage Structure (Ministry of Health, Labor and Welfare of Japan), various years.

under the age of 45, but by the 1990s, only 8% of department heads were under 45. The ratio of young managers declined more rapidly than the ratio of young workers in the workforce, and the ratio of young executives declined even faster than that of young managers. This is because, in general, the promotion of managers and executives is more or less related to seniority, so the effect of an aging workforce will be magnified in the age composition of management and executives as a result. It becomes a vicious cycle, because as the management of the firm becomes older, they will make promotion criteria more conservative and seniority-based to protect their power and influence. As a result, young workers in Japan occupy more junior positions, have less managerial experience, have less financial and social capital, and thus have lower entrepreneurial capability.

In Chapter 2, I showed that 30-year-olds tend to be the most able potential entrepreneurs because, at this age, they have accumulated industry experience and social connections, yet are still risk-taking, hard-working, and quick to adapt to new technologies. In an aging country, 30-year-olds are not only few in number, but also have less entrepreneurial ability because they occupy lower positions in the work environment; hence, they have less experience and social capital with which to start a new firm.

In a slow economy, typically a firm has no growth and hires very few people. This increases the risks for entrepreneurs. In such an environment, when a startup fails, it will be very difficult for the employees in the startup firm to find regular jobs in other firms. Consequently, young people are reluctant to join startups; as a result, startups usually have a hard time attracting talented workers, making them less competitive and less likely to succeed.

Japan is a good case study of this phenomenon. Figure 6.4 shows the number of new Japanese firms that emerged between 1966 and 1999. The firm-formation rate dropped from 6–7% in the 1960s to only 3–4% in the 1990s.

Compared with the United States, the entrepreneurial rate in Japan is much lower; in fact, the Japanese overall entrepreneurial rate is the lowest in the world, as shown in Figure 6.5.

FIGURE 6.4 Firm formation and exit in Japan from 1966 to 1999

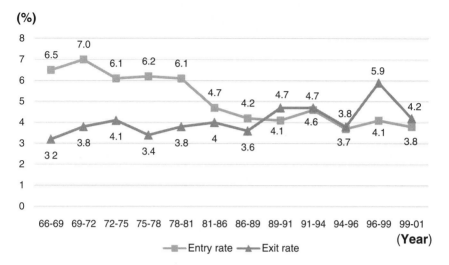

Data Source: MPHPT, Establishment and Enterprise Census of Japan.

New firms are crucial in high-tech sectors, such as software and Internet sectors. Let's compare the top 10 high-tech companies in the United States and Japan as ranked by Forbes in 2010 (Table 6.2). The table also shows information on the founders of these companies. Of the top 10 companies

FIGURE 6.5 Entrepreneurial rate of different countries

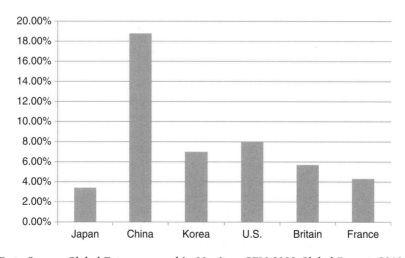

Data Source: Global Entrepreneurship Monitor, GEM 2009 Global Report, 2010.

TABLE 6.2 Top high-tech companies in Japan and the United States

United States	Age	Company founded	Age of founder	Japan	Age	Founded year	Age of founder
IBM	died	1911		Nintendo	died	1889	
HP	died	1939		Sony	died	1946	
Microsoft (Bill Gates)	61	1975	20	Panasonic	died	1918	
Apple	died	1976		Hitachi	died	1910	
Cisco (Leonard Bosack)	64	1984	33	Toshiba	died	1875	
Oracle (Larry Ellison)	72	1977	32	Kyocera (Inamori Kazuo)	84	1959	27
Google (Larry Page)	43	1998	24	Fujitsu	died	1935	
Intel (Gordon Moore)	87	1968	39	Sharp	died	1912	
Facebook (Mark Zuckerberg)	32	2004	20	NEC	died	1898	
Amazon (Jeff Bezos)	52	1995	31	Nikon	died	1917	
Average time of establishment: 43 years				Average time of establishment: 100 years			

in the United States, eight were founded during the last 30 years. In Japan, none of the high-tech companies were founded over the last 40 years.

Six out of the 10 founders of top U.S. high-tech companies are still alive today. Their average age when they founded the company was 28. Bill Gates founded Microsoft at the age of 20; Steve Jobs founded Apple at 21; Leonard Bosack and Sandy Lerner founded Cisco at 33 and 31, respectively; Larry Ellison founded Oracle at the age of 32; Larry Page and Sergey Brin founded Google at the age of 24; and Michael Dell founded Dell at the age of 22.

These six high-tech U.S. companies had a market capitalization of US$600 billion in 2010. Because the shareholders of these companies are mostly founders, employees, and other U.S. nationals, these six companies have generated an enormous amount of wealth for the United States over the last 30 years, equivalent to 5% of the country's GDP in 2010. On the other hand, the value of existing Japanese firms has not grown significantly over the last 30 years. The superior performance of the U.S. economy in recent years is mostly due to the aforementioned high-tech firms, especially new high-tech firms.

One interesting observation is that the leading Internet websites in Japan are either run by professional managers of foreign multinationals or large syndicate firms. For example, the biggest search engine is Google Japan, the largest portal and auction site is Yahoo Japan, and the largest social networking site is Line, which was originally a subsidiary of a Korean company. But in the United States, China, or even Korea, almost all the Internet companies were founded by young local entrepreneurs. This is another piece of evidence pointing to the lack of entrepreneurship in Japan.

The Aging of Japanese Firms

It is not just entrepreneurial firms that are lacking in Japan, even established firms are slow and clumsy at competing with U.S. firms in the area of innovation.

A few years ago, executives from my company Ctrip.com visited a leading travel company in Japan. The top executive teams of the two companies sat on opposite sides of a large meeting table. Even though the two companies are of similar size, the contrast was vivid as the executives of the two companies were from two different generations. On the Ctrip.com side all were 30-something men and women. On the Japanese company side all were men aged 50 or above. Occasionally during the meeting there would be young employees coming in and out of the meeting room, but they were secretaries and assistants to the management of the Japanese firm.

Typically, after a young college graduate joins a Japanese firm, he is gradually promoted based primarily on seniority, and he remains with the same firm until retirement. I use "he" because most women quit the workforce after marriage. Once I had a conversation with one of my Japanese friends, who commented that the seniority culture continues to be both strong and prevalent. To give one example, young workers need to address the senior workers differently. I inquired whether a young worker would need to change the way he addresses an older worker were he to be promoted to a higher position than the older worker. My friend thought about that for a while and said that as far as he was aware, this has *never* happened in his department. I asked why such a suffocating seniority-based culture continues to persist in firms. He said it is because senior positions are all occupied by older employees, who really do not have any incentive to change.

Many economists think that an aging workforce, combined with an ossified promotion system, sapped the vigor out of Japanese firms and caused them to lose the race of innovation against young U.S. firms. For example, Japanese firms once dominated the semiconductor industry. In the 1980s, Japanese firms had over half of the world's market share. NEC and Toshiba were the top two semiconductor firms in the world. Half of the top 10 semiconductor firms were from Japan. However, 20 years later, only two of the top 10 semiconductor firms are Japanese. The number one and two firms are Intel and Samsung from Korea (Table 6.3). The reason for the

TABLE 6.3 Top 10 semiconductor makers, market share by region (excluding foundries, US$bn)

Rank	1993		2000		2006		2016		1Q17	
1	Intel	7.6	Intel	29.7	Intel	31.6	Intel	57.0	Intel	14.2
2	NEC	7.1	Toshiba	11.0	Samsung	19.7	Samsung	44.3	Samsung	13.6
3	Toshiba	6.3	NEC	10.9	TI	13.7	Qualcomm (1)	15.4	SK Hynix	5.5
4	Motorola	5.8	Samsung	10.6	Toshiba	10.0	Broadcom (1)	15.2	Micron	4.9
5	Hitachi	5.2	TI	9.6	ST	9.9	SK Hynix	14.9	Broadcom (1)	4.1
6	TI	4.0	Motorola	7.9	Renesas	8.2	Micron	13.5	Qualcomm (1)	3.7
7	Samsung	3.1	ST	7.9	Hynix	7.4	TI	12.5	TI	3.2
8	Mitsubishi	3.0	Hitachi	7.4	Freescale	6.1	Toshiba	10.9	Toshiba	2.9
9	Fujitsu	2.9	Infineon	6.8	NXP	5.9	NXP	9.5	NXP	2.2
10	Matsushita	2.3	Philips	6.3	NEC	5.7	MediaTek (1)	8.8	Infineon	1.9
Top 10 Total ($B)	47.2		108.1		118.2		202.1		56.0	
Semi Market ($B)	108.8		218.6		265.5		365.6		99.6	
Top 10% of Total Semi	43%		49%		45%		55%		56%	

Data Source: Research Bulletin of IC Insights, 2017.

downfall of Japanese firms is that during the 1990s, there were major innovations in the semiconductor industry. Intel captured the opportunity of using microprocessors for personal computers, and Samsung captured the market in memory chips for personal computers. In contrast, Japanese firms were very slow in reacting to new opportunities; instead, they continued to focus on perfecting the mainframe chips, and did not transition to the personal computer market; as a result, they lost out to U.S. and Korean competitors.

Another example is the software industry. In the 1990s, many enterprise resource planning (ERP) software companies emerged in the United States and Europe. ERP refers to software that helps large manufacturing firms to manage their operations. The leading ERP software makers, Oracle and SAP, have become some of the largest software companies in the world. Smaller firms include Baan, which is based in the Netherlands, and PeopleSoft, which is based in the United States. It is immensely puzzling that Japan, which has the world's largest and most advanced manufacturing companies, does not possess even a single global ERP software company. The reason is that Japanese firms, in comparison with U.S. firms, were very slow to adopt new information technologies. The adoption level of ERP software is only half the level it is in other developed countries (Whittaker and Cole, 2006). The adoption of CRM software (a type of ERP software) in Japanese firms was one-third lower than in U.S. and European firms, and even significantly lower than in Korean and Taiwanese firms. A survey examining the reason for the low level of adoption of ERP software found that Japanese management had a low level of understanding of IT and were generally reluctant to change their existing business processes (Miyoshi and Nakata, 2011). Slow adoption of new information technologies was related to the conservative mentality of Japanese executives, who were considerably older than their U.S. counterparts.

Other high-tech industries in Japan, such as telecommunication equipment, were also slow to adapt to new IT. Overall, not only does Japan lack new entrepreneurial firms, but its established firms have also become conservative, slow, and rigid. When the pace of technology innovation and adoption accelerated globally, the older Japanese executives had a hard time catching up.

The Aging of Japanese Society

I often discuss the predicament of the Japanese economy with Japanese economists; many of them agree that the low fertility rate and aging society are the root cause of the problem. The question is what the Japanese government has done to raise the fertility rate. As I discussed in Chapter 5, the budget allocated for pro-fertility policy measures is low compared with other developed nations with low fertility rates. Currently, Japan's fertility rate is only

1.4, still one of the lowest in the world. I asked one economist why Japan did not spend more money to raise the fertility rate. The answer I received was: "The main constituents of the Japanese government are the elderly."

As Japan ages, there are more old people and there are even more old voters relative to young voters, because the elderly turn out at the voting booth at a much higher rate than the young. In 2003, the voter turnout ratio of people aged between 60 and 69 was 77%, whereas the turnout ratio of people aged between 20 and 29 was only 35% (Coulmas et al., 2008). Because the elderly dominate the voting booth, public policies naturally lean toward the elderly. With an ever-growing budget to support the elderly, the Japanese government does not have the will or means to allocate more money to subsidize child-raising young couples.

Over the last few years, as Japan experienced a recession with stagnant wages, the benefits for the elderly have remained stable, while young workers have been hurt disproportionately. Moreover, the unemployment rate of young workers is much higher than that of the middle-aged or elderly. Deflation in the Japanese economy also helps the old at the expense of the young, because even with no nominal raise, the incumbent old workers' real wages keep rising, and firms are reluctant to hire or give raises to young workers. Figure 6.6 shows the wage trends of different cohorts. It shows that the wages of recent young cohorts grew much more slowly than their parents' generation, whereas the wages and benefits for the older cohorts were largely unaffected (Coulmas et al., 2008).

FIGURE 6.6 Japanese wage trends of different age cohorts

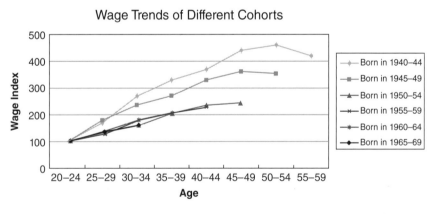

Data Source: Basic Survey on Wage Structure (annual edition), Ministry of Health, Labor and Welfare; Consumer Price Index, Ministry of Public Management, Home Affairs, Posts and Telecommunications.

As the population ages, more social resources and attention are tilted toward the elderly. Last year, as I was filling out a form at a Japanese hospital, three presbyopia glasses with different magnification levels were provided. No wonder Japan is said to be a paradise for the elderly. The benefits and perks enjoyed by the elderly after retirement are the envy of the world. After retirement, Japanese workers receive 70% of their pay, much higher than the average salary of young workers. The government transfers a large sum of income from the young to the old via the tax and benefit system.

It is not necessarily unfair to transfer income from the young to the elderly, because eventually every young person will be old. But just like when old people occupy more management positions, the firms become less innovative, when older people have more wealth and power relative to the young, the government and society become more conservative. Japanese politicians tend to be older than their U.S. counterparts, and they adopt more conservative economic policies. In the 1990s, when the real-estate bubble burst, the Japanese government adopted a zero-interest policy, a very conservative approach that allowed the badly managed banks or firms to survive. Many Western economists did not understand why the government did not let these low-productivity firms fail, so that more productive firms could expand and new firms emerge, thus releasing the much-needed energy of creative destruction. This policy choice might also be related to the aging of the workforce. The median age of Japanese is 45 (whereas the median age of Americans is 35). If the government allowed these firms to fail, it would have been much more difficult for an average 45-year-old employee to learn new skills and find a new job after being laid off, in comparison with an average 35-year-old. Maybe the Japanese government made the right choice in allowing these low-productivity firms to survive, because the adjustment cost for the elderly employees would have been too heavy to bear in the context of society as a whole.

For similar reasons, the Japanese government is too conservative in its immigration policy. The immigration policy is still very restrictive, because the Japanese government worries too much about the short-term burden on public resources or the short-term pain of assimilating immigrants. But again, from the point of view of the elderly who control the votes, this is a rational choice, because the elderly care only about the short term—the period of time in which they will live. In an aging society, public policy tends to be conservative and short-term focused. Young people's interests are marginalized, because they are politically marginal.

The marginalization of the young also has a negative impact on marriage and the fertility rate. More young people have to live with their parents in order to save money. The parents, typically wealthier, are also happy to have their children at home and provide additional financial support. A word has been coined for these young men who live with their parents: "herbivore." These "herbivore" men typically have temporary jobs or no job, and are financially

TABLE 6.4 Unmarried rate of Japanese women and first marriage age

Year	15–19	20–24	25–29	30–34	35–39	40–44	45–49	50	First marriage age
1950	97	55	15	6	3	2	2	1	23.6
1955	98	67	21	8	4	2	2	2	24.7
1960	99	68	22	9	6	3	2	2	25.0
1965	99	68	18	9	7	5	3	3	24.8
1970	98	72	18	7	6	5	4	3	24.7
1975	99	69	21	8	5	5	5	4	24.5
1980	99	78	24	9	6	4	4	5	25.1
1985	99	81	31	10	7	5	4	4	25.8
1990	98	85	40	14	8	6	5	4	26.9
1995	99	86	48	20	10	7	6	5	27.6
2000	99	88	54	27	14	9	6	6	28.6
2005	99	89	59	32	18	12	8	7	29.4

Data Source: The Institute for Research of Social Guarantee and Population in Taiwan, 2008.

dependent on their parents. Because their career prospects are slight, they have neither the motivation to work hard, nor the motivation to pursue a marriage partner who might complicate this comfortable arrangement. A best-selling book entitled *The Herbivore will Change Japan* (in Japanese, available from http://bookclub.kodansha.co.jp/product?isbn=9784062725354) estimates that two-thirds of men between the ages of 20 and 34 are "herbivores." By traditional standards, it is increasingly hard for Japanese women to find suitable husbands; consequently, many Japanese women remain single. The percentage of single Japanese women in all age groups has increased rapidly in recent years, as shown in Table 6.4. The percentage of single women in the 30–34 age group increased from 10% in 1985 to 32% in 2005, and many of them will never marry; late marriage or no marriage at all further reduces the fertility rate. The marginalization of the young further exacerbates the problem of low fertility, forming a vicious cycle.

To sum up, Japan is deeply mired in the low-fertility trap. The aging workforce has contributed to the lack of entrepreneurship and innovation. Japan was routed by the United States and other emerging countries in the race of high-tech innovation. The effect of an aging society is self-reinforcing; an aging society makes it more difficult for the young to break away from their shackles, because the elderly control the voting booth and company management positions. As a result, the young are in a weaker position in an aging society and face numerous challenges, including a diminished likelihood of getting married and having children.

CHAPTER 7

China

O ne of the best sellers in 2011, *Battle Hymn of the Tiger Mother* (Chua, 2011), tells the story of an extremely demanding Chinese American mother pushing her children academically. The story was not a surprising one in the United States, as Chinese students there are known to be very hard working and have excellent grades. In elite U.S. colleges, the ratio of ethnic Chinese students far exceeds their ethnic ratio. Why did this book create such a stir in the United States? I think it is because the release of the book coincided with the emergence of China as a real world power. Americans may well feel threatened that China will have access to the largest and best talent pool in the world if all Chinese moms are like the Tiger Mom in the book!

Recently, another piece of news underlined that concern. On the PISA test, which tested over 1 million students in 65 countries, Shanghai high-school students scored at the top, a notch better than students from the top-scoring Asian countries (i.e. Singapore, Japan, and Korea), and much better than students from European countries and the United States (Figure 7.1). Shanghai was the only city tested in China, but PISA believed other large Chinese cities would have similar scores. No doubt, China has the smartest high-school students in the world. Fifty years ago, American parents often used the "starving Chinese kid" to urge children to finish their food; these days, parents are more likely to say: "If you do not study hard, Chinese kids will take your job."

The concern was well grounded. As China becomes wealthier, the quality of its education will be at least on a par with that of other developed nations. And China will likely overtake the United States economically, because it has a much larger talent pool.

Will the Twenty-First Century be the Century of China?

The most important event of the twenty-first century is the emergence of a vibrant Chinese economy. Per capita GDP in China has reached US$7,500

FIGURE 7.1 Comparison of student performance on the PISA test in 2009

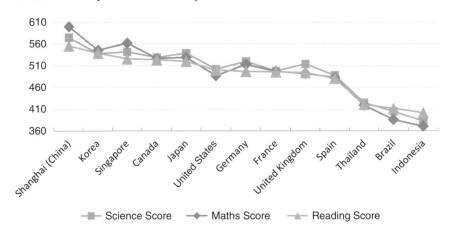

Data Source: OECD Program for International Student Assessment 2009 Database.

and the total GDP of China is $11 trillion, about 60% that of the United States and much larger than that of Japan, which is the world's third-largest economy. On a PPP basis, the Chinese economy is already larger than the U.S. economy.

The Chinese economy is still growing at about 6.5% annually, much faster than the 2% growth rate in the United States. If the Chinese economy continues to grow at 6% per annum over the next five years, its per capita GDP will reach US$10,000. After 2020, if it continues to grow at about 5–6% per year, its per capita income will reach US$16,000–20,000 by 2030. Even though its per capita GDP is only one-quarter to one-third that of the United States, its overall GDP will certainly be larger than that of the United States. After 2030, if the Chinese economy continues to grow faster than that of the United States, it will become the largest economy in the world and remain in this position throughout most of the twenty-first century.

Can China sustain a 5–6% growth rate over the next 10–20 years? If it can sustain this growth rate over the next 20 years, China will become a high-income country. But many economies, including those of many Latin American countries, after reaching the middle-income level (around US$10,000), stop growing and remain stuck at this level of affluence; this is the so-called "middle-income" trap. Only four Asian Tiger economies have successfully escaped the "middle-income trap" and continued to grow rapidly: Korea, Taiwan, Hong Kong, and Singapore. Today they are rich economies with a per capita GDP of well over US$20,000. Is China more like contemporary Latin American countries or more like the East Asian Tiger economies of 20 years ago?

FIGURE 7.2 Comparison of saving rates of selected countries

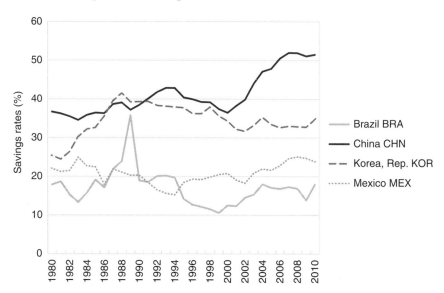

Data Source: World Bank, gross savings (% of GDP), 2010.

Let's compare the economies of Latin America, the Asian Tiger economies, and China.

First of all, let's look at the savings rate. A high savings rate is required for capital formation and infrastructure investment, both of which are essential for a developing economy to grow wealthy. During the takeoff period of the Asian Tiger economies, their savings rates were much higher than those of Latin American countries (Figure 7.2). High savings rates allowed them to invest heavily in infrastructure and key manufacturing industries. What does China's savings rate look like? The Chinese savings rate is even higher than that of the Asian Tiger economies when they took off. This is one of the reasons why China has built an infrastructure and manufacturing industry that is the envy of the world.

Secondly, let's compare their export capabilities (Figure 7.3). Export capability is a measure of a country's competitiveness and innovation. When Asian Tiger economies escaped the middle-income trap, their export capability was much higher than that of comparable Latin American countries; consequently, they had a large trade surplus and a stable and appreciating currency during their takeoff period. In contrast, the Latin American economies usually had a large trade deficit on non-resource trade, with unstable currencies and frequent financial crises. China's economy is clearly more like the Asian Tiger economies, as it has a huge trade surplus.

FIGURE 7.3 Historical trends in high-technology exports of selected countries

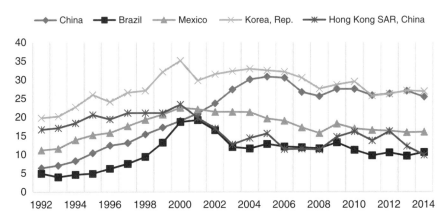

HIGH-TECHNOLOGY EXPORTS (% OF MANUFACTURED EXPORTS)

Data Source: World Bank, high-technology exports (% of manufactured exports), 2014.

Next let's compare the technology capabilities. Asian Tiger economies, after the initial stage of developing labor-intensive industries, successfully climbed up to capital-intensive and technology-intensive industries, and built many exporting high-tech firms such as Samsung. In contrast, most Latin American countries' exporting firms are resource-related. Chinese exports still have a significant portion that is labor-intensive, but in recent years, Chinese exports have become more aligned with those of economies like Taiwan and Korea, whose exports contain a large high-tech component. The share of electronics and equipment in export has risen from 17% in 1993 to 48% in 2008, whereas the share of textile exports has dropped from 29% in 1993 to 12% in 2008. Overall, high-tech exports as a share of total exports have risen to 30%, a level that is far higher than in Latin American countries, and a level similar to that of other developed countries.

Some people argue that the high-tech exports in China stem mostly from the operations of multinationals rather than from indigenous Chinese companies. In reality, many multinationals have moved at least a part of their research and development to China, and, with a large tangible presence in China, they are no different economically from local companies. Moreover, in the electronics and equipment industries, indigenous companies such as Huawei and Xiaomi have become world leaders in their respective industries. Clearly, in this regard, China is a lot more akin to Korea in the 1990s than to Mexico either then or now.

Last of all, and most fundamentally, let us look at human resources. The absolute number of college graduates in China is 7 million a year, which is a much larger total number than that of any other country. On a per capita level, the college graduation rate of nearly 40% is similar to that of Latin American countries. However, the quality of Chinese college graduates is much higher; one way to look at this is to look at the ethnic mix of graduate students in U.S. PhD programs. U.S. universities have the best PhD research programs in the world, so the best college graduates all over the world compete for PhD slots in U.S. universities. The share of PhD candidates from a particular country could be deemed to reflect the quality of the college graduates of that country. As shown in Figure 7.4, in 2010, Chinese PhD students accounted for 30% of all foreign PhD students in science and technology fields in U.S. universities. European and Indian graduates accounted for 11% and 17%, respectively, while all the Latin American students combined accounted for only 5%, representing one-eighth of the total of Chinese students.

FIGURE 7.4 Non-U.S. citizens awarded doctorates in science and engineering by country, 2010

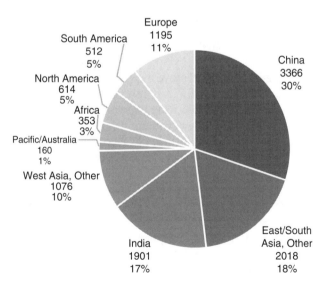

Note: A total of 25 degrees were awarded to non-U.S. citizens from unknown countries.

Data Source: National Science Foundation, Science and Engineering Doctorate Awards: 2009–10.

Let's look at another measure of high-end human capital: the number of people engaged in research and development. Even though China's per capita GDP is still lower, the number of people engaged in research and development in China per million people is far higher than in Latin American countries. And this is against the background of research and development spending as a percentage of GDP in China being far higher than in other developing countries, currently at around 1.5% (which is still half the level of Korea, but growing rapidly). The number of patents awarded to Chinese companies is already second only to the United States.

In addition, Chinese companies have the advantage of tapping into a large stock of Chinese engineers who once worked for U.S. high-tech companies. Just as the returning Taiwanese engineers jump-started the high-tech industries in Taiwan, these returnees have been crucial to the rapid development of Chinese high-tech industries. No other developing country (except India) has this advantage.

In summary, the Chinese economy is similar to the East Asian Tiger economies of 20–30 years ago, and will likely continue to grow by 5–6% per year, surpassing the United States to become the largest economy before 2030.

Pessimists often point to the potential risks of the Chinese economy; I will analyze the most commonly cited risks below.

Risk of Transiting from Manufacturing to Service

By 2020, China's per capita GDP will reach US$10,000, which is five times the level of low-income countries such as India, Vietnam, and Pakistan. Chinese companies and multinationals will move their labor-intensive jobs to these low-income countries. Robots will be widely used in China, which is already the largest market for robots. Will this create mass unemployment in China?

The answer is that these extra workers will be absorbed by the service sector. The service sector in China currently accounts for about 50% of GDP, which is much lower than that of other middle-income countries or developed countries; it is even lower than that of India, where the service sector accounts for 60% of GDP. China's service industry can grow from its current low level to a more normal 60–70% of GDP, creating more than enough jobs to absorb these extra workers.

Some people would argue that the Chinese economy is structurally unhealthy, with too much investment, too much manufacturing, and too much reliance on export. When investments and exports inevitably slow down, the economy will also follow suit. No doubt, investments and exports as a share of the total economy will eventually have to come down, but the fact that they are still very high is a sign that the Chinese economy has a much higher potential than other middle-income economies.

The high investment rate is a result of the high savings rate and a high potential return on investment. For example, the Chinese government invested heavily in infrastructure projects, such as airports, high-speed railways, and subways, which generate good social and economic returns. The high investment rate also reflects the vibrant level of entrepreneurial activities. For example, according to the Global Entrepreneurship Monitor, China has the most entrepreneurs per capita among middle-income and high-income countries, and the money invested by Chinese entrepreneurs from retained earnings or personal savings (instead of from banks and other financial institutions) was 11% of China's GDP in 2011, the highest in the world. This shows that the return on investment in China is still relatively high.

Similarly, a high level of manufacturing and export is a sign of Chinese companies' competitiveness. In recent years, Chinese companies have been able to export more high-tech manufacturing goods, demonstrating their progress in terms of being innovative. A high level of investment, exports, and especially strong manufacturing are strengths of the Chinese economy rather than weaknesses. Latin American countries would love to have these "problems."

As China grows wealthier, demand for services will inevitably grow. The health-care, travel, financial, and education industries will grow faster than manufacturing. Expanding these industries is much easier than building a manufacturing base, because the service industry is typically not constrained by patents or proprietary technology. A hospital can import state-of-the-art medical equipment, and grow its business as long as there is local demand; in contrast, manufacturers of things as complex as medical equipment almost always need to compete in the world market. This is just one structural reason why the service industry will naturally grow faster, while the manufacturing and export industry slows down.

Risk of a Widening Income Gap

For the last 30 years, the income gaps between urban and rural residents and between highly skilled and unskilled workers have increased in China (Figure 7.5). Up until the early 2010s, China had a surplus of rural labor, who became migrant workers in cities, and their income remained low while the income of highly skilled workers continued to increase. The Gini coefficient reached 0.46 in early 2010, and some people worried that this widening income gap would threaten the stability of Chinese society.

However, as I explained earlier, the one-child policy reduced the birth cohort size in the 1990s so dramatically that by around 2010, China finally ran out of surplus rural labor and the wages of unskilled migrant workers

FIGURE 7.5 Monthly income growth of rural workers in China

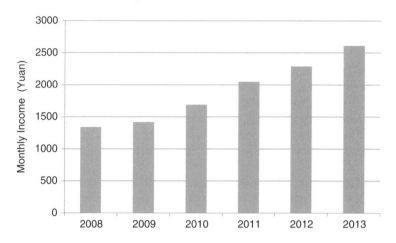

Data Source: China's National Bureau of Statistics, Monitoring Report of Rural Workers in China, 2013.

rose sharply; an increase that has been particularly noticeable over the last few years. The income of farmers who remained in villages also increased, because they have more land to work with. As a result, the Gini coefficient has stabilized. The expansion of college education has also helped to reduce the income gap between highly skilled and unskilled workers, because the wage increases of graduates were slowed by the large increase in their supply.

China's inequality is mostly a rural/urban phenomenon, which is mainly a result of the government's long-standing policy of restricting urban and rural migration. China's urbanization rate was only 50% in 2015, much lower than that of other middle-income countries, and even lower than that of India. As a result of the reform, hundreds of millions of farmers have escaped abject poverty by becoming migrant workers, but they still face discrimination in housing, education, and health-care services in large cities. In the future, many of these migrant workers will settle in cities, and thus the problem of urban–rural inequality will eventually be mitigated (assuming, of course, that the government further relaxes its restrictions on internal migration). China's inequality problem is not as difficult to resolve as that in other countries, because internal migration is relatively easy (the Chinese population has a relatively homogeneous culture and ethnicity): 90% of Chinese are Han Chinese with a culture of valuing education, and the children of new urban residents generally tend to be much better integrated than their parents.

Risk of Political Reform

Political reform is a very complicated subject, which warrants a separate book. In general, the quality of a country's political institutions and level of democracy depend on the level of economic development and human resources. Governments of low-income countries, such as those in Latin America and Africa, are democratic in form, but are often corrupt, unstable, and economically inefficient. On the other hand, most high-income countries, such as Korea, can make the transition from an authoritarian government to a democratic government, and remain stable and functioning democracies.

Today, for many people in China, the Chinese one-party system is a better fit compared with a democratic multiparty system, partly because of the fear of a "tyranny of the majority" and partly because, at this stage of its development, China needs to build a significant volume of infrastructure, something an authoritarian government does well. However, when China becomes a high-income country and an innovation-driven economy, it is quite possible that China will also transition to a more democratic system, as have other wealthy Asian economies. Transition to a democracy in a high-income country can be politically quite chaotic, but it generally does not cause much damage economically, and usually results in a stable and functional democracy, albeit often after a few years of political turmoil. Korea experienced a rough political transition to a democracy when it reached an income level of US$10,000 per capita, but during the chaotic political transition, the growth of its economy was almost unaffected.

Environmental and Natural Resource Risk

I have argued in previous chapters that the constraint stemming from the availability of natural resources is no longer an important factor in modern economies. Even with China's voracious and growing appetite for natural resources, the world, as a result of continuing innovation, has an increasing number of choices of abundant renewable resources, with the help of new energy technologies. It is not a coincidence that the price of oil and other commodities has consistently declined in recent years.

Moreover, China is not a resource-poor country. China has more resources per capita than most Asian countries, such as India, Japan, Korea, and Vietnam. It is estimated that its reserve of shale gas is more abundant than that of the United States. In agriculture, China has more than enough farm land to feed its 1.3 billion people. Despite this, China will likely remain a net importer of food, because—as Chinese workers become more expensive—it will not be to China's comparative advantage to grow all the food it needs.

With the fast growth of its cities and industries, some Chinese cities (such as Beijing) have become among the most polluted cities in the world. Beijing smog has made headlines all around the world. However, as I have demonstrated in previous chapters, the pollution problem usually peaks at a per capita GDP of US$8,000, which China has already exceeded. As China grows more affluent, it will invest more money and make more efforts to reduce pollution—both because it can afford to do so and because doing so will drive growth. As manufacturing growth has slowed down and tougher environmental standards have been enforced recently, the smog situation in wealthy coastal regions has improved.

The Demographic Advantage of China

As discussed above, most of the commonly cited risks regarding the Chinese economy are unfounded. The main strength of the Chinese economy is its enormous scale. China has the largest market for almost any goods. For example, it has 900 million Internet users, three times more than the population of the United States, making China a fertile ground to nurture some of the best Internet companies in the world.

China also has the largest pool of human resources. It has more college graduates and PhD graduates than the United States today, and is catching up very quickly with the United States in terms of number of researchers (Figure 7.6). Of course, the quality of research is lower in China, and per

FIGURE 7.6 Number of researchers in China and the United States

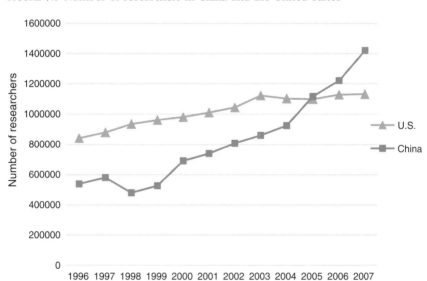

Data Source: World Bank, number of researchers in R&D, 2007.

researcher spending is also lower than that of the United States, so it is unlikely that China will challenge or surpass the United States in this area in the short term. Nonetheless, over the next 10–20 years, overall research and development spending will exceed that of the United States, and it is likely that China will have at least one high-tech innovation center like Silicon Valley.

Some economists question the quality of Chinese innovation. Chinese innovations have, in the past, been mostly low-cost imitations, but that is perfectly normal for the current stage of China's development as an innovator. When Korea was catching up with Japan, and when Japan was catching up with the United States, and when the United States was catching up with the United Kingdom (in the late 1800s), the pursuers always imitated and absorbed the technologies of the leaders first, and only later were able to create frontier innovations. It is unsurprising that many Chinese firms have recently started to take frontier innovations to market. For example, Huawei has become one of the leading global innovators for communications equipment. Moreover, Chinese firms are now catching up fast with the United States in the number of patents (although the quality of patents filed is admittedly still lower than that of those originating in the United States).

Some would also point to the fact that very few Chinese consumer brands have developed into global brands. This is also perfectly normal at this stage of an innovative economy's development. Usually, it is business-to-business brands that develop first, because, on the whole, businesses are more objective decision makers. It takes longer to build a consumer brand, because it is more difficult to convince consumers of a product from a historically backward country. Many years ago, Korean cars already demonstrated better quality than American cars; however, it is only recently that Korean automobile brands have achieved a reputation for quality and penetrated global markets in a meaningful way. Chinese equipment products such as Huawei have already become successful business product brands, and it is only a matter of time before Chinese consumer products become global consumer brands.

Another argument made by the pessimists over China's future is that China does not have many leading universities or Nobel Prize winners, but that's also normal, because the award of the Nobel Prize usually comes many years after a discovery has been made. The United States was already the leader of innovation in the early 1900s, but its universities became globally recognized as cutting edge only after the 1940s. Top universities in China, buoyed by the government's enormous education budget, are already able to afford and attract the best scholars in the world; furthermore, the number of academic publications by Chinese scholars is catching up very quickly with that of U.S. scholars. It is likely that it will be another 20–30 years before we see more Chinese Nobel Prize winners.

The scale advantage of Chinese firms will continue to drive more innovation. The largest talent pool and the largest market will likely make at least some of the mega cities in China high-tech innovation centers like Silicon Valley. By 2040, not only will China's economy surpass that of the United States, but it will also catch up with the United States in terms of innovation.

This should not be surprising, since China has been the largest and wealthiest economy for most of the last 2,000 years. With the enlightened economic policies adopted after 1978, it will take roughly two generations for China to catch up with other developed nations in terms of productivity. The Asian Tigers achieved this in two generations; India is likely to do the same some two generations after the economic reform of the 1990s. However, China will achieve it faster and more spectacularly, due to its scale advantage.

Some people would undermine the advantages intrinsic in being a big nation by asking: "Why has China for the last 500 years been consistently much weaker and poorer than the smaller European countries?" First, historically, China has not always been the country with the largest population. The Roman Empire ruled more people than the Han dynasty in China, and was wealthier than China on a per capita level. After the collapse of the Roman Empire, Europe disintegrated into many smaller nations, and they became much poorer than the unified Tang and Song dynasties in China. China had the largest population in the world between the fifth and fifteenth centuries, making it the wealthiest and most technologically advanced nation of the world for about 1,000 years. However, after 1500, when the great voyage of Zheng He was called off by the emperor, China made the colossal policy mistake of pursuing an autarky trade policy, which basically cut China off from the rest of the world. On the other side of the Euro-Asia continent, the West discovered the American continent, which is much closer to Europe geographically than it is to China. The discovery of America, and new trading routes to Asia, allowed the West access to a much larger market, including Europe, America, and Asia. As a result, the West led the industrial and scientific revolution, while China became backward and vulnerable. It thus attracted invaders, became mired in wars, and, subsequently, was the subject of a doomed experiment in a Soviet-style command and control economy.

After the 1980s, a post-reform China was once again on a level playing field with other nations, with its scale advantage coming back into play. It startled the world with the fastest economic growth rate ever recorded in world history. The emergence and dominance of the Chinese economy is the single most important event in the twenty-first century, but the question is: How long can the dominance of the Chinese economy last?

The Aging of the Chinese Economy

Demographics will be China's Achilles' heel. Starting from 2040, the Chinese economy will be affected by the rapid aging of its population, which will be exacerbated by the one-child policy implemented from the 1980s to 2015. India will soon surpass China to be the most populous country and the fastest-growing economy. It is entirely possible that the United States, with its unrivaled ability to attract immigrant talent, will regain the innovation leadership by the late twenty-first century, after yielding it briefly to China.

The Great Demographic Transition of China

Like other developing countries, the demographic transition of China has followed a typical pattern. It had a very high fertility rate and rapid population growth during the 1950s and 1960s. As shown in Figure 7.7, its fertility rate was as high as 6.0 throughout this period (except for a sharp drop from 1959 to 1969, when the Great Famine occurred). Meanwhile, the state of public health greatly improved, leading to a substantial decrease in the infant mortality rate, and, as a result, the population grew rapidly at an annual rate of 2–3%, expanding from 500 million in the 1950s to 800 million in the 1970s.

At the same time, the government implemented a Soviet-style central planning economic policy, which turned out to be a total failure. China's economic growth stagnated in the 1960s, and its agricultural production was a disaster from 1959 to 1962, causing widespread famine. As the population continued to grow rapidly in the 1970s, the government became concerned

FIGURE 7.7 Fertility rate in China, 1950–2010

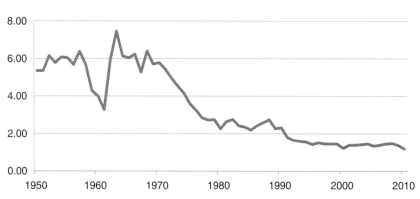

Data Source: China Population Census, fertility rate trend of China, 2010.

about food shortages. The government blamed overpopulation for its economic problems, and started advocating a family planning policy to curb population growth. The policy was initially voluntary, but became increasingly coercive and extreme; it eventually turned into the one-child policy, one of the most extreme forms of birth control ever recorded in human history. In hindsight, the harsh policy was largely unnecessary, because the fertility rate had already dropped to 2.2 when the policy began to be enforced.

The one-child policy took a variety of forms in different parts of China. In the cities, the enforcement of the policy became increasingly stringent throughout the 1980s. Between the 1980s and the 1990s, anybody who had a second child would lose his/her job, as the government was the only employer in many industries during this period. After 2000, as private firms became major employers, the threat of job loss began to lose its teeth. In response, the government imposed a steep fine of three times annual income. As a result, in the cities, where about 50% of the population live today, almost everybody had only one child after the 1990s. Only in 2015 was the one-child policy replaced by the two-child policy. The fertility rate in major cities such as Beijing and Shanghai was 0.7 in 2015, the lowest recorded rate in human history.

In rural areas, the situation was more complex. When the one-child policy was first enforced in rural areas, it induced such strong opposition that it was later changed to the one-and-a-half-child policy, which allowed a second child only if the first child was a girl. At that time, it was culturally and economically unacceptable for Chinese farmers to be without a son. Even with this one-and-a-half-child policy, many farmers still desired to have a son after having two girls. The strict enforcement of this policy sometimes led people to extremes. Forced abortions and destruction of property were not uncommon in the 1980s and 1990s. There was a small portion of the population that was exempt from the one-child policy. These were ethnic minorities, mostly in the Western part of China, who represented less than 10% of the overall population.

Currently, the fertility rate is 1.8 in rural areas and 0.8 in urban areas. Overall, the fertility rate has dropped below the replacement level since the early 1990s, below 1.5 in the 2000s, and most recently dropped to only 1.3, making China one of the ultra-low-fertility countries.

Drastic Demographic Change as a Result of the One-Child Policy

Owing to the unprecedented one-child policy, China's fertility rate declined rapidly, beginning in the 1980s; as a result, the age structure of the population has changed drastically, more so than that of any other country. Even though the total population is still growing in China, the working-age population (from 15 to 64) began to decline in 2015. The year 2015 was an inflection point. In the few decades preceding 2015, the working-age population grew about 1% a year, but from 2015 to 2025, the working-age population will not grow at all, and, after 2025, will shrink 0.5–1% per year. This partially explains why the Chinese economy experienced a significant slowdown in 2015, with the growth rate dropping from 10% to less than 7% a year.

The rapid aging of the Chinese population will impose a heavy burden on the Chinese economy and government. Figure 7.8 illustrates the change in the dependency ratio in China. The dependency ratio is defined as the number of dependents (the elderly and children) per worker. Starting from the 1980s, the dependency ratio has declined much faster in comparison with other developing countries, as the number of children needing to be supported dropped. But these missing children became missing workers 20 years later. By 2015,

FIGURE 7.8 Dependency ratio in China

Dependency Ratio (%)

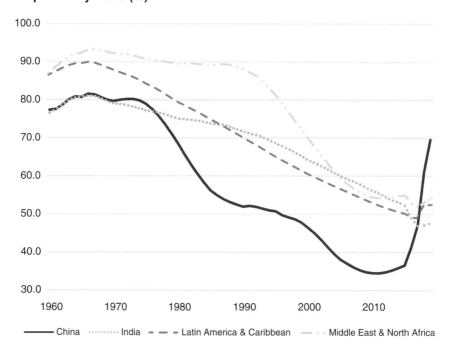

Data Source: Data for 1960–2015 is from the World Bank, 2015. Data for 2015–2050 on India is from the United Nations Population Division. The rest of the data is from the Department of Economic and Social Affairs, World Population to 2300.

FIGURE 7.9 Comparison of population structure of China in 2010 and 2040

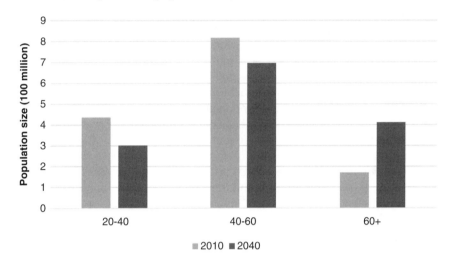

Data Source: U.S. Census Bureau, 2015.

the dependency ratio reversed and started to increase, and it is expected to rise rapidly after 2030.

The number of the elderly will increase rapidly relative to the working population after 2030. Figure 7.9 compares the population structure in 2010 vs. 2040. In 2040, the total population is expected to be roughly 1.4 billion, but the elderly population will increase from 171 million to 411 million. By 2040, the working population, aged between 20 and 60, will drop from 817 million to 696 million. The number of young people, aged between 20 and 40, will drop by 30%, from 436 million to 302 million. As a result of these changes, the age structure will be a top-heavy reverse pyramid shape (Figure 7.10).

Gender Imbalance

In addition to the problem of an aging population, China also has a severe gender-imbalance problem to deal with. Chinese farmers prefer sons to daughters. When the government limited the number of children to one or two per couple, from the 1980s, Chinese farmers selectively aborted unborn daughters with the help of ultrasound prenatal screening technology. So, from the beginning of the 1980s, the ratio of males to females rose from 1.05 in the early 1980s to 1.20 in the late 1990s, and remained high in the 2010s (Figure 7.11). A gender ratio of 1.2 at birth means that there are 20% more boys than girls; consequently, in the birth cohort of the 1990s and the 2010s,

FIGURE 7.10 Population structure of China, 2008–2040

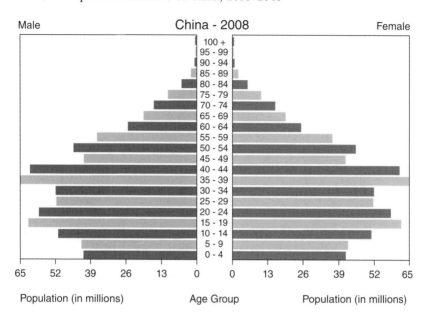

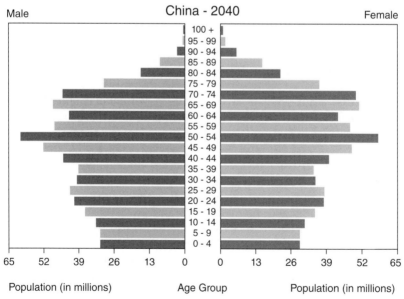

Data Source: U.S. Census Bureau, 2015.

FIGURE 7.11 Gender ratio in China

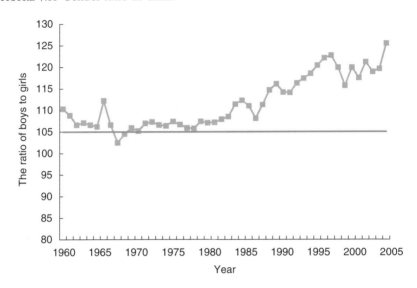

Data Source: World Bank, 2015.

about 20% of males will not have a corresponding female partner of their age.

The End of the One-Child Policy

In recent years, many scholars have urged the government to abolish the one-child policy. After receiving my PhD in economics from Stanford in 2012, I continued my research in aging and innovation. I noticed the absurdity of the one-child policy and its huge looming negative impact on the Chinese economy. I tried to communicate my research findings and policy recommendations to the public and to political leaders; however, up until a few years ago, any criticism of the one-child policy was forbidden in the Chinese media, and most economists and the media were not aware of the severity of the problem. China paid a huge price for this media censorship, which prevented rational public policy debate and delayed the reversal of a policy that clearly had a detrimental impact on the future economic health of the country.

Luckily, with the Internet and particularly social networking websites, I was able to attract a large audience for my research and policy recommendations; my blog attracted over a million followers. With my co-authors Wenzheng Huang and Jianxin Li, I published *China Needs More Babies*, which was the first book in mainland China to directly criticize the one-child policy (Liang et al., 2012). By

2013, the opinions of the mainstream media and the academic community shifted in favor of abolishing the one-child policy. This influenced the Chinese government to change the one-child policy to the two-child policy on October 29, 2015. The question now is what the fertility rate will be in the future.

Forecasting China's Fertility Rate

If we look at the fertility rates of other East Asian countries with similar cultural patterns, we will reach the conclusion that China will continue to experience very low fertility rates in the absence of meaningful policy intervention. The fertility rates of Japan, Korea, Taiwan, Hong Kong, and Singapore are around 1.1–1.4, the lowest in the world. Vietnam, similar to China culturally but at a much less advanced stage of development, has a fertility rate of 1.8 without the presence of a one-child policy. So, China's natural fertility rate will likely be only 1.6. As China grows wealthier, its fertility rate will continue to drop. Currently, the per capita GDP in China is US$7,500; it is expected to reach US $10,000 by 2020. When Japan and Korea reached the US$10,000 level, their fertility rate dropped to below 1.5.

What about the young rural Chinese? Will they have more children than their young urban counterparts and so help the overall fertility rate? The answer is that they are also unlikely to have many children, because they are mostly destined to become migrant workers in the cities and, as a result of their migrant status, face an even tougher burden economically to raise children.

Of course, in the first few years following the relaxation of the one-child policy, there will be a pent-up demand to have a second child; therefore, it is expected that there will be a surge of new births from 2016 to 2018. However, after this initial increase, China's fertility rate and new births will drop again. Table 7.1 shows the fertility rebound in several Asian

TABLE 7.1 Fertility rates of countries five years before and after birth policy changes

	Limiting population growth					Encouraging population growth				
	Year	−2	−1	Stop	+1	+2	Year	−2	−1	Begin	+1	+2
Japan	1974	2.14	2.14	2.05	1.91	1.85	1994	1.46	1.50	1.42	1.43	1.39
Korea	1996	1.66	1.63	1.57	1.52	1.45	2005	1.18	1.15	1.08	1.12	1.25
Taiwan	1990	1.86	1.68	1.81	1.72	1.73	2005	1.26	1.18	1.12	1.12	1.10
Singapore	1988	1.43	1.63	1.96	1.75	1.87	1988	1.43	1.63	1.96	1.75	1.87
Iran	2012	1.90	0.91	1.92	/	/	2012	1.90	1.91	1.92	/	/

Notes: Both Singapore's and Iran's population policy reversed immediately, to stop inhibiting and begin encouraging birth at the same time.

Data Source: Data pertaining to Taiwan is from the Department of Household Registration, MOI Taiwan. The rest of the data is from the World Bank.

countries after the abolishment of anti-fertility policies. Only Singapore experienced a 0.2 rebound in fertility, and this only lasted for a period of three years; none of the other countries experienced a significant rebound.

Based on the experience of these countries, the rebound in China will likely be slight and short-lived. From our analysis, the number of births is expected to increase from 16 million in 2015 to about 18 million between 2016 and 2018, and start to drop again after 2020.

China to Adopt Pro-fertility Policy

Sooner or later, China will need to completely reverse its anti-fertility policy and adopt a pro-fertility policy just like the other East Asian countries. However, there are reasons to believe that the job of raising the fertility rate in China will be even more difficult than it is in other Asian countries. Here are some of these reasons.

The first reason is a cultural one. The Chinese care about the educational achievements of their children more than the parents of any other culture. This is both a historical artifact (competitive examinations having been part of the Chinese culture for millennia) and a recent phenomenon (Chinese parents recognize that the global market prizes educational performance). The "Tiger Mom" style of parenting is quite common among Chinese parents. Extra-curricular activities and cram classes are costly and time-consuming for parents. Chinese parents are more concerned about investing resources to ensure the best educational outcomes for their children, rather than the quantity of their children. This naturally limits the number of children they believe that they can afford to have.

Second, Chinese women have more education and career demands than other countries. Chinese women are more educated and independent than in many other nations. Under Mao, almost all women worked and this trend has remained a strong one in post-reform China. Even today, the female labor force participation rate is extremely high by international standards.

Lastly, for demographic and cultural reasons, highly educated Chinese women will likely have both a low marriage rate and a low out-of-wedlock birth rate. Chinese women, like Japanese women, have a culture of not "marrying down." Consequently, many highly educated Chinese women have a hard time finding suitable husbands, and these so-called "leftover women" are increasingly common in large cities in China. On the other hand, it is still culturally unacceptable to have children out of wedlock. In Japan, China, and Korea, the out-of-wedlock birth rate is less than 3%, in comparison with 40% in Scandinavian countries.

In summary, Chinese women are more likely to be unmarried, career-oriented, and care more about the "quality" of their children than the quantity; therefore, it is likely that they will have fewer children than women in other countries, even should a robust pro-fertility policy be adopted in China.

During a recent survey conducted in China, the desired number of children per woman worked out at around 1.8, compared with 2 in Japan and 3 in the United States. Typically, the actual number of children per woman is 30% lower than the desired number of children. So, without any pro-fertility policies in place, China's fertility rate could be only 1.2, a rate similar to those in Singapore, Hong Kong, and Taiwan. In fact, even with the two-child policy, the urban fertility rate is likely to remain the lowest in the world.

Deterioration of Demographics

The number of births in the late 1990s was, on average, 16 million per year, which is almost 40% lower than in the 1980s (Figure 7.12). In 5–10 years, those born in the 1990s will become parents, and if they have a fertility rate lower than 1.5, then the number of new births will be only 12 million a year. India, in contrast, will have over 16 million new births a year. After 2040, China will have one of the most top-heavy demographic structures in the world, and its population will shrink by 10 million a year, which is an unprecedented decline in world history.

FIGURE 7.12 Forecast of number of newborns in China per year, 1950–2160

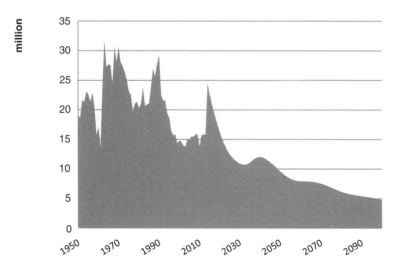

Data Source: Estimates based on the Sixth Population Census and the China Statistical Yearbook.

The Impact of Demographic Change on the Chinese Economy and Innovation

These abrupt demographic changes are very likely to have a large negative effect on China's economy, especially on its capability to innovate.

Currently, the Chinese are still relatively young demographically, because the birth cohort stemming from the 1980s is enormous, with an average of 25 million new births a year during that decade. They are now in their 30s, a golden age for both earning and consumption; their demand for housing and other items has been the main driver of the Chinese economy over the last 10 years. But over the next 20–30 years, they will grow old and retire. The 1990s birth cohort is 40% smaller than the 1980s cohort. When they reach the prime age of 30, something which is only several years away, domestic demand for goods and services will slow down. Of course, this will be counterbalanced by an increasingly affluent society. Nevertheless, the cohort size is such that it will have a considerable structural impact on consumption.

In terms of innovation capabilities, 30–40 is the most productive age group, and is also the best age group for entrepreneurship. Currently, the 30–40 age group is composed of the huge 1980 birth cohort. But in 10 years' time, when the much smaller 1990 birth cohort turns 30, the level of innovation and entrepreneurship will almost certainly suffer. As the size of the young population in China shrinks, the scale advantage of Chinese innovation will yield precedence to that of India and eventually to that of the United States.

Figure 7.13 compares the proportion of young workers (aged 20–39) of China to that of Japan. In Japan, the proportion of young workers has declined

FIGURE 7.13 Share of young workers (aged 20–39) in workforce (aged 20–59) in China and Japan

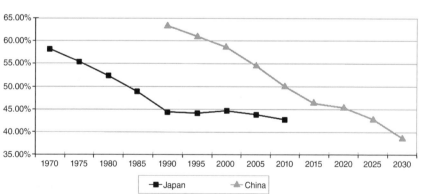

Data Source: U.S. Census, 2015.

rapidly from 55% in the 1970s to about 40% today. I have argued in previous chapters that an aging workforce will block the promotion opportunities of younger workers, making them less innovative and entrepreneurial. The lack of innovation and entrepreneurship caused by an aging workforce is one of the major reasons for Japan's economic stagnation over the last 25 years. The aging of the Chinese workforce will follow a very similar trend to that of Japan, albeit with a 35-year lag. By 2025, the Chinese workforce will be as old as the Japanese workforce in the 1990s, and by 2040, the Chinese workforce will be older than the Japanese workforce today. If Japan is a case study to learn from, then the Chinese economy will suffer as a result of a lack of innovation and entrepreneurship, beginning in 2025.

Policy Suggestions

China currently attracts next to no immigration and is unlikely to be able to attract a significant number of immigrants relative to its huge size, so it urgently needs to revamp its demographic policies.

1. To completely reverse its anti-fertility policies and help families raise more children. With a fertility rate of only 1.3, China should not only abolish its current two-child policy, but also adopt aggressive pro-fertility policies such as tax and cash benefits for families with children, more funding for daycare facilities, and educational reforms such as those discussed in Chapter 5.
2. To further relax internal migration and help more young college graduates and migrant workers to settle in big cities. China needs to abolish the "Hukou" (residency registration) system, which discriminates against non-residents in their ability to access public services. This policy has not only exacerbated the problem of urban–rural inequality, but also put a brake on the growth of large cities, reducing the potential agglomeration effect of innovation for its large cities.
3. To increase the size of its major cities, by facilitating more investment in housing, roads, subways, airports, schools, hospitals, and other public services in large cities. Recently, housing prices in major Chinese cities have risen quickly. But rather than increasing the land supply, infrastructure, and public services, the government has instead tried to further restrict migration to these large cities. This is clearly a misguided policy as China, simply because of its sheer size, needs to have the largest cities in the world to host the largest concentration of human resources in the world.

China will pay a heavy price for its demographic policy mistakes over the last 40 years; moreover, China has been very slow to adjust its draconian demographic policies. With the vibrant economy of today, the Chinese government certainly can afford to have a generous pro-fertility policy and continue to invest in infrastructure and public facilities in large cities, to accommodate a much larger urban population. Unfortunately, however, it seems that the Chinese government still sometimes views a large population as an economic liability rather than an asset. Mainstream economists still underestimate the advantages of a large, concentrated, young workforce. This is the main reason why China is unlikely to adopt the recommended aggressive pro-fertility policies any time soon.

Conclusion

China will benefit significantly from its large population size, and become one of the most innovative economies of the world in the early part of the twenty-first century. By 2040, the per capita income of China will stand at about half that of the United States, and its total GDP will possibly be larger than that of the United States and Europe combined. However, by 2040, China's workforce will be one of the oldest in the world, with a demographic cohort makeup similar to that of Japan today; as a result, its innovation and entrepreneurship capabilities will be much diminished.

By 2040, India, with a much larger population and a fast-growing economy, will emerge as one of the innovation centers of the world. By 2040, the United States will remain an innovation hotspot, with a growing population and a large influx of highly skilled immigrants. If this trend continues, the dominance of the Chinese economy and innovation will be short-lived. In the latter part of the twenty-first century, India and the United States will likely overtake China as the world's most innovative countries. The twenty-first century may not be the century of China after all, because of its self-inflicted demographic wounds.

CHAPTER 8

The United States of America

The emergence of the United States as a superpower has truly changed world history during the last century. The country has been hugely successful in terms of innovation.

A History of Innovation in the United States

By the late 1800s, the United States had already exceeded France, Germany, and the United Kingdom in the number of patents awarded, as shown in Figure 8.1. The most important innovations—such as electric light, telegraph, telephone, and mass-produced automobiles—were invented or first became commercially successful in the United States. In 1870, the per capita GDP of the United States was 30% lower than that of the United Kingdom, but by 1929, the per capita GDP of the United States was 30% higher than that of the United Kingdom. This growth was driven mostly by innovation.

This sudden rise in U.S. innovation was quite surprising, because in the 1860s, the United States had only just emerged from the Civil War. European countries, such as the United Kingdom, France, and especially Germany, seemed to have all the advantages required to succeed in innovation. They were much more industrialized, had the best incumbent firms, and the best universities in the world.

So how did the United States become so successful so quickly? Some say it was due to its railroads and territorial expansion following the civil war, but I would argue that ultimately it was due to the expansion of its population. Even its successful territory expansion was a consequence of population growth, which led to more people exploring the Western and Southern areas of the country (formerly Spanish territory), a move that eventually led to the defeat of Spain in the Spanish–American War. The construction of the railroads was also a consequence of population and territorial expansion. The rapid growth of

FIGURE 8.1 Patents statistics for France, the United Kingdom, the United States, and Germany, 1838–1945

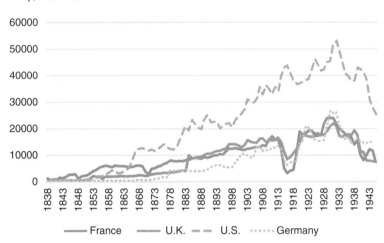

Data Source: B. Khan, *An Economic History of Patent Institutions.* EH.net Encyclopedia (ed. R. Whaples), March 16, 2008.

the population was ultimately what made the United States unique in the late 1800s.

From 1865 to 1925, the U.S. population grew from 30 million to 110 million. At the same time, the French population only grew from 38 million to 40 million; the U.K. population grew from 24 million to 45 million; and the German population grew from 38 million to 63 million. The United States was by far the largest immigrant country in the world during this period.

By the early 1900s, the U.S. market was already twice the size of France and the United Kingdom and 50% larger than Germany. Moreover, compared with other New World countries, the United States also had a much larger population. In 1870, when the United States already had a population of 40 million, Mexico and Brazil had populations of under 10 million, while Argentina had a population of under 2 million (Figure 8.2).

Although the United States was already an innovative country in the early 1890s, it still lagged behind Continental Europe in basic science and research. It is unsurprising, therefore, that the number of U.S. Nobel Laureates was far lower than those from Germany. However, despite the lack of world-class scientists, U.S. innovation surpassed Europe thanks to its huge market, which provided the greatest opportunities and incentives for inventors and entrepreneurs to focus on commercial innovations. Electricity was first discovered in Europe, but U.S. entrepreneurs such as Thomas Edison and Nikola Tesla

FIGURE 8.2 Historical population in the United States, Russia, Germany, the United Kingdom, and France (1801–2000)

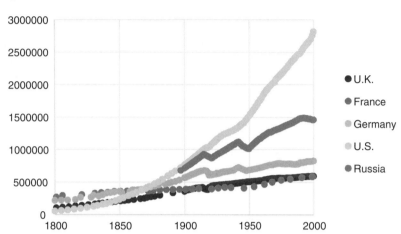

Data Source: B. R. Mitchell, *International Historical Statistics* (3rd and 4th edn); Statesman's Yearbook (1930–2001); Demographic Yearbook/United Nations (195X–); "Suomen tilastolinen vuosikirja" 1998; A Hundred Year (1890–1990) Database for Integrated Environmental Assessments/C. G. M. Klein Goldewijk and J. J. Battjes, 1997.

pioneered its commercial application. By 1925, New York became the world's largest city, with a population of more than 7 million, which was more than double the size of Paris and Berlin. Helped by the largest market, U.S. firms were able to achieve economies of scale earlier than European firms in the commercialization of new technologies such as electricity. Also, thanks to its large market, U.S. firms were the first to introduce the assembly line mass-production process. The first Ford Model T car was mass produced in 1908; as a result, the unit production cost plummeted and productivity soared, and U.S. automobile firms, capitalizing on their success, became the leading innovators of the world.

The advantage of scale not only helped in the innovation of consumer goods, but also capital goods. For example, with many potential manufacturing firms as customers, suppliers of machinery in the United States were able to develop specialized machinery and sell it in large volumes, ushering in many innovations in this sector during the early 1890s.

By the early 1890s, the United States already had more than twice the population of the next largest country in the Western world, and it became an economic superpower before the First World War. When the United States used its economic might in the context of a war effort, its scale advantage proved decisive. Its intervention and direct involvement won two world wars and changed world history. After the Second World War, the United States enjoyed an even greater advantage in terms of demographics. Many scientists, including Jewish scientists, joined U.S. universities, which helped the United States to surpass Europe in basic scientific research. Because the United States continued to attract significantly more immigrants than Europe, and had a higher fertility rate than Europe, by the 2000s, the U.S. population grew to 300 million, which is larger than the combined populations of the United Kingdom, Germany, France, and Italy, and three times larger than that of Japan. It was not until recently that China was able to match its market size. Not surprisingly, for most of the last century, the United States has had the best universities and the best companies, and it has dominated the world in terms of innovation.

Owing to its size advantage, the United States is far ahead of other countries in terms of information technology, financial services, the media industry, and military technology. The only exception is a number of European and Japanese companies that have retained a lead in several manufacturing industries. The reason that European and Japanese companies can still compete with the United States in manufacturing, with a much smaller home market, is because in manufacturing, product specification and quality performance is objective and observable, so it is much easier to export a manufacturing product than to export a service or a software product or film. For example, the Finnish company Nokia can achieve worldwide scale without a large home market. Nokia once had a very innovative and successful mobile phone product.

However, the share of the manufacturing industry in the modern economy is gradually eroding and giving way to service, software, and Internet industries. In these non-manufacturing industries, the product is not readily exportable, and perfecting a service product/technology involves joint creation between the firm and the customers. So, a large home market becomes a very important advantage. For this reason, U.S. companies disproportionately dominate the service and information technology industries. For example, the United States has the largest logistics companies, such as FedEx and UPS, the largest restaurant and hotel chains, as well as the largest financial services firms. The market share of U.S. firms in the global service industry is much larger than that of European or Japanese firms. Typically, these U.S. firms achieved scale and perfected their products in the U.S. market before they captured the markets of other countries and became successful global brands. Therefore, it is not surprising that U.S. software and Internet companies now dominate globally. When mobile phones became a service/software product rather than simply a manufactured product, United States-based Apple overtook Nokia.

Does the United States have an Inherent Advantage in Innovation?

The question now arises: Will the United States be able to successfully withstand the challenge from China? Vice President Joe Biden once said that the United States is hardwired for innovation while China is not. He also stated that the strength of the United States lies in three areas: the political system, the economic system, and the education system. I disagree—these three areas are not sources of U.S. strength in innovation.

First, the political system is not related to innovation, because many democratic countries are not successful innovators. Almost all European countries are democracies, but Southern and Eastern European countries have very low levels of entrepreneurship and innovation because of their small market size, aging population, and net negative immigration. During the 1970s and 1980s, Singapore, Taiwan, and South Korea were arguably not democratic, but they were quite successful innovators.

Second, the economic system is not a sustainable source of advantage either. The policy ingredients for innovation are trade liberalization, minimal regulation, good infrastructure, and good property protection (including intellectual property protection). Most countries understand these ingredients, and are capable of providing them. China has pursued a market-based economy, has an open economy with good infrastructure, and has started to enforce intellectual property protection laws. A good economic system is not unique to the United States.

Third, the education system is only partially an advantage for the United States. Although the United States has a very small number of elite private high schools, the overall U.S. high-school education can objectively be assessed as worse than that of most of the developed world, and significantly worse than East Asian countries on average. Some people say that due to their rote-learning school system, Chinese students are incapable of becoming innovators. This is a myth. Even though high-school students in China lead a miserable life with a heavy study load, there is no evidence that studying too hard hurts their creativity later in life. Japanese students have always endured the same kind of education as Chinese students, and yet they came up with the Walkman, video games, and many other great inventions during the 1970s and 1980s. Only recently has the capacity of the Japanese to invent suffered, as a result of its aging workforce. Korea has a similar education system to China, but Korea has been very successful in terms of innovation in the automobile industry, home appliances industry, and many other industries. Recently, many Chinese firms have become successful innovators in high-tech industries, and this has little to do with the system of education.

The United States still leads the world in higher education, especially in graduate and PhD programs, but this is because U.S. universities can attract the best students and scholars from around the world. If the United States has any hardwired advantage, it lies in its ability to attract more talent from the rest of the world, as well as, to a much lesser extent, a relatively high fertility rate for a developed country.

The Fertility Advantage

The much higher population growth in the United States is a result of a higher level of fertility and immigration. Let's first look at the fertility rate (Figure 8.3). The United States has the highest fertility among all the developed countries. Its fertility of 2.0 is near the replacement level, and is much higher than the European average of 1.5. Even if we just look at the Caucasian population, the fertility rate is higher than that of Europe (Figure 8.4).

Why does the United States have an exceptionally high fertility rate in comparison with other developed countries? Scholars are still debating this question. It seems that there is more than one reason. The first reason is religion; the proportion of religious people in the United States is higher than that in Europe, and religious people tend to value both marriage and large families (Figure 8.5). For example, the Mormons and Catholic Hispanics have high fertility rates when compared with the general population.

FIGURE 8.3 Overall fertility trend in the United States

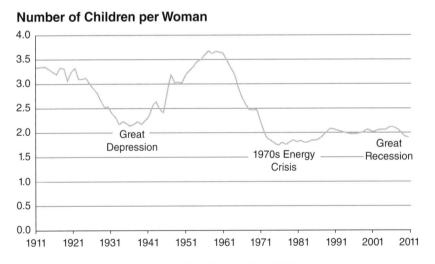

Number of Children per Woman

Data Source: National Center for Health Statistics, 2012.

FIGURE 8.4 Fertility by ethnic group in the United States

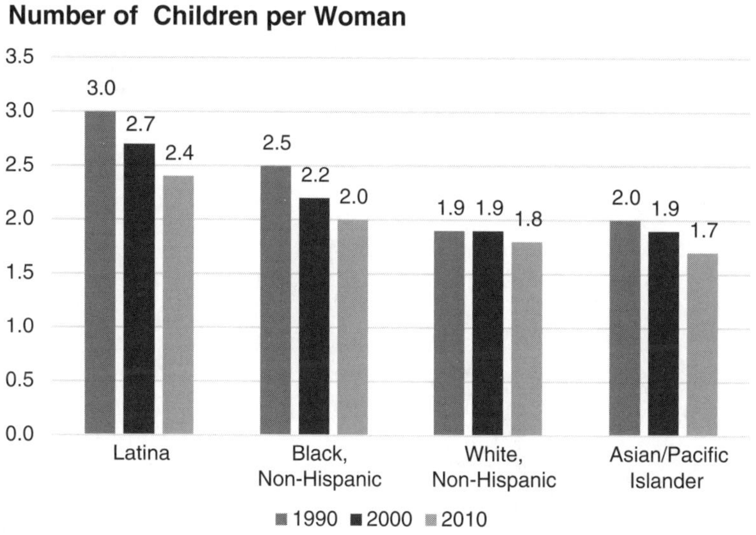

Number of Children per Woman

Group values:
- Latina: 3.0 (1990), 2.7 (2000), 2.4 (2010)
- Black, Non-Hispanic: 2.5 (1990), 2.2 (2000), 2.0 (2010)
- White, Non-Hispanic: 1.9 (1990), 1.9 (2000), 1.8 (2010)
- Asian/Pacific Islander: 2.0 (1990), 1.9 (2000), 1.7 (2010)

■ 1990 ■ 2000 ■ 2010

Data Source: National Center for Health Statistics, 2012.

The other reason is the country's relatively inexpensive housing. In contrast to East Asian countries, such as China, Korea, and Japan, most Americans live in suburban areas where the cost, per square meter, of housing is much lower, and space is usually not a constraint to having more children.

But is this fertility advantage sustainable? I think the fertility advantage will diminish over time because, with the globalization of media and culture, the younger generation will adopt a lifestyle and attitude on family size that is more similar to that of Europe. Also, more and more young Americans are moving to large cities, where real-estate prices are becoming more expensive due to the agglomeration effect.

Immigration Advantage

The ultimate sustainable innovation advantage enjoyed by the United States in contrast to the rest of the world is immigration. The United States became a superpower mostly as a result of consistent pro-immigration policies, which led to a constant influx of immigrants into the country. It will now have to rely on immigration again to sustain its leadership position on innovation. The United States currently attracts about 0.5 to 1 million immigrants a year (Figure 8.6). The skill level of the immigrants is polarized. On the one hand, most of the immigrants only have a high-school diploma or even less

180

FIGURE 8.5 Religiosity map of the world.

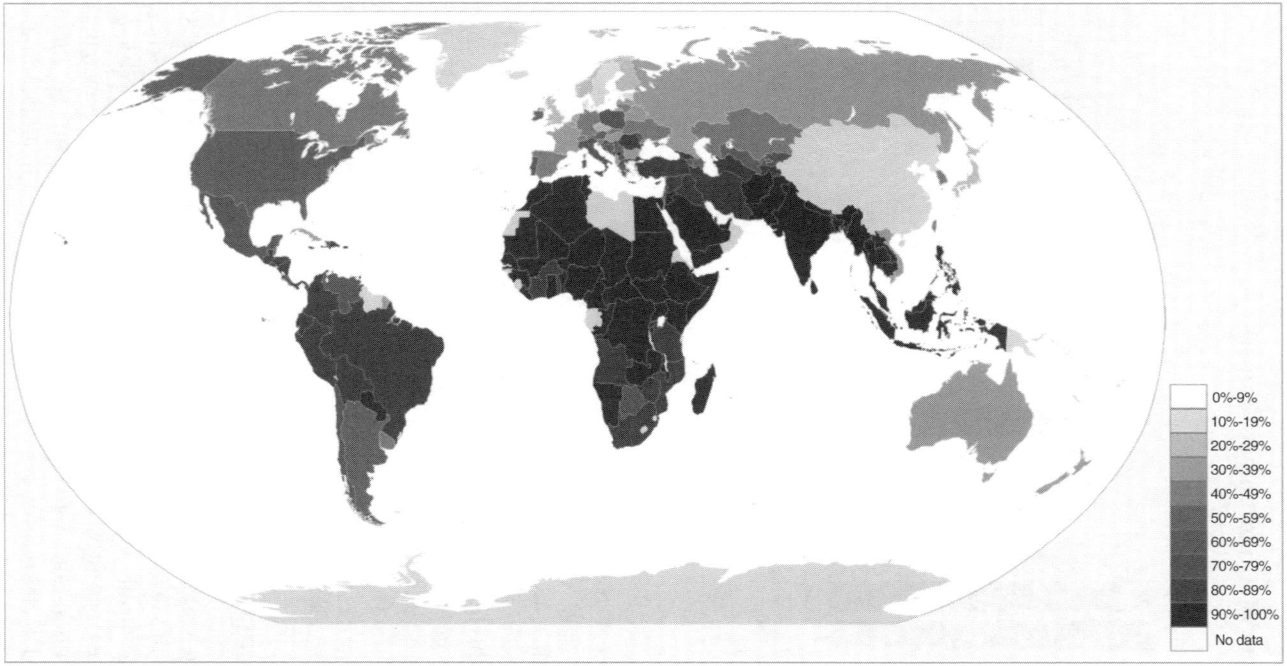

Note: Results of a 2008/2009 Gallup poll on whether respondents said that religion was "important in their daily life."

Data Source: Crabtree Steve, Religiosity Highest in World's Poorest Nations, Gallup Global Reports, Retrieved May 27, 2015.

FIGURE 8.6 U.S. net migration

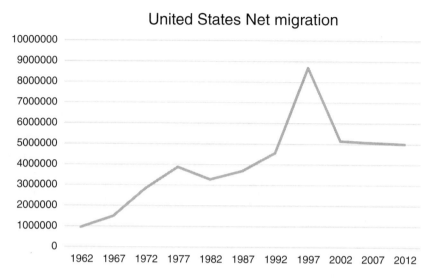

Data Source: World Development Indicators, 2012.

formal education; on the other hand, the share of master's degree/PhD holders is a lot higher than that of the native-born population. I define unskilled workers as those without a college degree, and highly skilled workers as those with a college degree or higher. Approximately more than half of these immigrants are unskilled immigrants, mostly from Latin America, but there are also a few hundred thousand highly skilled workers arriving yearly, mostly from Europe and Asia.

Many researchers have demonstrated that immigrants tend to be more innovative and entrepreneurial, and they have more children than natives, even when their education is taken into consideration. A highly skilled immigrant to the United States is on average twice as likely to hold a patent and 30% more likely to start a successful company (Hunt, 2010).

U.S. universities attract many talented students every year. The share of foreign-born PhD graduates ranges from 10% to almost 50%, depending on the major (Figure 8.7). In computer science and engineering majors, the percentages are 45% and 47%, respectively. Most of these PhD graduates stay and work in the United States for their entire career. They represent the best and brightest of their home country, and many of them later become leading researchers and entrepreneurs. About half of the successful high-tech companies in the United States have one or more immigrant founders. If we include the children of first-generation immigrants, more than half of the engineers in Silicon Valley are from immigrant families. In many high-tech

FIGURE 8.7 Share of foreign-born PhD candidates in U.S. universities (%)

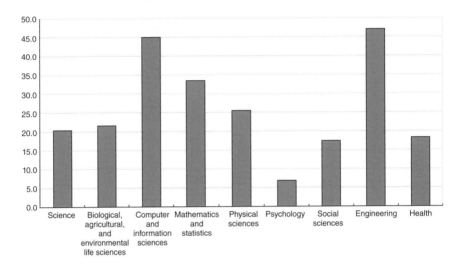

Source: https://www.nsf.gov/statistics/doctoratework.

firms, the share of inventions by ethnic Indian and Chinese has reached 20–40%, and is still growing (Kerr and Lincoln, 2010). Most of the ethnic Indian and Chinese are first- and second-generation immigrants.

The United States is uniquely successful at attracting immigrants, because it already has more immigrants than any other country in the world, which is an example of a classical network effect (Figure 8.8). This makes it easier for newcomers to leverage ethnic groups to find friends and jobs. Moreover, a growing population and a dynamic economy provide more jobs and innovation opportunities, which attract even more immigrants. Lastly, more immigrants will make the country more diverse and tolerant, culturally and politically (and thus more attractive to immigrants). This scale and network effect of immigration is an advantage that no other country has the ability to mimic any time soon. In contrast, China (as well as other large economies) has a relatively homogeneous population, and it is difficult to see China becoming a country that attracts a significant number of immigrants.

English is also an advantage for the United States because it makes it easier for newcomers to assimilate. English-speaking countries are the most popular destinations for immigrants and international students. Figure 8.8 compares the number of foreign students in four countries. Among all the English-speaking countries, it is clear that the United States is the most attractive to international students. Also, because it has the largest population and economy, the United States is able to offer many students the chance to stay and

FIGURE 8.8 International students in the United States, the United Kingdom, Canada, and Australia

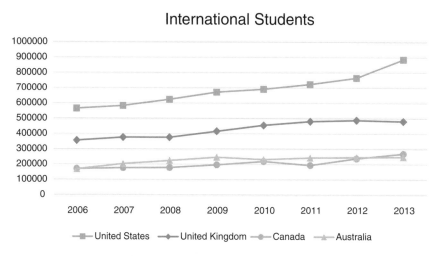

Data Source: Project Atlas Australia, International students in Australia, 2013.

work on completion of their studies. This is one of the reasons why many international students in the United Kingdom, Canada, and Australia end up working or attending graduate school in the United States after they finish their undergraduate studies.

Immigration is a unique advantage of the United States, but can this be a lasting advantage? I believe that it can, unless, of course, the United States self-imposes restrictions on immigration, like it did many times throughout its history. In U.S. history, periods of open immigration coincided with periods of prosperity and periods of low immigration preceded periods of decline. It is not a coincidence that before the Great Depression, in 1924, the United States introduced immigration laws to greatly reduce the number of immigrants. In periods of economic difficulty, politicians often scapegoat immigrants for problems such as unemployment and inequality.

Is Inequality a Problem?

In recent years, income inequality in the United States has worsened; the share of pre-tax income received by the richest 1% of Americans rose from 13.3% in 2009 to 14.6% in 2011. During 2012 alone, the incomes of the wealthiest 1% of Americans rose nearly 20%, whereas the incomes of the remaining 99% rose only 1% (Figure 8.9).

FIGURE 8.9 The U.S. Gini index

United States
Gini index (World Bank estimate)

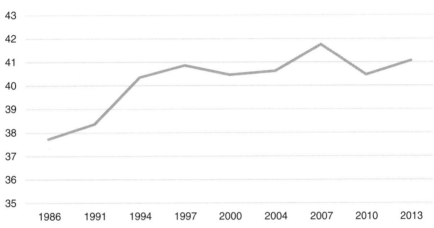

Data Source: World Bank, United States Gini index, 2015.

The United States ranks on the 30th percentile in income inequality globally, meaning that 70% of countries have a more equal income distribution.

Meanwhile, the United States has the strongest economy and the most dynamic IT industry among all developed countries. The rise in inequality and the rise of the IT industry are not just a coincidence. Information technology makes some workers more productive, and they are the IT engineers and other highly skilled workers with skills complementary to technology. Highly skilled engineers and entrepreneurs in the IT and related industries make a lot more money than they previously could, resulting in a widening income gap in the United States.

Income redistribution is not a good solution, because it will dampen the incentive for innovation and entrepreneurship. A better way to level the playing field is to raise the skill level of the poor, but this is also difficult to do. Throwing resources at the poor is unlikely to significantly raise their level of education, because there are complicating factors such as culture.

As explained in Chapter 5, highly skilled immigration can help solve the inequality problem. Increasing the number of highly skilled immigrants will increase the supply of highly skilled workers, hence reducing the wage premium paid for their skills. At the same time, more highly skilled workers will increase demand for unskilled jobs, as highly skilled workers will demand more gardeners, plumbers, maids, and so on. This increased demand will also increase the wages for unskilled workers and further drive down inequality.

China vs. the United States

In about 10 years' time, China will be a wealthy nation with an economy larger than that of the United States and a population four times its size. China will certainly have a home market larger than that of the United States, but because of the immigration advantage and the language (English) advantage, the United States may still have a chance to come out on top.

For some markets, such as the gaming and entertainment industries, the market boundary is not national borders but rather language or cultural boundaries. For example, a Chinese film has a market size of 1.3 billion, but an English film has a market size of close to 2 billion (with most people in Europe and India also being potential customers). Most service products, such as Internet or software products, are like the movie industry, where the boundaries are culture and language, rather than national borders.

In terms of talent pool size, China will have a much larger pool of college students and researchers than the United States. However, in terms of the quality of students or researchers, the United States will continue to enjoy an advantage over China, since graduate schools at U.S. universities will still be a magnet for the best undergraduate college students around the world. This means that the United States will effectively have a global talent pool that it can draw upon that is several times larger than that of China.

Also, the U.S. population will be much younger than that of China, because of the much higher fertility and immigration rate. For example, by 2040, the median age of the Chinese will be over 45, but only 40 in the United States (Figure 8.10). As I explained in Chapter 2, an aging country is likely to be much less innovative and entrepreneurial.

Policy Recommendations

The United States should try to attract more international students to study and work in the United States upon graduation.

1. Offer more working visas to international students upon graduation from U.S. universities.

    It is estimated that there are more than 1 million international students in the United States. Most of them pay full tuition fees, and desire to stay in the United States after graduation. The United States should allow these students to work and pay tax upon graduation with no conditions

FIGURE 8.10 The prediction of population structure in 2040

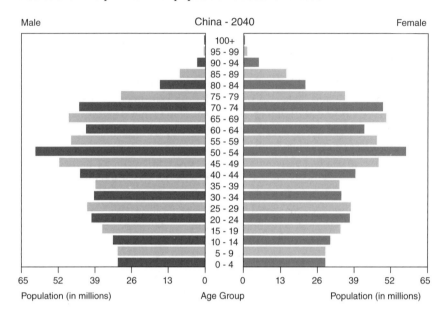

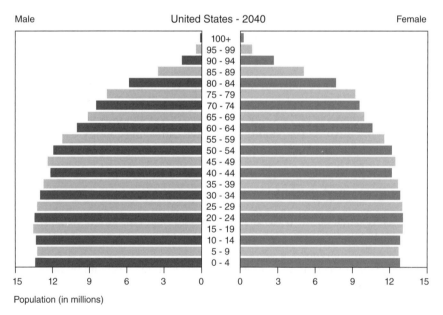

Data Source: U.S. Census Bureau, 2015.

attached; it is the sending country that should believe itself at a disadvantage and be concerned about a brain drain.

2. Expand both undergraduate and graduate programs.

The demand for U.S. education is high; it is estimated that the number of students from China alone will triple over the next 10 years. Similarly, as Indian parents become wealthier they will also send more of their children to study in the United States. Soon, there will be huge capacity shortages in U.S. colleges, primarily due to increasing demand from India and China alone. Let's do a back-of-the-envelope forecast of demand from China. It could well be that 10% of the college student cohort in China would want to study outside of China for undergraduate or graduate study (i.e. 10% of 8 million college students each year). Of the 800,000 million Chinese international students a year, I estimate that 50% will want to study in the United States (which is by far the most popular choice of destination). Therefore, 400,000 Chinese students will apply for U.S. colleges every year. Other countries, such as India, Korea, and Vietnam, will also see huge increases in the number of students who want to study in the United States. Currently, U.S. colleges grant about 2 million bachelor's degrees a year. Unless the United States is prepared to grant 20% of its college degrees to students from China alone, there will be a huge shortage of supply for college education in the United States.

If higher education were a private industry, the colleges would be very happy to continue to grow their business, but unfortunately, most educational institutions are not-for-profit entities. Universities brag about low admission rates and exclusivity, and unlike companies who seek to maximize profit, they are very reluctant to expand. I am not sure what the solution will be, but high demand for U.S. education will be a happy problem for the United States to solve (if the best American universities can somehow meet the growing demand by either expanding their facilities or allowing more online instruction). Such expansion would be a great boost for the education sector and the economy in the long run.

3. Allow more highly skilled immigrants into the United States.

If we define highly skilled immigrants as those with at least a college degree, the United States can admit about 400,000 highly skilled immigrants each year. However, the H1 B (employment visa) is capped at only a little over 100,000 a year. The United States should take all the highly skilled immigrants that it can get.

Many economists think that the United States should allow all international students with a college degree to work and live in the country. The United States currently grants about 2 million bachelor's degrees a year. If 20% of degrees are awarded to international students and 80% of them want to stay and work, this amounts to 320,000 college graduates (20% × 2 million × 80%). Therefore, a 100,000 employment visa quota is less than one-third of the potential highly skilled immigrants who are likely to be available simply by way of the higher education system. When I worked at Oracle in the 1990s, because of the long queue for H1 visas, Oracle and many high-tech firms in Silicon Valley were forced to open large research and development centers outside the United States. This was detrimental to the U.S. economy, both in the short and long term!

The United States should dramatically raise the availability of employment visas to around 600,000 per year, including 300,000 for recent graduates and 300,000 for experienced, highly skilled workers. Assuming that each highly skilled worker will bring one relative on average, this would double the size of the current annual immigration from 1 million to 2 million. Two million a year in absolute terms will be the largest immigration figure in the history of the United States, but as a ratio of the total population, it is only 0.7% a year (a much lower ratio of immigration compared with that 100 years ago). At 0.7% a year, the United States easily has the capacity to absorb and provide basic public services for these newcomers. A total of 600,000 highly skilled workers a year would be a great boost for U.S. competitiveness, with the added bonus of helping to reduce inequality.

4. Expand infrastructure and public services.

In order to gain broad public support to admit many more immigrants a year, the United States needs to build more infrastructure such as roads, hospitals, and schools. This is certainly achievable given the relatively modest size of the immigrant pool vis-à-vis the total population. Moreover, infrastructure investment will boost the economy and generate more employment, particularly for the unskilled labor pool (once again contributing to the reduction in inequality).

Predicting the Effects of Donald Trump's Presidency

Donald Trump ran on the platform of anti-globalization, a platform that supposedly would help unskilled workers, but one that is clearly bad for both businesses and the economy. On the other hand, Donald Trump also has a traditional conservative agenda of lower taxes and a smaller government, something that is good for both businesses and the economy. These are seemingly conflicting agendas, trying to achieve what seem to be polar opposite goals.

I would argue that an anti-globalization agenda, even if implemented successfully, is not going to help the affected workers much, because the manufacturing jobs that Donald Trump wants to return to the United States are unskilled jobs that will soon likely be replaced by robots in any case. It is quite ironic that Trump wants iPhones made in the United States but at the same time Foxconn, the company that employs millions of workers (mostly in China) to produce iPhones for Apple, is pushing hard to replace Chinese workers with robots. Do we really want American workers to compete with robots in China?

The answer is no. Instead, Donald Trump should be fighting to have more robots that are made in the United States. This requires the United States to have the best scientists and engineers in the world. The key to increasing the number of American jobs is to attract the best talent—including engineers, professors, and students—to stay and work in the United States. It seems contradictory that to create more jobs we need more immigrants but, as explained in this book, immigrants (especially highly skilled immigrants) create additional highly skilled jobs due to the agglomeration effect, which will further strengthen the United States as the pre-eminent center of global innovation. Moreover, highly skilled immigrants also create demand for unskilled jobs (such as gardeners, waiters, and barbers), and help close any emerging inequality gap. If one understands the economics of innovation and immigration, allowing more high-skill immigration is an easy policy choice. It remains to be seen, of course, whether Donald Trump's presidency will be a sensible one.

The Thucydides Trap: A Conflict between China and the United States

The Thucydides trap, named after the Ancient Greek historian, refers to the prediction that an incumbent superpower (such as the United States) will almost always wage war with an emerging superpower (such as China). The newly elected U.S. president has promised to "get tough" with China. The territorial dispute in the South China Sea seems to be escalating to a standoff between China and the South East Asian nations, which are often backed by the U.S. military.

Obviously, a military conflict between the United States and China would be disastrous for both countries and the world. Unfortunately, historically the new and old have all too often ended up in conflict, whether this was Germany and Britain, Athens and Sparta, or America and Japan.

However, I would argue that this time will be different. During the agricultural and industrial ages, countries went to war to compete for land, labor, and natural resources. Today, innovation and technology are the most important factors in an economy, and they reside in people's brains. In other words, the innovator's mind is the key resource. Even in the event of a war, a country can be victorious over another country and possess all of its natural resources, and yet it cannot suborn its human resources or the minds of its people. For example, in the unlikely event of a foreign army successfully occupying Silicon Valley, innovation there would stop almost immediately. Engineers at Google would simply leave the war-torn country and start a new search engine elsewhere. One cannot force people to be creative. When human resources and innovative minds become the most valuable asset, the motives for traditional war disappear.

Today, economic competition is not a war for resources, but rather a war for talent. A war for talent is not a war but a beauty contest, where countries compete to provide the most beautiful and safest cities, with the best public services and infrastructure, to attract the most talented minds. Today, the best minds are also very mobile. Any aggressive military standoff will create fear and insecurity, causing the most talented people to emigrate to countries they deem to be safer. Aggressors are unlikely to be able to capitalize on their belligerence.

Even though China will soon be the largest economy globally, its military power is still years behind that of the United States. In addition, by 2040, the Chinese economy will have an aging population; typically, an aging country becomes very conservative in terms of domestic and foreign policy. China's innovation capacity will also suffer as a result of an aging society. The United States, on the other hand, with its growing population and a constant inflow of talent from around the world, will likely regain the leadership in technology and innovation in the latter part of the century.

CHAPTER 9

Europe

Europe is not a single country, so let us analyze the largest countries in Europe (i.e. the United Kingdom, France, and Germany) as potential contenders for leading nations in innovation. Even though the EU has created a single custom trading bloc and a single currency, each European country has its own language, culture, law, and public institutions. The degree of integration in terms of the goods and labor market is not nearly as complete as that of the single market in the United States. Therefore, in terms of scale, even the largest European countries (such as Germany, France, and the United Kingdom) are far smaller than the United States, China, India, or even Japan. Moreover, Europe, on average, is aging rapidly, with a fertility rate of 1.6, which is much lower than that of the United States. Hence, it is in a weaker position demographically compared with the United States. These factors will almost certainly prevent even the largest European countries, or the bloc as a whole, from challenging the United States and China for the leadership position in innovation.

The Historical Innovation Champion

Europe was once unified under the Roman Empire (if we view the Roman Empire as a predecessor to Europe, although geographically the Roman Empire did not cover exactly the same region as modern Europe). The Roman Empire was geographically and demographically the largest country in the world during this period, even significantly larger than the Han dynasty in China. It is estimated that the Roman Empire had a population of 80 million, 30% larger than the population of contemporary China. Rome was the largest city in the world, with a population of a million, double the size of Chang'an, the largest city in China. Just like China, language was a unifying element; the official languages were Greek and Latin, and the exchange of goods, people, and ideas was vibrant among the Roman provinces across the Mediterranean Sea. The Roman Empire was also the global leader in innovation and science. Its engineering, military, navigation, and transportation technologies were at the forefront of its time. Unfortunately, due to both internal and external factors, many of which are still being argued about by historians, the Roman Empire collapsed around 400 AD and was broken up into many smaller states. At the same time, China's Han dynasty also collapsed. However, a few hundred years later, China was united again during the Tang and Song dynasties. China was the world's leading innovator for the next 1,000 years, until the 1500s, when the Chinese emperor made the fateful decision to close China to international trade.

Meanwhile, several European countries, particularly those in Western Europe, started to experiment with navigation technologies to explore the Atlantic Ocean; they had a lucky break when they discovered the New World. These Western European countries were of small and medium size, including Portugal, the Netherlands, Spain, and the United Kingdom. Owing to their limited size, these nations had a strong incentive to explore the ocean to find new trading routes to link to the lucrative markets of West Asia and China. This explains why it was these four smaller nations that took the lead in exploring the Atlantic rather than France or the Austro-Hungarian Empire, which were much larger. The discovery of the New World allowed these countries to access natural resources, and the new trading routes also allowed these countries to access new markets in Asia, making them wealthier. Their per capita income was much higher than that of the other non-trading nations in Europe. During the late 1700s, after a series of conflicts, the United Kingdom, the largest country of the four, with a superior navy, secured supremacy of the high seas and became the dominant player in world trade and the most successful colonizer.

During this period, the United Kingdom was the most advanced nation in the world. Even though its population was smaller than that of France, the United Kingdom had access to a much larger market, including India and China. As a result, it enjoyed one of the highest living standards in the world (second only to the Netherlands, which was much smaller), and had more entrepreneurs and engineers than other European countries. This was one of the key factors that led to the Industrial Revolution in the late 1700s in the United Kingdom. During the late 1700s and early 1800s, the United Kingdom was the undisputed dominant power and a leader in innovation in the world.

The Industrial Revolution started in the United Kingdom, but quickly spread to the rest of Europe and the United States. For a brief period, France was the largest country in Europe, with the largest population and the largest GDP, but multiple wars caused significant population loss and destabilized its political system; further, repeated revolutions led to internal disruption and a low fertility rate. On the other hand, Germany, following its unification, soon had a population larger than those of France and the United Kingdom. The scale advantage started to favor Germany on the global stage, and it became a leader in the Second Industrial Revolution that started in the late 1800s. German scientists founded modern chemistry and German companies became world leaders in the modern chemical industry. By the early 1900s, Germany's per capita income was one of the highest in the world.

In the early twentieth century, Germany may have been the largest country in Europe, but it was still much smaller in population than the United States. As a matter of fact, Germany was not quite the largest in Europe either, if we count Russia as a European country. Soviet Russia had a much larger, faster-growing population than Germany, and it was catching up quickly in terms of both industrialization and innovation. By the time of the Second World War, Nazi Germany greatly underestimated the strength of the Soviet Union; in fact, the Soviet Union was a much stronger power than France, with three times its population. The direct result of this was the German defeat at the hands of the Soviets; of course, with the help of the United States (an even bigger country), the fate was sealed for Nazi Germany right from the start.

A common pattern in European history is that a small country can have a lucky break in the innovation of new technologies or organizational forms, and enjoy the fruits of their success for a short period of time. However, in the long term, the technology and organization innovation will spread and reach larger countries. Once larger countries catch up, their scale advantage will be overwhelming, and they will usually win the innovation race by becoming the center of innovation.

Is it Too Early to Write Off Germany?

Germany became a superpower in Europe following its unification in the 1800s. It had the largest population in Europe, and for a brief period in the late 1800s, it had the largest population of the Western world before it was surpassed by the United States. During this period, Germany led the world in terms of technology, innovation, and scientific research. Recently, with its reunification with East Germany, Germany has once again become the largest and strongest economy in Europe, and a leader in many industries (especially high-end manufacturing). There are many high-tech German multinationals, such as Mercedes and Siemens. Germany, much like Japan, will likely continue to be a strong player in high-end manufacturing. Unfortunately, the problem is that manufacturing will be less important in the future. The industries of the future are information technology, entertainment, and high-end services; these industries will represent an ever-increasing share of the economy. In these vibrant and innovative industries, it is the size of the home market that matters, and the United States and China will enjoy an advantage.

Let us look at the Internet industry. There are almost no European home-grown Internet companies. In the service sector, Accor is the only large hotel chain brand and, not surprisingly, it was created in France, which was the largest market in Europe before the reunification of Germany. There are very few large software companies too; the only exception is SAP, which is a manufacturing software company. Nokia was a very successful mobile phone manufacturer, but when phones effectively turned into computers in the mobile Internet age, Nokia was no match for Silicon Valley companies such as Apple. In the entertainment industry, Continental European countries lag far behind the United States. The only exception is the United Kingdom. Thanks to English, the United Kingdom essentially has the whole English-speaking market as its home market; it is for this reason that it is able to create global media sensations such as Harry Potter.

Why has Europe failed to innovate in the service, information technology, and entertainment industries? Again, market size is the critical factor here. A website or mobile app built for a single European country simply cannot compete with the United States or China in terms of research and development expenditure. In the manufacturing industry, where product quality specifications are objective and easily measured, an innovative firm can enjoy the scale of the world market by exporting its products around the world. However, in services, and the software and Internet industries, a firm's service offerings need to be co-created with its customers, so having a large and sophisticated home market to experiment with is a big advantage. The exceptional success of the German software giant SAP was primarily because its software was aimed at manufacturing companies. Many of its manufacturing customers are based in Germany and other parts of Europe, so SAP was able to take advantage of a sophisticated home market.

The scale advantage is especially important in the Internet industry, where speed is everything. The ability to capture early adopters of a new technology is critical to gaining a head start in the race. Hypothetically, let's assume that 1 million users is the critical mass for a social networking website. Facebook only needs to wait for the penetration rate to reach 0.25% in the United States, but in the United Kingdom, with less than one-quarter of the U.S. population, any potential native social networking website will need to wait for the penetration rate to reach 1.3%. Thus, Facebook, the U.S. social networking website, has an early head start, giving it enough time to launch and perfect its product in the United States first and enter the U.K. market later, dispatching any indigenous competitors. In contrast, such ruthless action may not be possible in China, because it has a larger indigenous market than that of the United States. Native Chinese companies can imitate U.S. companies almost immediately as a result, and can research and trial their own groundbreaking technologies and developments.

TABLE 9.1 Venture capital in Europe, China, and the United States (2009)

	US$ millions
United States	180,000
China	15,285
United Kingdom	7,174
Italy	2,958
France	2,786
India	2,765
Germany	1,363
Russia	1,308
Japan	1,100
Spain	879
Korea	711

Data Source: EVCA Yearbook, 2011.

The abysmal performance of indigenous European companies in the software and Internet industry is reflected in venture capital statistics (see Table 9.1).

The other problem for Europe is the lack of entrepreneurship. The most disruptive technologies, such as the Internet and e-commerce, usually come from new firms. Some people say that the dearth of European entrepreneurship is a result of culture. Maybe so, as the United States has a more entrepreneurial culture on account of its immigrants, who are self-selected for their enterprising potential, but I don't believe that this is the main reason for the lack of entrepreneurial drive in Europe. The main reason is again the scale of the market; in a smaller country, the prize of winning is smaller. If somebody wants to start a French travel website, the incentive is five times smaller than establishing a U.S. travel website, not to mention that U.S. travel websites have a much better chance of tapping users in other countries and capturing a portion of the world market, for the reasons explained earlier. The disadvantageous risk-to-reward ratio is one of the most significant reasons for the lack of an entrepreneurial culture. The situation for China is the complete opposite; culturally, it is less individualistic than Europe, but in China's huge market, even a very small niche product can generate a large profit. As a result, entrepreneurship is very attractive to anyone willing to take a risk in China.

The third problem is that the labor market is not as competitive. Visibly, Europeans are more laid back than Americans—they work fewer hours per week and take longer vacations. But I would argue that this is also due to the size of the market. Despite unrestricted labor mobility across EU countries, labor is not completely mobile due to language and cultural differences. A French professor in a typical French university is effectively only competing with other French-speaking professors, not with a much larger English academic community in the world. The same is true for other highly skilled workers. Therefore, highly skilled workers in Europe are less driven than their comparable American counterparts, because they have less competition. This is the same reason why residents in large cities work harder; in other words, diligence increases with city size.

Is the United Kingdom Different?

In this regard, the United Kingdom is an exception among other European countries, mainly because of the continuing dominance of English globally. The United Kingdom has a smaller market, but its labor market is effectively connected with other English-speaking countries (visa is not a barrier, as most countries welcome highly skilled immigrants). Some people argue that German and French people can speak English well, but in order to be an effective business leader, author, or script writer, English as a native language is a distinct advantage for highly skilled positions in English-speaking countries.

The English language factor has both pros and cons for the United Kingdom. On the one hand, British talent can move to countries such as the United States more easily, further bolstering this already strong competitor. On the other hand, in certain easily exportable industries such as the entertainment industry, U.K. firms can take advantage of the large English-speaking market. Moreover, being English speaking is also advantageous in attracting immigrants. Lastly, it is easier for U.S. multinational firms (and even Chinese multinational firms) to relocate their research and development facilities to the United Kingdom because of English being the indigenous language.

Overall, having English as the first language is a significant advantage for the United Kingdom and for other English-speaking countries such as Canada and Australia. These countries effectively enjoy the scale advantage of a much larger English-speaking product and labor market. Theoretically, they can be as successful as any U.S. region or city, but the key is probably to be closely integrated with the United States and other English-speaking countries.

Is Russia a Part of Europe?

At the opposite end of the spectrum to the United Kingdom is Russia. Although it is geographically within Europe, it is not a part of the EU, which means it is isolated from the EU market. Moreover, culturally and politically, it is quite different from Western Europe, but similar to Eastern Europe. After the Second World War, the Soviet Union had a population that was even larger than that of the United States. Even with a centrally planned economy that forbade entrepreneurship, innovation was strong in certain areas under direct state control, and the Soviet Union launched the first satellite into space. However, like all other centrally planned economies, without the incentives for private entrepreneurship, innovation withered and the economy eventually collapsed. After the breakup of the Soviet Union, this huge country lost almost half of its population. Currently, Russia has a population of only 150 million, less than half that of the United States and only slightly higher than Japan. To make matters worse, it has a low fertility rate, currently standing at 1.6, making the country's prospects appear quite bleak. The abundance of natural resources is not helpful, and actually could pose a problem (the "resource curse"), as commodity prices fluctuate and possibly even decline in the future. As argued earlier in this book, the possession of natural resources is not a positive factor for economic development or innovation. A resource-rich country is typified by an unstable government, ineffective institutions, and inadequate property protection laws, all of which are detrimental to the nurturing of innovation. It seems that Russia has exactly these problems.

The Prospect of Innovation in Europe

The prospects for Europe becoming an innovation powerhouse are poor. The integration of Europe as a single market will not be complete in the short term, due to inherent cultural, political, and language barriers. Furthermore, efforts to raise the fertility rate have had mixed results. Immigration might be an option, but Continental Europe is a much less attractive destination for highly skilled workers compared with the United States (primarily because of language). Hence, overall, Europe will likely be a secondary player to the United States or China when it comes to innovation.

Fertility and Aging

On average, Europe has a fertility rate of 1.6 (i.e. 25% below the replacement level), but there are a few bright spots (see Figure 9.1). The high-fertility countries include the United Kingdom, France, and the Northern European countries. The United Kingdom has a fertility rate of 1.9 and France has a fertility rate of 2.0. The low-fertility countries are Germany and Southern and Eastern European countries.

The strongest economy, Germany, has a fertility rate of 1.4, one of the lowest in the world. Germany has a zero or negative population growth, even with a large annual inflow of immigrants. It is not surprising that many Germans do not want to have children, as this is a common problem of all

FIGURE 9.1 The current fertility map of Europe

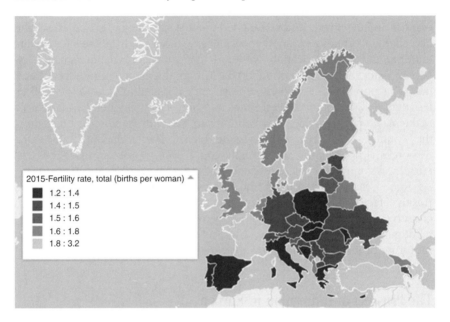

Data Source: World Bank, 2015.

wealthy industrialized nations. To make the fertility situation worse, German women are among the most educated and therefore more likely to focus on career over children, and historically the government has not provided generous child-support benefits compared with other wealthy European nations. Germany, with a strong economy, certainly can afford to increase benefits for families, and recently the government has increased spending on family-friendly policies; time will tell whether or not this yields results.

Other low-fertility-rate countries are Southern and Eastern European countries. Italy has a fertility rate of 1.5, and both Spain and Poland have a fertility rate of 1.4. Consequently, the populations in these countries are aging rapidly. In contrast to Germany, these countries have underdeveloped economies, and are not attractive immigration destinations. In fact, they are losing many talented young people to the United States and other EU countries. Furthermore, unlike Germany, these countries are financially weak and do not have the resources to offer subsidies to large families, so there is little hope for these countries becoming centers of innovation.

At the opposite end of the spectrum are the high-fertility countries, such as the United Kingdom, France, and the Scandinavian countries. The United Kingdom has a fertility rate of 1.9, France 2.0, and Sweden 2.0. It begs the question: What is the difference between high-fertility countries and low-fertility countries?

What is Causing the Difference in Fertility Rates?

The difference seems to be that the governments of the high-fertility countries offer generous financial support and other pro-fertility benefits, such as free daycare centers. On average, spending directly on supporting families accounts for 3–4% of GDP in high-fertility countries, compared with an average of 1–2% in low-fertility countries. In general, there is a positive relationship between family support spending and a higher fertility rate. Of course, this is hardly good news for most low-fertility countries, because most Southern and Eastern European countries have a weak economy with tight government budgets.

The other difference is the attitude toward marriage and out-of-wedlock births. With the rise in female education and employment, the marriage rate has declined universally. The decline of the marriage ratio is not a problem for fertility if the out-of-wedlock fertility rises. However, out-of-wedlock birth rates in the low-fertility countries are typically much lower than those in the high-fertility Scandinavian countries, for example. The reason for the low out-of-wedlock birth rate could be cultural—these countries still value the traditional family and therefore they frown upon single-parent families. It could also be a result of economic policy; as explained earlier, low-fertility countries spend less on family support, making it harder for a single woman to raise a child independently. If the reason is the latter, then Germany still has a chance to raise its fertility rate by spending more to support larger families, as well as single-parent families.

Immigration

The United States has benefited a great deal from immigration, especially highly skilled immigration. Can European countries rely on immigration as a way out of their demographic doldrums? Let us look at the numbers. Figure 9.2 shows the number of immigrants in major EU countries and North America.

From this data, we see that the major Western European countries are accepting just as many immigrants as the United States, and some even more as a share of the total population.

But What About the Skill Level of Immigrants?

Comparing immigration numbers with the United States is a bit unfair for individual European countries. The EU can be considered as one country, and

FIGURE 9.2 The net immigration for major countries (annual average from 2005 to 2010)

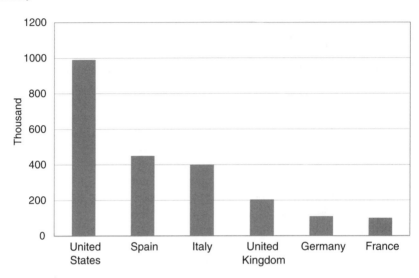

Data Source: UN, World Population Prospects (the 2010 Revision), New York, 2011.

inter-EU migration can be thought of as moving from one state to another in the United States. Table 9.2 breaks down the immigration numbers into EU immigrants and non-EU immigrants.

From Table 9.2, non-EU immigrants are much higher in number—almost twice the number of inter-EU migrants. Actually, the number of inter-EU migrants is much smaller than inter-state movement in the United States, which means that labor mobility between EU countries is lower than labor mobility between states in the United States. This is another excellent reason why this book still treats the EU as a collection of countries rather than a single economic entity. Approximately two-thirds of the immigrants to EU countries are from non-EU countries, and they tend to be unskilled.

Are large European countries taking in highly skilled innovators just like the United States? For Germany, France, and Spain, the share of immigrants with a college-level education is lower than the native population, as shown in Figure 9.3. Moreover, the share of college graduates is just a part of the total picture; the United States attracts a far larger proportion of top talent (e.g. those with PhD degrees) than do European countries.

In a sense, European countries seem to be attracting the wrong type of immigrants. Obviously, immigration policies can be designed to attract the right type of immigrants. Canada's points system, which prioritizes immigrants

TABLE 9.2 Migration into and out of the European Union

Country	Total population 2010 (1,000)	Total foreign-born (1,000)	%	Born in other EU state (1,000)	%	Born in non-EU state (1,000)	%
European Union	501,098	47,348	9.4	15,980	3.2	31,368	6.3
Germany	81,802	9,812	12.0	3,396	4.2	6,415	7.8
France	64,716	7,196	11.1	2,118	3.3	5,078	7.8
United Kingdom	62,008	7,012	11.3	2,245	3.6	4,767	8.1
Spain	45,989	6,422	14.0	2,328	5.1	4,094	8.9
Italy	60,340	4,798	8.0	1,592	2.6	3,205	6.5
Netherlands	16,575	1,832	11.1	428	2.6	1,404	8.5
Greece	11,305	1,256	11.1	315	2.8	940	8.3
Sweden	9,340	1,337	14.3	477	5.1	859	10.2
Austria	8,367	1,276	15.2	512	6.1	764	9.1
Belgium	10,666	1,380	12.9	695	6.5	927	7.3
Portugal	10,637	793	7.5	191	1.8	602	5.7
Denmark	5,534	500	9.0	152	2.8	348	6.3

Data Source: Eurostat, Migration and migrant population statistics, 2013.

FIGURE 9.3 Tertiary educational attainment, by place of birth, 2011 (% of population aged 25 and over)

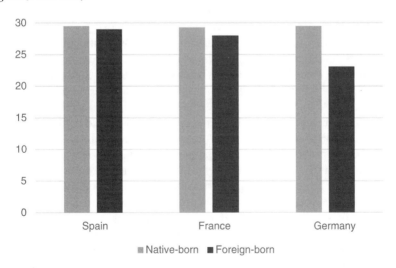

■ Native-born ■ Foreign-born

Data Source: Eurostat (lfsa_argacob and census hub HC34 and HC45), 2011.

based on education, skills, and age, is being adopted by more countries around the world. However, in general, the attractiveness of Western European countries for the most innovative workers is much lower than that of the United States, because these countries do not have the best universities or innovative companies (not to mention the English factor).

Muslim Immigration

One hundred years ago, the United States was also admitting immigrants with a lower level of skill and education than the native population. However, the children of these poor Irish, Chinese, and Indian immigrants are well integrated into society, and actively participate socially and politically; many of them became entrepreneurs and innovators.

Some people worry that Muslims have difficulty in assimilating, and their high fertility rate will turn Europe into a Muslim continent. This worry might be premature.

Currently, Muslims only make up about 6% of the European population (Figure 9.4). The fertility rate of the Muslim population is about 50% higher on average than that of the native population, which means that it will take one generation (2050) for the Muslim population to make up 10% of the population, and three generations (2100) to make up 20% of the population (Table 9.3). Even at 20%, Muslims would remain a minority. Despite this, and because of the highly visible nature of the Muslim presence in some countries and cities, where the Muslim population already exceeds 10%, this growth of the Muslim population is a source of friction and worry for the native populace.

These projections are all made under the assumption that all Muslim immigrants' fertility will remain much higher than that of native women, even in the second or third generation. As discussed in Chapter 1, the main reason for the higher fertility of Muslim women is their low level of education and work force participation rate. The big question is, will these Muslim women in Europe, in their second and third generations, be more like natives in having more education and careers instead of more babies?

Eighty years ago, Catholics, to a large extent devout, were perceived to be just as radical as the Muslims of today. This was particularly true in the United States. Look at how this perception has changed in two or three generations. All around the world, people are becoming more secular, and women are pursuing more education and careers. In many parts of the world, Muslim fertility rates are also falling, with urbanization and rising income. Iran already has a fertility rate below the replacement level. The fertility rates of European Muslims will likely be similar to those of the native population in the future. So, by 2100, two generations from now, the Muslim share of the European population will more likely be 15% rather than 20%. The growth in the Muslim

FIGURE 9.4 Percentage of Muslims in European countries

Data Source: Pew Research Center, 2014.

population is therefore unlikely to rescue the low-fertility European countries from their demographic trap.

In Europe, the fertility rate of Muslim women is not much higher than the replacement level. The problem is that the native population only has a fertility rate of 1.6. The challenge is how to encourage the native population, which typically has higher education and income, to have more babies. Singapore,

TABLE 9.3 Muslim fertility rate compared with native-born population

	All religions	Muslims	Difference
Sub-Saharan Africa	4.8	5.6	0.8
Middle East/North Africa	3.0	3.0	0.0
North America	2.0	2.7	0.6
Asia-Pacific	2.1	2.6	0.4
Europe	1.6	2.1	0.5
World	2.5	3.1	0.6

Note: Differences are calculated from unrounded numbers. Only regions for which there are sufficient data are shown.

Data Source: The Future of World Religions: Population Growth Projections, 2010–2050.

with a significant Muslim population, once had a policy to give fertility cash bonuses only to women with a college degree. This particular policy is politically a non-starter in democratic countries (it lasted only a year, even in Singapore), but other ways of providing fertility benefits to working women—such as long maternity leave and tax exemptions—should be considered, to help higher-income families have more babies.

Brexit and the Future of the European Union

Britain's exit from the EU is a huge blow to the bloc. Envious of the enormous size advantage of the U.S. market, the EU was founded out of the ambition to form a large single market with a population larger than that of the United States. Ideally, the EU should be a "United States of Europe," but the reality is that the EU is more like a free-trade bloc made up of many different independent entities. First, due to difference in language and culture, labor is not nearly as mobile as in the United States. More importantly, the development levels of different European countries are much more varied than the development levels of different states in the United States. The wealthy Western and Northern European counties have a per capita income five times that of the poorest countries, such as Romania. In contrast, the richest U.S. state (New Jersey) has a per capita income only twice that of the poorest U.S. state (Alabama). I think the EU has been overly ambitious trying to include too many countries in a short period of time; rather, it should have worked more slowly to just include the wealthy countries first. With such a large difference among its members, it's hard to have a one-size-fits-all policy. When the voters of a country think the EU policies are consistently suboptimal for them, they have an incentive to leave.

One of the major reasons behind Brexit was that U.K. voters did not like the EU's overly generous immigration and social policies. Most economists say that the cost of leaving the EU is high, because the United Kingdom's exports to the EU might be hurt by a tariff. However, the United Kingdom is unique in that its goods exports to the EU are small compared with its service trade, and the United Kingdom imports a lot more goods from the EU than it exports to the EU. More importantly, the United Kingdom is a financial powerhouse, with large service exports to the EU and the world. The EU has vowed to punish the United Kingdom for the exit, because Brexit sets such a bad example for other countries, which may well choose to follow in the U.K.'s footsteps; but keep in mind that taxing U.K. exports will not only hurt the United Kingdom, but also hurt the EU, because it further reduces the size advantage of a single market. Moreover, I am not sure how the EU could hurt Britain's prominent status as a financial center in Europe. Right now, there is no other European city that is even close to having the status of London, which has attracted a huge network of world-class firms and highly skilled workers in the financial industry.

The United Kingdom's highly skilled labor market and financial market is actually more integrated with the United States than with other EU countries. Furthermore, the United Kingdom was also the favorite European country for the Chinese (and other countries) to do business with and invest in, because it is a relatively open and free economy, and because it is more accessible as a result of the English language. Recently, Ctrip.com made a £1.4 billion investment into a United Kingdom-based Internet company serving the European market. I am still quite optimistic about the post-Brexit United Kingdom, especially if it can form a tighter relationship with the United States and China, and continue to be a financial gateway to Europe.

Policy Recommendations

The country that has the best chance of raising its fertility rate is Germany, which is the only large and wealthy country with a low fertility rate (the United Kingdom and France have a high fertility rate). Germany has a lot to learn from the Scandinavian countries, which spend about 2–4% to support large families. Germany certainly has the financial resources to do the same.

On the subject of immigration, while countries should remain open to all kinds of immigrants, they should design policies to attract more highly skilled workers. Continental European countries should try to be more English-friendly, and should stop at nothing short of creating a dual official language system just like Singapore. This will likely make the countries more attractive to highly skilled immigrants whose first or second language is English.

For Germany, the focus should be on high-end manufacturing, where market size does not matter as much as it does with the service industry. Also, a generally good strategy for smaller countries is to be more tolerant and pro-active about promoting promising yet controversial technologies such as genetic engineering and driverless cars; in contrast, larger countries are typically slow to adapt their laws and regulations to controversial new technologies. For example, while the United States is still working on its laws on driverless cars, Singapore just announced that it will implement driverless cars within the next five years.

The United Kingdom, with the advantage of having English as its first language, has carved out niches not just in manufacturing, but in high-end services. It can act as a gateway between Europe, the United States, and the rest of the world. It is already the financial center for Europe, and also a first stop for U.S. and Chinese multinationals to get into Europe. So, the trick is to integrate both with Europe and with the United States; and if this strategy works, the United Kingdom will continue to be one of the strongest economies in Europe.

Other Developed Countries

To be a gateway economy, a country might not need to be very innovative in technology, but it is important to be innovative in terms of regulations and institutions. Hong Kong was a gateway to China for the second half of the last century, and although it was not a great innovator in terms of technology, its gateway status made it very prosperous. Singapore is also a good example; it is rapidly becoming a gateway between South East Asian countries and the rest of the world. In fact it is more successful than Hong Kong, because South East Asia, which is relatively more backward than China, relies on Singapore more than China relies on Hong Kong. As a part of the gateway strategy, both Singapore and Hong Kong correctly pursued very open and free market-oriented policies, with low taxes and low welfare; moreover, both emphasized English as the official language. These policies are good ingredi-ents for the gateway strategy, and also essential to attract the right type of immigrants.

Outside Europe, East Asia, and North America, there are only a few wealthy countries. Some are gateway city states, which are very rich and small, such as Singapore. Others are resource-rich English-speaking countries, like Australia and Canada. Some people attribute their success to their abundant resources, but there are many poor resource-rich countries in South America and the Middle East. The resource-rich English-speaking countries are differ-ent because they have highly developed human capital and good institutions, and are very well connected to other wealthy countries because of the common English heritage and language. However, the disadvantage of these countries is still large: they are too small to have a critical mass of talent.

Israel is a special case. It has very high-quality human capital and is very innovative but because of its small size, it cannot build very large companies. Most of its technology innovations are sold to U.S. or Chinese companies after the initial stage of development. With the emergence of China and India as competitors, it will feel the pressure of losing talent to the United States, India, and China.

Conclusion

Europe, because of its fragmented market, low fertility rate, and language barriers, will be much weaker economically and much less innovative than the United States or China in the future. However, if European countries are more open to highly skilled immigration from the rest of the world, more English-friendly, and increase financial support to raise the fertility rate, the prospect of innovation remains promising, especially in high-end manufacturing industries.

CHAPTER 10

India

Let us start our analysis of India by discussing Figure 10.1, which shows the number of foreign PhD students in U.S. graduate schools by their country of origin. A country's share of foreign PhDs in U.S. graduate schools is a good proxy of the relative strength of human capital in each country. The figure shows that the number of doctorates awarded to Chinese students is almost twice the number awarded to European students.

The number of Indian students is much bigger than those of any single other country, except for China; even bigger than Europe and non-U.S. America. Using this as a predictor for future GDP, India's innovation should rank only after that of China and the United States. After a country reaches the middle-income level, its ability to move further up to the high-income level depends on its innovation capacity, which is determined by the size and quality of human capital, so this graph should be a predictor of the distribution of the GDP of the major countries in the future.

Other economists have made the same projection. Bloomberg predicts that the Indian economy will grow at about 7% a year over the next 15 years, quadrupling its current size to reach a per capita income of US$8,000 by 2030. This will make India the third largest economy on the planet, surpassing Japan and Germany. Similar to China, as India reaches the middle-income level, with hundreds of millions of middle-class consumers and a very large educated workforce, India will begin to be a more fertile ground for innovation itself. The long-term outlook for India is even brighter. After 2030, India will still be relatively poor but, unlike China, with a much larger, younger, and growing population it will continue to enjoy the "catch-up" advantage, allowing it to grow faster than the United States and China. Two generations from now, India will have a much larger workforce than China, and the number of young workers will be twice as large as in China. It is possible that by late this century, India's economy will surpass that of China and the United States to become the largest in the world.

FIGURE 10.1 Non-U.S. citizens awarded doctorates in science and engineering by country of citizenship, 2010

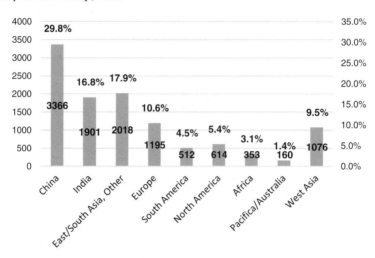

Note: A total of 25 degrees were awarded to non-U.S. citizens from unknown countries.

Data Source: National Science Foundation, Science and Engineering Doctorate Awards: 2009–10.

It seems far-fetched today when I forecast that India's economy will be the largest in the world in 80 years, but look at how quickly China and the Asian Tiger countries grew their per capita GDP after going through industrialization. After the Second World War, the per capita income of the Asian Tiger economies increased from a meager 5% of U.S. per capita GDP to 50% of per capita GDP in less than 50 years—and U.S. GDP was growing at the same time! China's growth has been even faster. Since the 1980s, the per capita GDP in China grew from 5% of the U.S. level to 20% in 30 years; moreover, it will likely reach 50% of U.S. GDP per capita in less than 50 years. There is no reason to believe that China will be the last country to join the wealthy-country club. The next country, following in its footsteps as a result of having a large quantity of high-quality human capital, will be India.

History of India

How do we explain the fact that India is still one of the poorest countries in the world? Historically, India had great ancient civilizations—just like China—and for the last 60 years, it has been a stable and functioning democracy. So why is India such a latecomer when it comes to industrialization?

For most of its history, India was not a single country. Instead, it was a collection of many small independent kingdoms. I have explained why the Industrial Revolution occurred in the West earlier than in the East. After the Second World War, the rest of the world started the race to catch up. But, unlike Japan, South Korea, and Taiwan, which took the market/open economy approach, India and China took a socialist/autarky approach.

Even though India's government was not a Soviet-style totalitarian regime politically, economically it embraced a Soviet-style central planning system until the 1990s. It possessed all the features and weaknesses of a centrally planned economy, which put a heavy shackle on innovation and entrepreneurship. In the notorious "license Raj" system, to operate any business, an entrepreneur needed to obtain a license, which was often very costly and sometimes almost impossible. Furthermore, a law supposedly designed to help small businesses required special government approval for any business wanting to expand in size beyond a few hundred employees. There were many other onerous regulations that deterred Indian firms from growing larger. One of the laws required special approval to lay off workers for any business with more than a few hundred employees. So, if a business became successful and expanded, suddenly it could not fire anyone! For any business owner, it is a terrifying thought not to be able to fire any workers. (Not that we enjoy doing it, of course, but it is an essential tool in making certain that the business remains both productive and competitive.) As a result of these regulations, businesses in many industries stayed small, and many businesses had to resort to the illegal practice of hiring temporary workers, something not conducive to long-term growth.

This regime basically killed off incentives for innovation and entrepreneurship. The motive for being an entrepreneur or inventor is to create and grow a successful business and, hopefully, make a lot of money. When a firm cannot grow, smart people will find alternative employment. Also, restrictions on business size annihilate India's biggest advantage, which is the scale advantage of its huge market. I once compared the textile firms in China with the textile firms in India and found that the average firm size of Indian companies was much smaller than those in China. What compounds the problem is that the productivity of a firm strongly relates to the size of the firm. The largest textile firms were much more productive than the smaller firms. The large Chinese firms had tens of thousands of workers. The productivity of these Chinese firms was competitive even by global standards, and they were also large exporters as a result. In contrast, there is almost no large Indian textile firm. When I asked Indian business owners why they were unable or unwilling to expand, the answer was that the laws and regulations favored small enterprises, making it very costly to expand beyond a certain size. Consequently, unlike China, India does not have a large, labor-intensive, exporting manufacturing industry.

The other mistake that the Indian government made before the reforms of the 1990s was that it pursued a very restrictive trade policy rather than an open trade policy. This is partly because its firms could not grow bigger or compete on the global market. To protect its favored small businesses, the government imposed a heavy tariff on imported goods. Foreign direct investment into Indian companies was capped below 50%, which discouraged many multinational firms from investing in India. Like in many Latin American countries that tried to implement it, this important substitution policy failed miserably. Indian firms did not compete or interact extensively with other firms in the world, further slowing down their ability to keep abreast of developments, catch up, and innovate. Lastly, by cutting itself off from the global market, these restrictive trading policies slowed down the exchange of people, ideas, and technology with the rest of the world; another heavy blow to innovation and economic growth.

Prior to the reforms in the 1990s, the Indian economy grew on average only 3.9% from 1950 to 1990, compared with the Korean economy, which grew 9.6% on average from 1960 to 1990. After the Second World War, India's per capita income was roughly the same as that of South Korea, but by 1991, India's per capita income was only one-tenth that of South Korea. India was not the only place where ill-conceived economic policies did great damage. North Korea and pre-reform China performed even worse. The fact that post-reform China achieved spectacular double-digit growth in the 1980s was in stark contrast to the performance of the Indian economy before 1991.

In the early 1990s, after 10 years of watching China's rise as a result of its reforms, India launched its own reforms. But, with a functioning democracy, the pace of its reforms has been much slower than that of the reforms in China. It was not until an economist, Manmohan Singh, became the prime minister in 2004 that the pace of reform sped up. Under his helm, the "license Raj" system was mostly dismantled. Tariff and other trade barriers were reduced dramatically. Limits on foreign ownership were lifted in most industries. With the new economic policy, India's economic growth started to accelerate (Figure 10.2). The GDP growth rate has accelerated by an average 6–7% in recent years, and is projected to grow 8–9% over the next two to three years. Moreover, its exports and foreign reserves have also grown rapidly.

Is India's Growth Sustainable?

As argued in this book, human capital and market size are fundamental factors that drive innovation. India has been able to greatly expand its stock of human capital in recent years. The college enrollment rate has increased from 6% to 10% since the reforms in the 1990s. India now produces over 2 million college graduates a year. The quality of the college students must be relatively high, as India represents one of the largest sources of graduate students for the

FIGURE 10.2 India's GDP growth rate

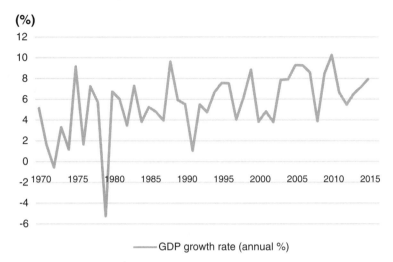

Data Source: World Bank, 2015.

best U.S. graduate schools. The Indian Institute of Technology is a world-renowned university, graduating thousands of top students in engineering and science every year.

Leveraging its large human capital, India has developed a world-class IT outsourcing and service industry. IT service exports have grown from US$5 billion in 2000 to over US$20 billion in 2010 (Hyvonen and Wang, 2012). India's innovative index ranking is also ahead of most economies at the same level of per capita income. India's venture capital has grown from US$718 million in 2006 to US$4.4 billion in 2015 (Figure 10.3).

The Scale Advantage

With a population of 1.2 billion, India possesses an advantage of scale that is very much like that enjoyed by China. It has the second largest mobile phone and Internet market in the world, which allows India to develop indigenous Internet companies capable of competing head-on with multinational heavy-weights (Figures 10.4 and 10.5). For example, Flipkart, an e-commerce giant, is leading the race against Amazon in India. Olacab, a taxi and car ordering company, is competing fiercely with Uber. The emergence of these home-grown Internet companies would not be possible in smaller countries.

However, India's metrics for innovation—such as research and development per capita and patents per capita—are still very low compared with

FIGURE 10.3 Indian venture capital

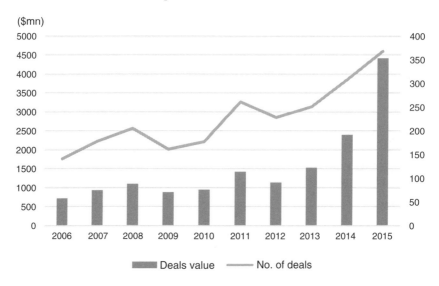

Data Source: Snigdha Sengupta, "10 years of venture capital investing in India: Time to pause, reflect & correct."

FIGURE 10.4 India's mobile users

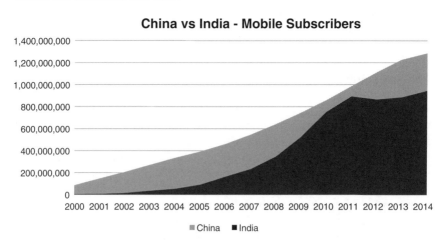

Data Source: Official data from Indian and Chinese regulators to October 2012.

FIGURE 10.5 India's Internet users

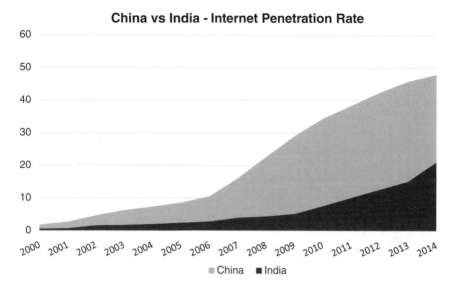

Data Source: International Telecommunication Union, World Bank, and United Nations Population Division.

high-income countries. This is because India is still mostly in the catch-up stage of development. At this stage, the main task is to adopt and adapt existing technologies, which also requires entrepreneurship and innovation, but does not require a huge amount of original research and development. For example, to meet the needs of India's poor, local phone maker Mircomax was able to lower the cost of its smartphones to about US$100; as a result, the company has become one of the top 10 mobile phone makers in the world. Ola, the local competitor to Uber, began offering rickshaw-ordering services in addition to its taxi-cab services, and is now bigger than Uber in India. A local version of Airbnb, Oyo Hotel, not only lists properties such as hotels, but also helps property owners to renovate and manage these. Makemytrip, the local competitor to Expedia, offers train and bus ticket services in addition to hotel and air ticket booking services. These are all examples of innovation in adapting technologies or business models to fit the local Indian market, and the speedy commercialization of these adaptions has been helped by India's colossal market size.

India's Infrastructure Problem

Many people worry that India's infrastructure is a bottleneck that is hampering economic growth. There is some truth to this, as India's infrastructure is indeed

FIGURE 10.6 Savings rate in India

Indian Household Saving Rate

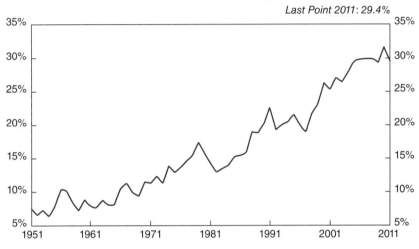

Data Source: Ministry of Statistics and Program Implementation, 2012.

very poor, primarily due to insufficient investment. But all poor countries have poor infrastructure when they start to take off. As their economies grow, savings and investment rates will increase, and so will infrastructure spending. This is exactly what happened in China. In India, the savings rate has been climbing, along with the infrastructure investment (Figure 10.6). Anybody who has recently been to Delhi can clearly testify to the fact that the freeways and the airport are improving (Figure 10.7).

Export and Balance of Trade

The problem with many Latin American economies is that their exports are primarily commodities or natural resources. Whenever there is a slump in commodity prices, their balance of trade suffers and their currency value collapses, which often leads to financial crises and macro instability. India, on the other hand, has a growing export industry and a very competitive IT outsourcing industry. In recent years, the balance of trade has been improving (Figure 10.8). In 2007, it reached a record foreign reserve level of over US$200 billion.

Political System

Some people argue that democracy slows down with the development of a large country like India. This is partly true. When India adopted a

FIGURE 10.7 Infrastructure investment in India

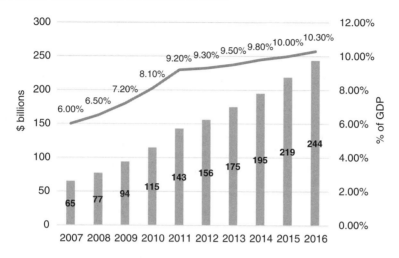

Data Source: Citibank Macro Economy Report, 2012.

market-based economy in 1991, it moved slowly, much slower than China. Only recently has it started to match China in terms of trade openness and ease of doing business, and only recently has it invested heavily in infrastructure, which is why India's growth rate is only now beginning to catch up with that of China.

FIGURE 10.8 India's foreign reserves

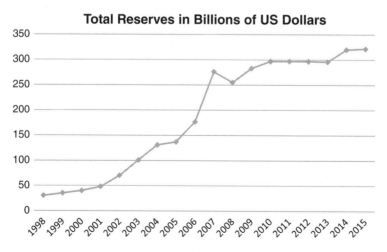

Data Source: Reserve Bank of India, 2015.

But there is also a benefit in being slow and at the same time being responsive to voters. China's top-down government made a huge mistake in adopting the draconian one-child policy in the 1980s; further, its strong enforcement of the one-child policy made matters worse. With a tightly controlled press and top-down political process, only recently did the Chinese government realize its mistake and begin to relax the one-child policy. India, in the 1970s, also tried to control the population. Indira Gandhi even tried to implement forced sterilization for men with two or more children, but it proved to be unpopular and politically impossible to implement in a democratic society. Today, India's growing and young population is widely regarded as an asset rather than a burden, so in hindsight, India avoided an absolutely critical policy error precisely because of its democratic political system.

Poverty and Inequality

With a rapidly growing economy, inequality usually rises, because the income of those who are very successful (such as entrepreneurs or IT engineers) grows more quickly than that of the rest of the working population. This is actually healthy, as high rewards for success induce people to work hard and take risks. Before the reform, the highest marginal income tax rate was as high as 80% in India; this punishingly high tax rate guaranteed that everybody would be equal, but equally poor. Now the top marginal income tax rate is 40%. There will be some super-rich individuals, but the rising tide will lift all boats. As its economy has expanded and continues to expand, India has lifted hundreds of millions of people out of poverty. In the future, there will be hundreds of millions of people moving into the middle class. India has a system whereby people are judged by their caste, but with more people in the middle class, even the caste system is fading as people are primarily judged by their education, job, and income instead.

Brain Drain or Brain Gain?

Some people argue that although India's universities produce excellent engineers and researchers, many of them move to the United States following their graduation, leading to a brain drain out of India. Every year there are about 100,000 college graduates going abroad to work and study, but this represents only about 0.5% of the total annual graduating cohort. One half of a single percentage point is not a significant dent in the overall pool of human talent in India; rather, this 0.5% is potentially a "brain gain." As soon as the Chinese economy started to take off, many members of the diaspora started to return to their home country, bringing with them all their education, experience, and the capital they had gained overseas. It is estimated that approximately 50% of the Chinese diaspora has now returned to China. Moreover, those who do not return can also help their home country in many ways. Many multinationals are setting up research and development facilities in India and China, partly because their executives are originally from India or China. Executives of Indian descent are highly successful in multinational firms. The current CEOs of Google and Microsoft, for example, are Indian immigrants to the United States, and these multinational firms are likely to continue to expand their presence and research/development activities in India.

Natural Resources

Just like China, India will consume a large amount of natural resources and energy as it industrializes. As I demonstrated in Chapter 4, there is, globally, a sufficient amount of resources to sustain a world population of 10 billion. In terms of agriculture, even though India has a population of over 1.2 billion people, after the Green Revolution to adopt modern agricultural technologies, it actually has more food than it needs, and has become a major exporter in the world food market.

India is a major importer of oil and has benefited greatly from low oil prices. I predicted earlier in this book that due to innovations in shale gas, solar, and battery technologies, oil and energy supply generally will continue to be abundant, and this is very good news for India's economy. On the demand side, China has already moved into the next stage of development to focus on developing its service and high-end manufacturing industries, and its appetite for energy and resources will likely slow down in the near future. This slump in demand will also help to keep prices down—and this is just what India needs as it industrializes.

The Environment

There is some bad news here; India's environment will get worse before it gets better. The general pattern is that a country's environment will improve after it reaches a per capita income of US$8,000–10,000, at which point the country will have both the means and the will to improve its environment. In the case of India, it may not need to reach this US$8,000, because the technology for eliminating and controlling pollution will be cheaper and more advanced in the future, driven by developments in other countries. But in the short run, India's environment will certainly get worse, unfortunately much worse than it is today. It will, however, improve when India reaches the next stage of development.

Future Economic Outlook

India certainly has all the ingredients for a high-income country: a stable government, an open and free market, high-quality education, a growing export industry, and most importantly a young and growing population. Obviously, China also has these very same ingredients, including (still) a growing and young population; however, very soon it will have a shrinking and aging population. In this light, India's economy may have the chance to get the upper hand over China in the long run.

Let us compare the population age structure between India and China.

Compared with India, the population problem facing China becomes quite obvious (see Figures 10.10 and 10.11). India has an almost perfect population pyramid today. Its median age is 28, compared with a median age of 38 in China. The fertility rate in India is around 2.4, compared with China's 1.3 (i.e. almost 70% higher). The number of newborn babies in India is about 22 million today, compared with only 16 million in China. This means that today, the number of newborn babies in India is 40% higher than in China; further, as a result of continuing declines in the fertility rate in China, it is estimated to be 60% higher in about 10 years' time.

When India reaches the middle-income level by 2040, it will have the largest population and the largest scale advantage in the world. India also has the advantage of being an English-speaking country. Compared with China, India's companies will have an easier time accessing the global market and

FIGURE 10.9 Photo of myself and children in Bombay during my research trip to India

Photo Credit: James Liang.

FIGURE 10.10 Population pyramid 2016

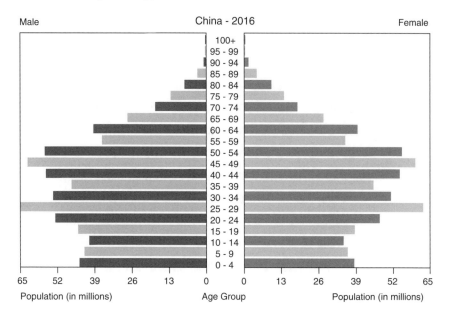

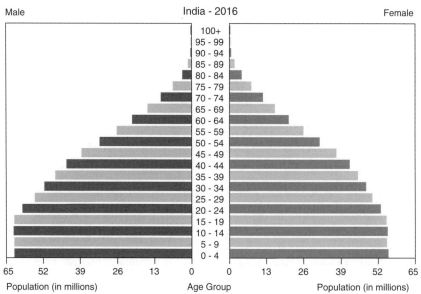

Data Source: U.S. Census Bureau, 2015.

FIGURE 10.11 Population pyramid 2040

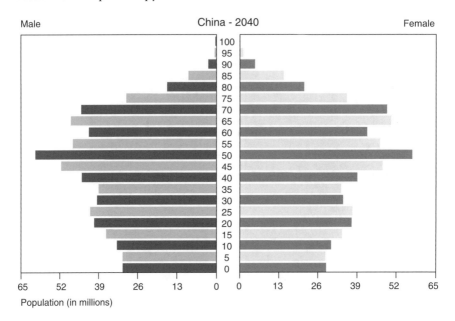

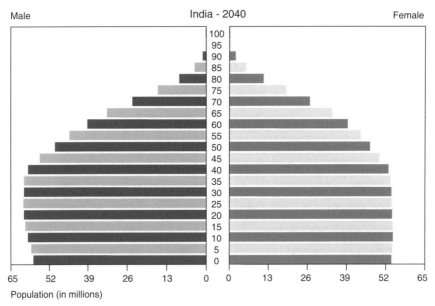

Data Source: U.S. Census Bureau, 2015.

FIGURE 10.12 Young worker population forecast, India vs. China

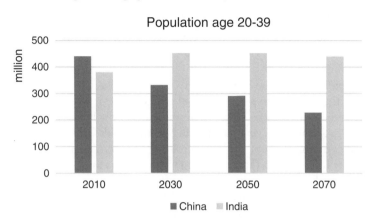

Population age 20-39

Data Source: U.S. Census Bureau, 2015.

operating around the world. Its academic community will have an easier time integrating with the rest of the world. In addition, India will be able to attract more immigrants than China, because of their ability to speak English.

By 2040, India will still be growing faster than China, further closing the gap between the two countries in terms of per capita GDP. At the same time, India's fertility rate will continue to be significantly higher than that of China. As a result, by 2080, India will have a population of 1.6 billion, 30% larger than the projected population of China (1.2 billion). India will also have a working-age population of 0.8 billion compared with China's 0.5 billion. This is almost 60% higher than the working population of China. So, even if India achieves only two-thirds of the labor productivity of China, India's economy will be larger than that of China, and much bigger than that of the United States.

If we look at the number of young workers in the longer run, then by 2080 India will have more than 0.4 billion workers between the ages of 20 and 39, twice as many as China (Figure 10.12). I have previously argued that young workers are the most creative and entrepreneurial part of the work force. Not only will India have a larger young cohort, but also the future Indians will likely be more innovative and entrepreneurial than their young Chinese equivalents, who will be handicapped by the blocking effect of an aging economy, something we have discussed in detail in this book. It is therefore very likely that by the late twenty-first century, India will be more innovative than China.

In summary, China will be the largest economy after 2025, surpassing the United States; however, in less than 60 years, India will take over as the largest economy in the world. The demography of each country is the main driver behind the dynamics of the relative strength of these three leading economies.

Other Developing Countries

India will certainly not be the only poor country capable of moving to the middle-income level over the next 20 years. Many poor countries, such as Burma and Vietnam, will also catch up. With the appropriate economic policies, these countries could grow quite rapidly and reach the middle-income level (close to US$10,000) in two generations.

Nevertheless, I believe (everything being equal) that such small countries will necessarily grow more slowly than their larger rivals. For example, while India can grow by 7% a year (everything being equal), smaller countries can only achieve a maximum growth of 5–6% a year. The reason for this is simple. The quantity and quality of human capital and the size of the domestic market do not favor growth in these small countries in the same way as they do in India; consequently, innovation and entrepreneurship are likely to be less vibrant. At the catch-up stage, what's important is not frontier innovation, but the absorption and adaption of technologies already invented by high-income countries. With a small market and a limited stock of human capital, the absorption and adoption process will necessarily be slower. A 1–2% difference in growth rate is quite significant over the long term. Mathematically, a 1.5% difference a year would add up to 34% over 20 years. At 7% a year, it would take about 20 years to quadruple the size of the economy, whereas at 5.5% a year, it would take a smaller country 25 years to quadruple the size of its economy.

One might say that an additional five years required in order to reach the middle-income level is not a significant difference, but the size advantage matters more after a country reaches the middle-income level. Increasingly, the size of the home market and the concentration of the talent pool are key ingredients in becoming a center of innovation, especially when it comes to frontier innovations. Other developing countries, with a low stock of human capital (both in terms of quantity and quality) and a smaller market size, will be no match for the three heavyweights: India, China, and the United States. It will be tough for smaller newcomers to compete. Korea, with its very high quality of human capital and relatively large size, has a chance to join the wealthy club, but Taiwan, with only half the size of Korea, is having a tough time becoming an innovation center. It is increasingly difficult for Taiwan to reach a critical mass of talent for any important industry, despite having a very high quality of human capital. Taiwan's talented young people are moving to larger innovation centers in the United States or China; its ultra-low fertility rate is not helping matters either.

Of course, many of these smaller countries are very nice places to live in or visit. For example, while Taiwan's economy is not as robust as that of Korea or China, its lifestyle is more relaxed and the quality of life is comparatively very good. However, these countries will take a back seat in the innovation and economic progress of the human race.

Conclusion

In this book, I have argued that the innovation capacity of a country is fundamentally determined by demographic factors, including the size, geographic concentration, and age structure of the population. The effect of demographics on innovation has been at work throughout history. I have surmised that the alternative rise of Western and Eastern civilizations throughout history can be partly attributed to demographic factors moderated by geopolitics and transportation technologies.

However, until recently, the effect of demographics on innovation has been underappreciated, partly because of the seemingly negative effect of a large, concentrated population on resources and the environment. Malthus was one of the most famous economists and demographers ever, and his theory was the theoretical foundation for the anti-fertility movement in many developing countries in the 1970s and 1980s. The effect of aging was underappreciated also because aging is a very recent phenomenon in just a few developed countries, such as Japan.

Going forward, I believe that the effect of demographics on innovation will be increasingly prominent for the following reasons.

1. As technology progress in the energy sector outpaces population growth, the resource/environment bottleneck is diminishing. The Malthusian worry of a large population is fading, and economists will focus increasingly on the positive side of a large population, especially its effect on innovation.
2. The emergence of service and information industries will amplify the scale advantage of a large population. Compared with manufacturing firms, firms in service and information industries benefit more from a large local market, because the innovators in these sectors need to be close to the customers. Moreover, in the field of artificial intelligence and robotics, firms in large markets benefit from the availability of a large amount of data to train machine-learning algorithms.
3. Even though routine jobs and processes can be carried out over the Internet, innovation still requires face-to-face communication, because innovation involves rich and intense interactions between the researchers, suppliers, and customers. Even though the growth of the global trade volume of goods has slowed down, air travel (especially international air

travel) has increased globally in recent years. The mega cities of the world will become innovation hubs in high-technology and high-value-added service industries.

4. Fertility in many countries will continue to drop, primarily due to the increase in women's level of education and career, in spite of strong pro-fertility policies. As a result, the aging problem will spread from just a few countries to many rich and middle-income countries, including China. The negative effect of aging on the economy, and particularly on innovation and entrepreneurship, will be more visible.

The three big heavyweights—China, India, and the United States—will be the leading nations of innovation. China will surpass the United States in terms of innovation between 2030 and 2040, but its innovation capacity will be in decline after 2040, as a result of aging. The United States will likely regain leadership by 2050, thanks mostly to its unmatched ability to tap into the global talent pool. The large metropolitan areas of China and the United States will continue to attract the most creative innovators and entrepreneurs. The race between China and the United States will be an interesting one to watch. The stakes are high, because these innovation hubs will increase in importance and wealth due to the network effect. India will be the fastest growing economy for years to come, thanks to its large population, and it will become a serious competitor in innovation in the second half of this century.

The race of innovation will be a race of human capital development. The winners will be those countries or cities that can nurture and attract a large stock of highly skilled workers. To keep fertility from falling further, most countries will need to design and implement generous pro-fertility policies. The education sector needs to take advantage of the latest technology and the lifelong learning trend to mint more potential innovators and entrepreneurs cheaper and faster.

Moreover, the race of innovation among countries (and cities) will be like a beauty contest to attract highly skilled immigrants. Highly skilled workers are increasingly mobile within a country and internationally, partly because English has become the language of the academic and research community. Consequently, the competition to attract talent will be fierce (but not destructive), and actually will generate a lot of common good, since the government will work hard to improve public services, infrastructure, and the environment in order to attract talent. In a way, each government is like a hosting company competing for customers (i.e. innovators on the effectiveness of its political and economic institution).

Lastly, it is my view that globalization will continue, reflected not so much in the trading of goods, but in cross-border cooperation in innovation. An increasing share of patents today have co-authors from different countries (Witze, 2016). Any nation that restricts the international flow of people, ideas, or capital will run the risk of isolation. Therefore, isolationism and populism will be increasingly more costly when innovation is not only more important, but also more international, Of course, there will always be occasional rises of populism and anti-globalization sentiment, but the competitive pressure among countries to foster and attract the best talent and companies in the world will be an effective counterbalance.

Epilogue: Historical Competition Among Civilizations: An Essay on Transportation Technology, Demographics and the Race of Innovation

The key ingredients of an innovative and progressive civilization are a large market for the exchange of goods and a large number of minds to facilitate the exchange of ideas. For this reason, the centers of innovation lie at the hubs for the movement of goods and people. Throughout history, the locations of such hubs have changed as a result of technological advancements in transportation and communication. The change of hub locations caused by technological change can explain the rise and fall of major civilizations, including the rise of the West.

Three thousand years ago, when sea navigation technology was still primitive, the geographic center of the Eurasian and African continents was Egypt and the Middle East. Both places became the homes of the most advanced civilizations and the centers for innovation. They were also the birthplace of the world's major religions. Later, when sea navigation technology progressed, the Mediterranean Sea became a freeway for goods and people. Greece and Rome, located at the center of the Mediterranean Sea, became the center of traffic for goods and people, and thus the center of global innovation.

Later, both the Roman Empire and the Han dynasty collapsed into smaller countries, each of which had a much smaller population and trade volume. Europe remained divided during the Dark Ages. China, after a period of division, reunited during the Tang and Song dynasties at around 800 AD. The Tang dynasty was estimated to have a population of 80–100 million, while the Song dynasty was estimated to have 120 million people, far larger than any single country in Europe. Not only did the Song dynasty have the largest domestic market, it also traded extensively with South East Asian nations.

During the Song dynasty, China had over 20 trading sea ports and a tariff revenue that at one point accounted for more than 15% of fiscal revenue. China became the leader in technology innovation, with inventions like gunpowder and block printing.

Later, during the 1400s, sea navigation technology further progressed to the extent that crossing the Atlantic Ocean was possible. Western Europe, strategically located at the forefront of the trading route across the Atlantic Ocean and to Africa, became the center of the world in terms of innovation and trade. China's sea navigation technology during the 1400s was actually more advanced, but still not good enough to cross the Pacific Ocean, which is much larger than the Atlantic Ocean. Unsurprisingly, the famous Chung Ho failed to discover the American Continent ahead of European explorers. Later, when Chinese emperors adopted an autarky trade policy which effectively cut off the exchange of goods and ideas with the rest of the world, China very quickly forfeited its leadership position in innovation to Western Europe.

After Western Europe became the trading hub of the world, countries in this region competed for global leadership. The general pattern is that a small country can build a lead in technology or organization in the short run, but a large country can take over the leadership when it catches up. In the beginning, the Portuguese and Spanish were the leading countries, with populations of only a few million people each; they were later replaced by the United Kingdom and France, each of which had populations in the tens of millions; later again, they were overtaken by Germany, with an even larger population. Eventually, Germany was replaced by the United States, with a population of over 100 million.

After the Second World War, only India, China, and the Soviet Union had a population larger than that of the United States. Unfortunately for these three countries, they all chose to follow ill-fated central-planning economic policies. Japan, with its population exceeding 100 million, raced up the standings in the race of innovation and was second only to the United States, but quickly fell behind as a result of an aging population. Russia, as a remnant of the much larger Soviet Union, had only half its original population and with a low fertility rate had no chance of competing with the United States on innovation. European countries, even when considered as the European Union, are not a single market for talent due to their different languages and cultures. In addition, many European countries—especially Southern European countries—have a severe low-fertility and aging problem. The only countries that have a meaningful chance of competing with the United States on innovation are China and India.

Today, with modern communication and aviation technologies, traveling from one end of the globe to the other is only a matter of a day's flight, which is why natural geographic hubs are nonexistent in the world today. India, China, and the United States are on a level playing field. Although both China and

India have a much larger population than the United States, the United States has the unique advantage of attracting the most talented innovators from around the world. The world will be a very different place when China, India, and the United States become the centers of innovation, because these three countries will account for nearly half of the world's population. With half of the human race competing with and learning from each other in the race of innovation, human civilization will be elevated to new heights.

References

Acht, J., Stam, J., Thurik, R., and Verheul, I. (2004) Business ownership and unemployment in Japan, Discussion Papers on Entrepreneurship, Growth and Public Policy No. 0904, Max Planck Institute for Research into Economic Systems.

Chua, A. (2011) *Battle Hymn of the Tiger Mother*, Penguin Press, Harmondsworth.

Coulmas, F., Conrad, H., Schad-Seifert, A., and Vogt, G. (2008) *The Demographic Challenge: A Handbook about Japan*, Brill, Leiden.

Ehrlich, P. (1968) *Population Bomb*, Sierra Club/Ballantine Books, San Francisco, CA.

Grossman, G. and Krueger, A. (1995) Economic growth and the environment, *Quarterly Journal of Economics*, 110 (2): 353–377.

Hedden, T. and Gabrieli, J.D.E. (2004) Insights into the ageing mind: A view from cognitive neuroscience, *Nature Reviews Neuroscience*, 5: 87–96.

Humphreys, M., Sachs, J.D., and Stiglitz, J.E. (Eds) (2007) *Escaping the Resource Curse*, Columbia University Press, Columbia, OH.

Hunt, J. (2010) Skilled immigrants' contribution to innovation and entrepreneurship in the United States. Open for Business Migrant Entrepreneurship in CECD Countries: 261–262.

Hyvonen, M. and Wang, H. (2012) India's services exports. http://www.rba.gov.au/publications/bulletin/2012/dec/pdf/bu-1212-4.pdf.

Jones, B.F. (2005) Age and great invention, NBER Working Paper No. 11359.

Jones, B.F. (2009) The burden of knowledge and the "death of the renaissance man": Is innovation getting harder?, *Review of Economic Studies*, 76 (1): 283–317.

Karlin, R. (2013) The entrepreneurship vacuum in Japan: Why it matters and how to address it. http://knowledge.wharton.upenn.edu/article.cfm?articleid=3145.

Kerr, W. and Lincoln, W. (2010) The supply side of innovation: H-1B visa reforms and US ethnic invention, Harvard Business School, Boston, MA.

Lazear, E. (2005) Entrepreneurship, *Journal of Labor Economics*, 23: 649–680.

Liang, J., Li, J., and Huang, W. (2012) *China Needs More Babies*, China Social Science Publishing, Beijing.

Liang, J., Wang, H., and Lazear, E.P. (2014) Demographics and entrepreneurship, NBER Working Paper No. 20506. http://www.nber.org/papers/w20506.

Lu, M. (2016) *Great State Needs Bigger City*, Shanghai People's Press, Shanghai.

Malthus, T.R. (1798) *An Essay on the Principle of Population*, J. Johnson, London.

Miyoshi, H. and Nakata, Y. (2011) *Have Japanese Firms Changed?: The Lost Decade*, Palgrave Macmillan, Basingstoke.

Piketty, T. (2014) *Capital in the Twenty-First Century*, Belknap Press, Cambridge, MA.

Porter, M.E. (1990, 1998) *The Competitive Advantage of Nations*, Free Press, New York.

Romer, P. (1990) Endogenous technological change, *Journal of Political Economy*, 98 (5): 71–102.

Schumpeter, J. (1942) *Capitalism, Socialism and Democracy* (2nd edn), Impact Books, Floyd, VA.

Smith, A. (1776) *An Inquiry into the Nature and Causes of the Wealth of Nations*, University of Chicago Press, Chicago, IL.

Van Den Bergh, J.C.J.M. and Rietveld, P. (2004) Reconsidering the limits to world population: Meta-analysis and meta-prediction, *BioScience*, 54 (3): 195–204.

Whittaker, D.H. and Cole, R.E. (2006) *Recovering from Success*, Oxford University Press, Oxford.

Witze, A. (2016) Research gets increasingly international, *Nature*. DOI: 10.1038/nature.2016.19198.

Further Reading

Becker, G. and Posner, R. (2011) Yes, the earth will have ample resources for 10 billion people. http://www.becker-posner-blog.com/2011/05/yes-the-earth-will-have-ample-resources-for-10-billion-people-becker.html.

Becker, G., Murphy, K., and Topel, R.H. (2011) On the economics of climate policy, *The B.E. Journal of Economic Analysis and Policy*, 10 (2). DOI: 10.2202/1935-1682.2854.

Benjamin, J. (2010) Age and great invention, *Review of Economics and Statistics*, 92 (1): 1–14.

Bergh, J. (2004) Reconsidering the limits to world population: Meta-analysis and meta-prediction, *BioScience*, 54 (3): 195–204.

Ge, J., Zhao, W., and Xie, S. (1988) *The History of Chinese Demography*, People's Publishing House, Beijing.

International Air Transport Association (2017) Another strong year for air travel demand in 2016, Press Release No. 5.

Porter, M.E. (1985) *Competitive Advantage*, Free Press, New York.

Zhao, W. and Xie, S. (1988) *Zhongguo renkou shi [Population History of China]*, Renmin chubanshe, Beijing.

Index